THE HISTORY OF THE OLD 2/4th (CITY OF LONDON) BATTALION THE LONDON REGIMENT ROYAL FUSILIERS

MAJOR-GENERAL SIR ARCHIBALD PARIS, K.C.B.

THE HISTORY *of the* OLD 2/4th (CITY OF LONDON) BATTALION THE LONDON REGIMENT ROYAL FUSILIERS

1919
THE WESTMINSTER PRESS
LONDON
W

FOREWORD

IN the History of the 2/4th Battalion no attempt has been made at literary effect. It simply describes the story of one of our Battalions, raised at the beginning of the War and broken up after nearly two years' service, owing to the exigencies of the Campaign.

The 2/4th may without demur be described as a very happy Battalion, for, although discipline was strict and a high degree of efficiency was aimed at, it is our proud boast that not a single Court Martial was ever held on any man belonging to the Battalion.

While every care has been taken to give a correct account of each man's service, mistakes must necessarily have occurred in its preparation ; it is hoped that any detail wanting or incorrectly recorded will be attributed to the unavoidable errors that must take place in dealing with the information forwarded for such a large number of men. The official returns were not available for reference.

The thanks of the Battalion are due to Capt. F. W. WALKER, D.S.O., for editing the letterpress, and to Capt. F. C. J. READ for that of the personal services of each man.

That this history has been illustrated by maps and photographs is due to the kindness of Capt. G. NOEL HUNTER, 2/2 London, who has not only superintended their reproduction by the Sun Engraving Company, but has borne the whole of the expenses connected therewith.

THE HISTORY OF THE FOURTH (CITY OF LONDON) BATTALION THE LONDON REGIMENT (ROYAL FUSILIERS).

THE TOWER HAMLETS was represented as a military body as far back as 1643, when the Tower Hamlets Regiment of Trained Bands took part in a muster held on the 26th September, 1643, during the absence from London of certain other of the Trained Bands at the Parliamentary Wars.

The Tower Hamlets Regiment on the day of the muster consisted of 849 Muskets, 385 Pikes, and 70 Officers, making a total of 1,304, with 7 Ensigns or Colours. The Commanding Officer was the Lieutenant of the Tower, and the Regiment was recruited within the limits of the " Hamlets " belonging to the Tower.

The London Trained Bands were re-organised as Volunteers in 1794.

In 1860 the Tower Hamlets Rifle Volunteer Corps was raised, and this consisted of 12 Rifle Corps, which were numbered 1-12.

In 1868 the 2nd and 4th Corps amalgamated, and were afterwards known as the 1st Corps, and the title of " The Tower Hamlets Rifle Volunteer Brigade " assumed.

The uniform was grey, with red and blue braidings, and the head-dress was a demi-shako, with " Cheese-cutter " peak.

In 1874 the 6th Tower Hamlets Rifle Volunteer Corps (The North-East London Rifles) were incorporated with the 1st Corps, and the regiment known as The Tower Hamlets Rifle Volunteer Brigade was complete.

The United Corps consisted of 16 Companies, with two Lieutenant-Colonels and the usual number of Officers. Lieutenant-Colonel J. HOLT was Commanding Officer, and Lieutenant-Colonel J. H. MAPLESON was junior Lieutenant-Colonel.

The Headquarters of the Brigade were at 112, Shaftesbury Street, Hoxton.

At the latter end of 1874, the War Office reduced the

establishment to 12 Companies, and on October 31st, 1874, the four Companies returning the lowest percentage of efficients were transferred to other Companies.

The Regimental Badge was the White Tower of the Tower of London.

The uniform was changed to scarlet on the 14th November, 1874, when it was notified in Orders that the new scarlet uniforms had been approved by the War Office.

In undress, the Officers wore black frockcoats, very similar to the Guards, black trousers with an oak leaf pattern braid stripe, and cap with peak. The Officers' Mess uniform, when the Battalion was in grey, was a black jacket with rolled collar, red open waistcoat, black trousers with oak leaf braid stripe. This was changed to scarlet jacket, fastened at the collar, and blue waistcoat. A rolled collar jacket was adopted in 1897.

In July, 1894, the Glengarry cap worn in undress was replaced by the field service cap, which has been altered to meet the various changes from time to time.

In 1877 the localization scheme underwent revision, and the T.H.R.V.B. became a Volunteer Battalion of the Rifle Brigade. For purposes of drill and discipline, however, it—with the other Metropolitan Corps—formed part of a Volunteer Brigade, under the Colonel commanding the Scots Guards, as Brigadier. In 1889 it was transferred to the Grenadier Guards, and formed one of the Battalions of the East London Volunteer Infantry Brigade. In 1902, the Brigades were re-arranged, and the Battalion was posted to the 2nd London Volunteer Infantry Brigade, under the Irish Guards.

Colonel MELIOR, who had been appointed Honorary Colonel, 20th February, 1867, having died in June, 1886, Colonel G. H. MONCRIEFF, formally commanding the Scots Guards, now Lieutenant-General, was gazetted Honorary Colonel 24th July, 1886.

Lieutenant-Colonel J. HOLT resigned the command of the Battalion on the 30th June, 1876, and Lieutenant-Colonel J. H. MAPLESON assumed command.

On 2nd November, 1888, Lieutenant-Colonel J. H. MAPLESON retired from the command of the Battalion, and Lieutenant-Colonel C. WIGRAM took over the command.

On 22nd November, 1890, Colonel WIGRAM retired, and Colonel E. T. RODNEY WILDE succeeded to the command.

Major Vickers Dunfee was gazetted Lieutenant-Colonel on 2nd January, 1901.

Regulations were made in 1896 that Commanding Officers should hold command for four years only, all those then serving being considered as having been appointed in 1896. Colonel Wilde's term of command thus expired in November, 1900, when it was extended for a further two years, to 22nd November, 1902.

Colonel Vickers Dunfee was gazetted to command the Battalion on 4th February, 1903 ; he resigned on 3rd November, 1908.

In the Battalion Orders of the 23rd December, 1899, Volunteers were called for the City of London Volunteers, and the Battalion supplied 1 officer and 38 rank and file.

Two officers and 61 rank and file from the Battalion were also attached to other units in South Africa.

CHANGE OF DESIGNATION.
D.O., No. 105, 8th May, 1903.

It is notified for information that His Majesty the King has been graciously pleased to approve of the 1st Tower Hamlets Volunteer Rifle Corps being in future designated the 4th Volunteer Battalion, the Royal Fusiliers (City of London Regiment).

Authority : War Office Letter, No. V/10/94/238, dated 30/4/1903.

The Tower Hamlets Rifle Volunteer Brigade consequently ceased on 7th May, 1903, from which date it was known as The Fourth Volunteer Battalion, the Royal Fusiliers (City of London Regiment).

In January, 1904, the following Order was issued by the Army Council :

HONORARY DISTINCTIONS.

His Majesty the King has been graciously pleased to approve of the following Corps being permitted, in recognition of services rendered during the South African War, 1899-1902, to bear upon their appointments the words specified in each case :

4th V.B. The Royal Fusiliers (City of London Regiment)
South Africa, 1900.

These words now appear on the drums and colours

On 30th March, 1908, an ever memorable meeting was held at the Headquarters in Shaftesbury Street to celebrate the close of the Volunteer Force, and consequently the end of the Fourth Volunteer Battalion the Royal Fusiliers (City of London Regiment).

The strength of the Battalion was :

Officers	..	..	..	..	47
Sergeants	..	..	..	..	71
Rank and File	..	..	..	1,230
Total		..	..	..	1,348

The Territorial Army came into existence on 1st April, 1908, being formed from the old Volunteer Force, which had existed for nearly 50 years.

The Fourth (City of London) Battalion The London Regiment (Royal Fusiliers) was the title finally given, after several changes, to the organisation formerly known as the Fourth Volunteer Battalion Royal Fusiliers (City of London Regiment).

The Battalion was fortunate in keeping its number of " Fourth " and retaining the same Headquarters with its old historic associations.

On 30th September, 1908, the strength of the Territorial Regiment, including transfers and recruits, was :

Officers	..	..	..	..	32
N.C.O's. and Men		..	..	452

Many men transferred to the A.S.C. and R.A.M.C. and other mounted units then being formed.

On November 1st, 1908, Lieutenant-Colonel and Hon. Colonel VICKERS DUNFEE (Captain, Reserve of Officers) retired on completion of his period of service in command of the Battalion.

Colonel Vickers Dunfee, who had ably commanded the Battalion from February 14th, 1903, had carried out all the arrangements necessary on the change of designation to the 4th Volunteer Battalion Royal Fusiliers, and greatly increased the strength of the Battalion. He remained to give a satisfactory start to the Territorial Regiment.

Colonel Vickers Dunfee was a Military Member of the City of London Territorial Force Association.

Major HARRY DADE was promoted Lieutenant-Colonel on November 1st, 1908, and to command the Battalion

Major-General Sir D. Mercer, K.C.B.
Adjutant-General, Royal Marines

MRS. VICKERS DUNFEE

COLONEL VICKERS DUNFEE

MAJOR VICTOR H. SEYD

On June 19th, 1909, a representative detachment of the Battalion attended at Windsor to receive Colours at the hands of His late Majesty King Edward VII. These Colours are highly prized by every member of the Battalion.

FORMATION OF THE 2/4TH (CITY OF LONDON) BATTALION THE LONDON REGIMENT (ROYAL FUSILIERS).

On August 2nd, 1914, the 4th (City of London) Battalion the London Regiment (Royal Fusiliers) went into Camp at Wareham, in Hampshire, for its annual training, and arrived there at 2 p.m.

At 3 p.m. the same afternoon orders were received for the Battalion to return at once to Headquarters, 112, Shaftesbury Street, London.

With great promptitude the Battalion re-entrained, and eventually arrived at its Headquarters shortly after 1.30 a.m. on August 3rd.

The Battalion left London again at very short notice, and took up guard duties on a section of the London and South Western Railway, from Waterloo to Bentley Station, at 2 a.m. on August 4th.

These guard duties were carried out until August 31st, when the Battalion received orders to return to its Depôt and to be prepared to proceed overseas.

The Battalion left Shaftesbury Street at 1.30 a.m. on September 5th, and embarked for Malta.

A few hours before the Battalion left London, four officers were detailed by the War Office to remain at Headquarters to raise, train and equip a Reserve Battalion. The officers selected for this duty were Capt. E. H. STILLWELL, Capt. W. H. HAMILTON, Lieut. H. G. STANHAM, and Lieut. H. B. PARKHOUSE ; these officers, together with N.C.O's., formed the nucleus of the 4th Reserve Battalion, which was afterwards called the 2/4 (CITY OF LONDON) BATTALION THE LONDON REGIMENT (ROYAL FUSILIERS).

The duties devolved upon the officers left behind were such that it was necessary at once to organise their work. Capt. Stillwell took command as Senior Officer, Capt. Hamilton acted as Adjutant, Lieut. Stanham assisted Capt. Stillwell in training and organising the men, and Lieut. Parkhouse managed the canteen and other similar matters.

At the end of the first week 250 men had been enrolled in the new Battalion.

Recruits continued to flow in, and by September 15th (*i.e.*, a fortnight after the original Battalion had left for overseas) the numbers had increased to 500 men.

At this period it was found that the work to be done in training was impossible at the Depôt in Shaftesbury Street, and therefore the Executive sought to obtain larger premises and parade ground. After some preliminaries, the Authorities arranged that they should take over temporary quarters at Folly Farm, Hadley Wood.

It was also obvious that the four Officers already mentioned were inadequate in numbers to perform the work which had devolved upon them, and therefore they sought the guidance of friends and the assistance of the Territorial Association. The Association instructed them to carry on until 750 men had been raised and then doubtless a Colonel would be appointed.

When over 600 men had been enrolled, Capt. Stillwell and his brother officers felt that it was a pressing need to obtain the assistance of a Colonel and other officers as it was physically impossible to cope with the necessary work.

A friend, who knew that Colonel Vickers Dunfee had in previous years held the command of the Battalion, advised Capt. Stillwell to approach him and ask for his assistance and advice. Colonel Dunfee gave Capt. Stillwell a very sympathetic hearing, with an assurance that he would consider the matter and let him know what he thought was the best course to pursue.

The following announcements appeared in the *London Gazette :*

4TH (CITY OF LONDON) BATTALION LONDON REGIMENT (ROYAL FUSILIERS).

Lieut.-Col. and Hon. Col. Vickers Dunfee, Retired List (late of this Battalion) to be Lieut.-Col. with the Hon. rank of Col. (Temp.) September 6th, 1914.

Hon. Lieut. Edwin V. Wellby (late Lieut.-Col. 4th V.B. Royal Fusiliers, City of London Regt.) to be Capt. and Adjutant, October 6th, 1914.

Colonel VICKERS DUNFEE, V.D., took over command of the 2/4 (City of London) Battalion The London Regiment (Royal Fusiliers), and Capt. E. V. WELLBY was his Adjutant.

Colonel Vickers Dunfee, who is a member of the Court of Common Council of the City of London, commenced his military career many years ago as a Lieutenant in the well-known Royal London Militia, with which he served during two or three of its annual trainings ; he then resigned to take up a commission in the Tower Hamlets Rifle Volunteer Brigade. He was gazetted Lieutenant, September 6th, 1884; Captain, August 3rd, 1889 ; Major, December 15th, 1897 ; Lieut.-Col., January 2nd, 1901.

THE 2/4TH (CITY OF LONDON) BATTALION THE LONDON REGIMENT (ROYAL FUSILIERS)

September 23rd, 1914.

At 9 a.m., the Battalion, then about 500 strong, after having been inspected by the Lord Mayor, Sir T. VAN-SITTART BOWATER, left the Depot and marched to Folly Farm, New Barnet. Here the men were accommodated in marquees, and the officers were quartered in the farm buildings.

By the kind permission of the Corporation of London a Recruiting Depot was opened at the Guildhall. A special poster, in which the British, French, Russian, Belgian, and Japanese Flags were displayed in colours, was posted throughout the City, and recruits of a splendid type joined up.

September 24th, 1914.

Training was commenced at once. Reveille was sounded at 6 a.m., a two-miles' run or march, then breakfast ; drill, bathing parades, musketry instruction and minia-ture range occupied the mornings, with squad and platoon drill in the afternoons. An occasional night march finished a useful day's training.

A grant of £100 was made by the Corporation of London to the Battalion for expenses incidental to the establishment of the Camp.

Sir HOMEWOOD CRAWFORD presented the Regimental drum to the Band, and Mr. F. J. DICKINS presented the side-drums.

The Vintry Ward Club and many kind friends sub-scribed to cover the initial expenses of forming the Battalion.

7

October 19th, 1914.

The Battalion was now over 1000 strong, and was fully clothed in uniform, but no equipment had yet been issued.

Unfortunately only a few rifles were available for the Battalion, but these were judiciously allotted to each Company in turn, and all troops received instruction in arms, drill, etc.

October 20th, 1914.

The Commanding Officer was permitted to make his own arrangements for housing as the cold weather came on, and a fine mansion, " Littlegrove Barracks," was taken over through the kind assistance of its owner, Mr. W. A. Vernon, which accommodated about 500 men. This residence was at one time the property of David Woodroffe, a citizen and Alderman of the City, who had acquired it from Henry Parker, another City magnate, who had to sell it to pay debts incurred through the great fire of London.

Another mansion, " Beech Hill," was also used, and this accommodated about 450 men.

Both these houses were splendidly situated in large parks, which were well wooded, and gave excellent facilities for training troops.

A fine range of stabling with living rooms, etc., known as " Oakhill," was lent free of charge to the Battalion. " H " Company, under Capt. V. H. SEYD, was accommodated there.

The Battalion now took over its own catering, and, thanks to the experience of the Quartermaster, the men were excellently fed.

At Barnet the Battalion was received with the greatest kindness.

The local clergy opened resting rooms and halls for recreational purposes, lantern lectures, etc. ; ladies opened reading and refreshment rooms.

Norman Court School placed its swimming bath at the disposal of the Battalion.

Viscount and Lady Enfield and Sir Philip Sassoon lent their estates to the Battalion for drilling and training purposes, whilst the Enfield Rifle Club not only gave their range, but also supplied both instructors and prizes for the troops.

October 29th, 1914.

Col. Sir CHARLES WAKEFIELD inspected the Battalion at " Littlegrove Barracks," and after the inspection, addressed the Battalion. The following is an extract from his speech :

" I am greatly pleased with the inspection this morning. I have noticed that some inspecting officers pay a good deal of attention to boots and buttons ; I pay more attention to faces. I have been delighted to see the clean cut, determined and cheerful faces you all possess. I congratulate you very heartily on your soldierly bearing, and also upon having such a C.O. as my friend Col. Dunfee. He and I have been associated for many years with the Territorial movement. You have, I am sure, already found that the Colonel is a cheery commander. . . . I have often said that life at each stage has its recompenses. For the first time I envy you your youth ; most of us who have reached middle age have had a colourless and humdrum life, but you, in your youthful days, have an opportunity of making glorious history. You will be winners in a magnificent cause, and may you be richly blessed in your fight for your God, your Country, and your King."

November 9th, 1914.

A detachment of the Battalion, under Capt. LIMPENNY, took part in the Lord Mayor's Procession, and many of the officers of the Battalion were invited to the banquet at the Guildhall in the evening.

December 12th, 1914.

Orders were received for the Battalion to leave Barnet, where for over two months the troops had been undergoing strenuous training.

December 13th, 1914.

The Battalion attended Divine Service at Trent Church at 11 a.m.

C.O. inspected men's quarters after Church Parade.

Friends of the troops were allowed to visit " Littlegrove Barracks " on Sunday afternoons, and the large conservatory there was used for their reception.

December 14th, 1914.

The Battalion was inspected in the morning by the

Honorary Colonel of the Battalion, Lieut.-General G. H. MONCRIEFF.

At mid-day the Battalion entrained at East Barnet station in two special trains for Maidstone.

On arrival at Maidstone, officers and men were all billeted in private houses ; each Company was billeted as far as possible in the same road.

On leaving Barnet, the following letter was sent from the Battalion to the Chairman of East Barnet District Council :

" Sir,—In consequence of our sudden departure for another station, both officers and myself regret that we have not had time to call and personally thank the many friends we have made in this district for their great kindness to officers, N.C.O's. and men.

" The Battalion will ever remember with pleasure their stay in Barnet, and cherish pleasant memories of the consideration shown to all.

" I should also like to thank through you the members of the District Council and the Medical Officer for the ready assistance they have at all times accorded us.

" Yours sincerely,

" VICKERS DUNFEE, Colonel."

12th December, 1914.
LITTLEGROVE BARRACKS, EAST BARNET.

December 15th, 1914.

Orders were received that the Battalion was to be employed in the erection of earthworks and digging trenches for the defence of the South Downs.

All men not inoculated at Barnet underwent this protective treatment and were given 48 hours off duty.

December 17th, 1914.

Orders were received that the Battalion was to be medically examined for Foreign Service, and this examination took place at Maidstone Barracks.

Major-General W. FRY, C.B., C.V.O., inspected and addressed the Battalion.

A special train from Woolwich with new web equipment arrived for the Battalion ; this equipment was at once issued to all Companies, and instruction was speedily given in fixing this new kit together.

As the Battalion was shortly to proceed overseas, forty-eight hours' leave was granted to all ranks, and all took this advantage of saying " Good-bye " to their relations and friends at home.

December 23rd, 1914.

The Battalion entrained at Maidstone in two special trains, which left at 10 a.m. and 10.30 a.m. respectively, and proceeded via Redhill and Guildford to Southampton Docks. Dinner was served *en route*.

Kit bags and luggage of the Battalion were speedily put on board H.T. " Avon," which until recently had been running on the South American service of the Royal Mail Steam Packet Co., Ltd. Unfortunately no accommodation had been provided for officers' chargers, and these had to be left behind.

Lieut.-Col. TEMPEST STONE superintended the embarkation of the Battalion at Southampton. This officer had been Adjutant to the 1/4 Battalion, and he received a most cordial greeting from all his old friends.

General Sir IAN HAMILTON, G.C.B., D.S.O., sent the following telegram to the C.O. at Southampton :

" Had arranged to go down and see your Battalion ; unfortunately situation renders imperative my presence at H.Q. Can only therefore wish you best of good fortune and hope we may meet again."

The C.O. replied as follows :

" My Battalion greatly appreciates your kind message."

The following officers, for various reasons, were unable to sail with the Battalion :

Major W. H. HAMILTON.
Major E. H. STILLWELL.
Capt. E. V. WELLBY.
Capt. A. E. WOOD.
Capt. S. W. J. LIMPENNY.
2/Lieut. C. BISHOP.
2/Lieut. GATHERGOOD.

Before leaving Maidstone the following letter was sent by the Mayor of Maidstone to the Battalion :

" I should like to place on record my high appreciation of the splendid way in which the 3rd and 4th Battalions

City of London Regiment have conducted themselves during their stay in Maidstone, and I can assure you that I voice the townspeople when I say that I am sorry you are leaving us. In the name of the County Town I wish you all God Speed and Good Luck.

" Yours sincerely,

" W. H. MARTIN, Mayor.

" *December 23rd*, 1914.
" TOWN HALL, MAIDSTONE."

The C.O. replied to the Mayor of Maidstone as follows :

" The 3rd and 4th Battalions City of London Regiment have received such a hearty welcome and so much kindness from the inhabitants of Maidstone during the stay in their historic town, that both officers and men would not like to leave without expressing their warmest thanks for the hospitality and friendship so cordially extended to them, and I trust that the behaviour of all ranks has been such that should these Battalions again visit the town an equally warm welcome will await them.

" VICKERS DUNFEE.

" *December 23rd*, 1914."

The following statement appeared in the *Kentish Mercury*:

" On behalf of the inhabitants of Maidstone we can assure Col. Vickers Dunfee that the behaviour of the two Battalions created a highly favourable impression on the town."

At about 5 p.m. H.T. " Avon," with Capt. J. TRIGG, R.N.R., in charge, left Southampton Docks, and the Regimental Band played " Auld Lang Syne " and other well-known tunes.

In addition to the 4th Battalion London Regiment, half of the 3rd Battalion also embarked on the transport, making a total strength of 33 officers and 1,134 other ranks as follows :

| 2/4 Battn. | 27 officers | 889 other ranks. |
| 2/3 Battn. | 6 officers | 245 other ranks. |

Troops were divided up into messes of 15, and tea was served soon after leaving port ; after tea, troops drew blankets and hammocks from the stores at the bottom of

GROUP OF OFFICERS, 2/4 CITY OF LONDON REGIMENT, R.F., FLORIANA, 2nd MAY, 1915

Lt.H.W.Dennis. Lt.J.E.W.Lambley. Lt.F.R.C.Bradford. Lt.N.Il.Thomas. Lt.S.N.Davies. Lt.I.G.Lovell. Lt.W.A.Stark. Lt.W.R.Botterill. Lt.H.W.Vernon.
Lt.D.Giannacopulo. Lt.R.N.Keen. Lt.A.H.Simpson. Capt.H.G.Stanham. Capt.H.Morris. Lt.W.H.Stevens. Capt.W.N.Towse. Capt.F.C.Read. Lt.R.C.Dickens.
Capt.G.H.Moore. Major V,G.Seyd. Brig.Genl.Earl of Lucan. Col.V.Dunfee,V.D. Major R.F.Legge. Major J.F.F.Parr. Capt.L.C.Coates.

The Battalion marching past Sir Peter McBride, Agent-General, South Australia

Littlegrove Barracks, New Barnet

Quarter Guard. Littlegrove Barracks

the ship's hold ; hammocks were strung up from hooks on the rafters in the mess rooms.

The following appointments were made for the duration of the voyage out :

O.C. Ship	Col. Vickers Dunfee.
Ship's Adjutant	Capt. W. G. Hayward.
Ship's Q.-Master	Lieut. Lambley.

The following routine was strictly carried out during the voyage :

TIME.	BUGLE CALLS.	MEANING.
6 a.m.	Réveillé	Turn out and stow Hammocks.
6.30	Ration	Orderlies draw meal allowance.
7.15	Breakfast	Draw and sit down to breakfast.
7.45	Fatigue	All cleaning, fatigues parade. Troop decks cleared by police.
8.0	Guard fall in	Mount Guard.
9.30	Four G's.	Sweepers parade and sweep upper decks.
10.0	Assembly	General Parade and Inspection of Troop Decks.
10.30	Orderly Room	Orderly Room.
11.0	——	Issue of beer. Troops allowed below.
Noon	Dinner	Draw and sit down to dinner.
1 p.m.	Four G's.	Sweepers parade and sweep upper decks. Troop decks cleared and swept.
2.0.	——	Troops allowed below.
5.0	Tea	Draw and sit down to tea.
5.30	Four G's.	Sweepers parade and sweep upper decks.
6.0	Warning for Parade	Draw Hammocks.
6.30	——	Troops allowed below.
8.30	Four G's.	Sweepers parade and sweep upper decks.
9.0	Lights out	Stop smoking, and everyone except Guard and Police go below.
9.15	——	Rounds ; every man to be in bed
11.0	——	Lights out in Saloon.

13

GENERAL CALLS.

Stand fast	Silence—every one to remain still.
Continue	Carry on.
Retire	Everyone off upper deck but the Guard.
Four G's.	Sweepers.
4 G's. & Double	Swabbers.
Alarm	Man overboard.
Charge	Permission to smoke.
Lights out	Leave off smoking.
Fire Alarm	Fire and Collision.

December 24th, 1914.

At daybreak H.T. " Avon " picked up her escort, H.M.S. " Eclipse " and H.T. " Euralia," with the remaining half Battalion of the 2/3 Battalion and the whole of the 2/2 Battalion on board ; these three vessels kept together until the Mediterranean was reached.

The coast of Devon and Cornwall was visible to starboard during the morning.

Sea turned rather rough in the afternoon, and rain fell heavily.

Ship's run, 194 miles.

December 25th, 1914—CHRISTMAS DAY.

Sea was rough, and the boat rolled very badly.

Capt. TRIGG, R.N.R., took Divine Service on deck in the morning.

Greetings were exchanged between our sister transport and our escort.

Troops had Christmas dinner at mid-day, as follows :

Soup.
Roast Beef.
Cabbage, Cauliflower, Potatoes.
Christmas Pudding.
Oranges, Apples, Nuts.

The Christmas puddings were provided by the City of London, and were greatly appreciated. Unfortunately for the other transport, " Euralia," we had their puddings on our ship, so that this part of their Christmas dinner had to be deferred until we arrived at Malta.

In the evening the officers of the Battalions and those of the ship dined together. The menu was as follows :

CHRISTMAS DINNER.
Caviar à la Russe.
Clear Turtle.
Boiled Salmon, Geneoise Sauce.
Lamb Cutlets, Petit Pios.
Asparagus au Beurre.
Roast Beef, Yorkshire Pudding.
Turkey with Bath Chap.
Boiled and Baked Potatoes.
Cauliflower.

Plum Pudding.	Mince Pies.

Orange Jelly.

Welsh Rarebit.	Baked Chestnuts.
Cheese.	Dessert.

Coffee.

The C.O. gave the health of the Captain of the ship, and, in reply, Captain TRIGG expressed a hope that he would have the good fortune to take the Battalion home again after the war had been successfully concluded.

As all lights had to be shaded on board until the Mediterranean was reached, no concert could be held.

Ship's run, 276 miles.

December 26th, 1914.

Weather improved and sea was calmer. Troops paraded on deck by Companies.

The accommodation on board for the men was not good, and permission was given for some to sleep on deck at night.

Ship's run, 276 miles.

December 27th, 1914.

Weather turned very fine, and sun was getting quite warm during the day. Troops experienced a magnificent sunrise : the coloured tints of the morning clouds and the reflection of them in the sea were gorgeous.

Divine Service was held on deck in the morning ; Colonel Vickers Dunfee took the Service.

In the afternoon Portugal was sighted on our port bow, and the headland of Cape St. Vincent was quite visible.

15

Days were now gradually lengthening out, and it was possible for one to read on deck up to 5.30 p.m.

Ship's log registered over 280 miles for the day.

December 28th, 1914.

In the very early morning land was again visible on both sides of the boat ; on the port side Spain was seen, and to starboard North Africa. The atmosphere was very clear indeed, and Sirius, the Dog Star, appeared more like a moon than a star.

Transport passed Mt. Atlas at about 5.30 a.m., and the effect of the rising sun on this mountain was magnificent. At 7.30 a.m. the famous Rock of Gibraltar, standing grandly at the mouth of the Mediterranean, was approached. H.T. " Avon " dropped anchor for about two hours, and a signal that the transport carried despatches was run up at the masthead.

Who on board will forget the tale of how we landed our despatches ? It can be told, but it must not be written.

We weighed anchor at 9.30 a.m. and steamed practically due East, passing a fine range of mountains, tipped with snow, on the Spanish mainland.

Our escort, H.M.S. " Eclipse," did not accompany us farther than Gibraltar.

The sun was quite hot now, and bathing on deck took place in the afternoons, many officers and men taking advantage of a good " shower " of sea water from hoses attached to the ship's salt water tanks.

Sleeping on deck was now very agreeable, and hammocks were slung up in parts of the ship's rigging.

As the ship was now travelling East, the clocks on board had to be altered daily accordingly.

Troops were exercised in marching round the promenade deck and where space would permit, physical training was also carried out. Classes for officers were held, and the Adjutant, Capt. W. G. HAYWARD, took the opportunity of examining junior N.C.O's. with a view to promotion.

Lights were now allowed on deck at night.

December 29th, 1914.

Weather was inclined to be showery, but the temperature still remained comfortable. The Algerian coast was

Garrison Duties.   Parading at Sporting Club Camp, Alexandria

The Battalion under canvas, Chain Tuffieha, Malta

2/4 London Regiment R.F., on the Parade Ground, Floriana Barracks, *Valetta*, Malta

visible most of the day, and in the afternoon the sun broke through just as we were passing the town of Algiers. From the transport most of the houses and mosques appeared to be made of white stone and sand, and at this distance they looked quite nice and respectable ; the small railway there was also quite plainly seen.

In the evening a Concert was held on deck, and was greatly appreciated by both officers and men. The programme was as follows :

Selection	Regimental Brass Band 2/4th Battalion.
Pianoforte Solo	Pte. Maystone
" Little Grey Home in the West "	Pte. Press
" Songs of Araby "	Pte. White
" Spaniard that blighted my Life "	Pte. Heath
Song	Pte. Cogger
Child Impersonations ..	Pte. Parslow.
" Chesapeake Bay "	Pte. Tunstall.
" Friend of Mine "	Pte. Russell
" Asleep in the Deep " ..	Pte. Blofield
" Land of Hope and Glory " ..	Pte. Ratcliffe
" I followed her there " ..	Pte. Moseley
" The Trumpeter "	Pte. Flowers
Selection	Pte. Gollop
" Green Eye of the Little Yellow God "	Pte. A. Smith
Song	2nd Lieut. Davies
Song	Capt. W. G. Hayward
Song	2nd Lieut. Hartman
Accompanist	Pte. Knight

God Save the King.

December 30th, 1914.

Weather was fine and sun very hot. African coast was visible the whole of the day.

Troops paraded in full marching order, and marched round promenade deck.

The Captain of the ship made arrangements so that parties of officers and N.C.O's. could go all over the ship's engine-rooms and see how the twin-screws worked.

December 31st, 1914.

Weather was perfect.

All troops were awake very early, and as soon as light

permitted we sighted the Island of Gozo, and later Malta. For some time H.T. "Avon" lay outside the Grand Harbour of Valetta, but at about 12 noon she came in and anchored in mid-stream.

Inside the harbour we found a fleet of French warships, etc., and as we passed each boat we heartily cheered the "froggies," and they in return cheered us. Before even out transport had anchored, numbers of small boats crowded round us with all manner of fruits, sweetmeats, etc., for sale, and quite a good business was done by means of a small basket attached to a long rope.

Brigadier-General the Earl of Lucan came on board and greeted us, and during the afternoon officers were permitted to go ashore.

The men spent their time in watching the crowded harbour and in investing in souvenirs.

January 1st, 1915.

The troops remained on board all day.

The Commanding Officer, with the Adjutant and Company Officers, were received by the Brigadier at Brigade Headquarters.

January 2nd, 1915.

Orders were received for troops to disembark from the transport.

The half Battalion of the 2/3 Battalion left the ship first, and at 10 a.m. the 2/4 Battalion was taken on lighters to the landing stage ; on arrival the Battalion was formed up and marched to St. George's Barracks, about 4 miles distant along the coast. The Barracks were beautifully situated quite close to the sea, and on arrival there Companies were told off to their respective quarters, where every man made a minute inspection of his barrack room, and particularly his iron bedstead.

Major J. F. PARR, R.A.M.C., joined the Battalion for duty.

January 3rd, 1915.

Capt. R. N. ARTHUR and Lieut. V. W. EDWARDS, together with a number of men, left behind by the 1/4 Battalion, reported for duty ; this party made the Battalion up to 1,000 strong.

Long rifles and side-arms were issued to all ranks of the Battalion.

January 5th, 1915.
The Battalion commenced a Recruits' and Trained Men's course of Musketry on the Pembroke Ranges, which were situated quite close to the barracks. Physical drill was carried out before breakfast.

Sergt.-Instructor STACEY, R.M.L.I., and Sergt.-Instructor MASTERS, R.M.L.I., were attached to the Battalion as Musketry Instructors, and Bombardier D. H. COX, R.G.A., reported for duty as Bayonet Fighting and Physical Drill Instructor.

January 10th, 1915.
The Battalion attended Divine Service in St. Andrew's Barracks. After the service the Commanding Officer inspected the barracks.

The promotion of Capt. V. H. SEYD to Major was officially announced, and all ranks expressed their gratification.

January 17th, 1915.
Battalion attended Divine Service, which was held on the Battalion parade ground. After the service, the Commanding Officer inspected all barrack rooms, kitchens, etc. At this inspection all N.C.O's. and men had to lay out all their kit in uniform manner.

January 18th, 1915.
The Regimental Band commenced a class of instruction in ambulance work at St. Andrew's Barracks.

A Reading Room, with Library, was opened nightly, and stationery was provided for N.C.O.'s. and men under the direction of the Battalion librarian, Corp. ROBINSON.

Inter-Company League Football Matches were played with results as follows :

" A " Company, 1 goal *v.* " C " Company, 1 gaol.

" E " Company, 2 goals *v.* " G " Company, nil.

January 19th, 1915.
A lecture by the Brigade Major on " The Discipline and Brigade in Attack " was given to all officers, N.C.O's. and selected privates of the Battalion in the Recreation Room.

One or two short rifles were allotted to the Battalion
for instructional purposes ; great keenness was shown
amongst the troops over this new rifle, and voluntary
classes were held in the evenings under the Sergeant-
Instructors.

January 23*rd*, 1915.
The Battalion, which up to the present had been composed of eight companies, was reconstructed to comply
with a new War Office order that a Battalion should consist of four Companies. The following amalgamations,
therefore, took place :

" A " and " B " Coys. were amalgamated and comprised a new " A " Coy.
" C " and " D " Coys. were amalgamated and comprised a new " B " Coy.
" E " and " F " Coys. were amalgamated and comprised a new " C " Coy.
" G " and " H " Coys. were amalgamated and comprised a new " D " Coy.

Tom Burrows gave an exhibition of Club Swinging
to the Battalion ; he completed 1,400 revolutions in 14
minutes. The entertainment concluded with a Boxing
Competition, the Battalion putting up some light weights.

January 24*th*, 1915.
A Course of Instruction in Machine Gun Training
was commenced under Lieut. SIMPSON.
The Regimental bandsmen attended, under Major J.
F. PARR, R.A.M.C., for instruction in First Aid.
Col. VICKERS DUNFEE was invited to Admiralty House.

January 26*th*, 1915.
The Battalion, with bands, marched in full marching
order from St. George's Barracks to the Marsa, a flat, grassy
stretch of land, where platoon training was carried out.
In the evening Brigadier-General the Earl of Lucan,
with his Staff, dined at the Officers' Mess.

January 29*th*, 1915.
Capt. R. N. ARTHUR, with a detachment from the

Battalion, proceeded to Vadala to guard a large number of German prisoners, military and civil, who were detained there. These prisoners included Capt. Herr von Muller, Prince Hohenzollern, and the crew of the "Emden."

A football match took place on the Marsa between the right-half and left-half Battalion. The right-half Battalion won by 3 goals to nil.

At 7 p.m. a whist drive was held in the Recreation Room at St. George's Barracks.

February 1st, 2nd and 3rd, 1915.

A storm was experienced with very high seas ; ferry boats in the harbours stopped running.

February 4th, 1915.

A tactical march and outpost scheme were carried out. The Battalion left St. George's Barracks at 9 a.m. and moved in three columns to the old-fashioned town of Gargur, with its little narrow streets, and halted in the square in front of the church. From here companies moved out to the outpost line, where positions were taken up and dinners were cooked by the men themselves.

The Battalion returned to barracks at 7. a.m. the following morning.

February 6th, 1915.

Drivers from the Battalion Transport Section were sent by route march to MUSTA FORT and commenced a course of instruction in A.S.C. duties.

The Battalion played a football match against the Royal Navy, and won by 2 goals to nil.

February 9th, 1915.

The guard at the Governor's Palace, Valetta was found by the Battalion for the first time. Lieut. L. C. COATES was in charge. The Battalion also provided guards for the Wireless Station and other important Government depôts, etc., in the harbour at Valetta.

February 10th, 1915.

Anniversary of the shipwreck of St. Paul at Melita, and the day was kept as a general holiday, all shops and banks being closed in Malta. In Valetta religious processions of the various Religious Orders with banners, crosses, etc., took place, and were followed by a large statue of St. Paul, which was carried by 20 members of the Maltese nobility.

February 11th, 1915.

Réveillé was sounded at 5 a.m., and preparations were at once made to hand over St. George's Barracks to the 2/1 Battalion London Regiment. All rooms and kitchens were thoroughly cleaned, and the Battalion marched out at 9 a.m., and proceeded to Floriana Barracks, in Valetta.

On arrival at Floriana Barracks, the Battalion was formed up in mass on the parade ground and rifles were piled. The 2/1 Battalion was also on this parade ground and, on departing for St. George's Barracks, it was given an enthusiastic send-off.

All officers and men soon settled down in their new quarters.

February 12th, 1915.

The guard found from the Battalion at the Governor's Palace was relieved by another guard from the 2/4th, under Lieut. S. N. DAVIES.

In the evening, H. E. The Governor, Sir LESLIE RUNDLE, G.C.B., G.C.V.O., K.C.M.G., D.S.O., and Staff left Malta for England. The Malta Militia found a guard of honour, and the Garrison Artillery another. A salute was fired from the saluting battery and from a cruiser in the harbour.

February 14th, 1915.

The Battalion attended Divine Service at the Barraca Garrison Church at 11 a.m.

The new Governor, Field-Marshal LORD METHUEN, G.C.B., G.C.V.O., C.M.G., arrived with Staff and was received at the Palace Valetta.

The following constituted the Staff at Malta :
Field-Marshal Lord Methuen, G.C.B., G.C.V.O., C.M.G.
A.D.C. Lord Windsor.
Col. A.D.C. Capt. Castelletti, M.V.O.
G.S.O. Major A. J. H. Keyes.
A.A. and Q.M.G. Major W. S. W. Radcliffe.
O.C.R.A. Major-General J. S. S. Barker, C.B.
G.O.C.Inf. Brig.-General The Earl of Lucan.
O.C. Dockyd. Vice-Admiral A. H. Limpus, C.B., R.N.

A new hydroplane from a cruiser took a flight in the harbour, with not altogether successful results.

February 17th, 1915.
H.E. Lord METHUEN visited the Battalion and watched the training.

The Battalion played a football match against the Eastern Telegraph Company, and won by 3 goals to 1.

February 19th, 1915.
The Battalion was issued with khaki drill clothing and sun helmets.

Companies in turn went to Ghain Tuffieha for a course on trench digging, etc.

February 24th, 1915.
Capt. W. G. HAYWARD, the Adjutant of the Battalion, was admitted into Cottonera Hospital.

Large numbers of transports were arriving and leaving the harbour daily.

A class of instruction in map reading for officers and N.C.O.'s. under Schoolmaster BAKER, was commenced in Floriana School in the evenings.

February 27th, 1915.
In consequence of a strike at the Docks the Battalion was confined to barracks.

The Machine Gun Section of the Battalion, which was at Pembroke ranges undergoing a course of field training, was ordered to return at once to Valetta, and H.E. the Governor expressed his great pleasure at the smart way in which Lieut. A. SIMPSON brought this section to Floriana Barracks on receipt of the order that the Battalion might be required at short notice.

The guard of the Battalion, under Lieut. L. A. DICKINS, at the Palace, was inspected by H.E. the Governor.

March 4th, 1915.
The Battalion played a football match against the 2/2 Battalion. Each team included two officers, and Lieut. STEVENS and Lieut. BOWATER played for us. The match ended in a draw, 1 goal being scored by each team.

A Regimental Assault-at-Arms was held at the Gymnasium, Valetta, in the evening.

March 11th, 1915.

At this period Company training was being carried out on the Marsa, the artillery ranges at Pembroke and around villages near Valetta.

Some Maltese were prosecuted at Valetta for buying or stealing food, the property of the Battalion.

March 13th, 1915.

The Regimental Transport Section, under Lieut. DENNIS, was inspected by O.C. A.S.C. on the Floriana parade ground.

In the afternoon H.E. the Governor inspected the Malta Boy Scouts on the Palace Square, and presented them with Colours. The Palace guard, under Lieut. L. A. DICKINS turned out for the ceremony.

The Commanding Officer dined with Lord and Lady Lucan in the evening.

March 17th, 1915.

Lieut. L. A. DICKINS proceeded to the 2/1 Battalion to undergo a course of machine gun instruction.

H.E. the Governor and the Hon. Seymour Methuen gave a dinner party at the Palace, to which the following ladies and gentlemen were invited :

The Hon. T. Vella and Mrs. Vella, the Hon. E. Bonavia and Mrs. Bonavia, the Marquis and Marchioness Apap Bologna, Col. H. Spencer, Col. J. L. Francia, Mrs. Francia and Miss Francia, the Hon. Angela Baring, Col. Vickers Dunfee, Col. Bendall, Col. and Mrs. A. E. Weld, Major and Mrs. Radcliffe, Major and Mrs. Lewis Hall, Lord Windsor, A.D.C., Capt. Marchall Roberts, A.D.C., and Capt. the Contino Teuma Castelletti, Colonial A.D.C.

After dinner a musical programme was executed by Chev. C. de Lancellotti's Quartette and artistes of the Royal Opera.

March 18th, 1915.

Colonel VICKERS DUNFEE, as Commandant of the Garrison School, was present at the distribution of prizes to the children, Mrs. MORRIS, wife of Capt. H. MORRIS, of the Battalion, presented the prizes. After the distribution, Army Schoolmaster BAKER tendered the thanks of the School to Mrs. Morris for being present.

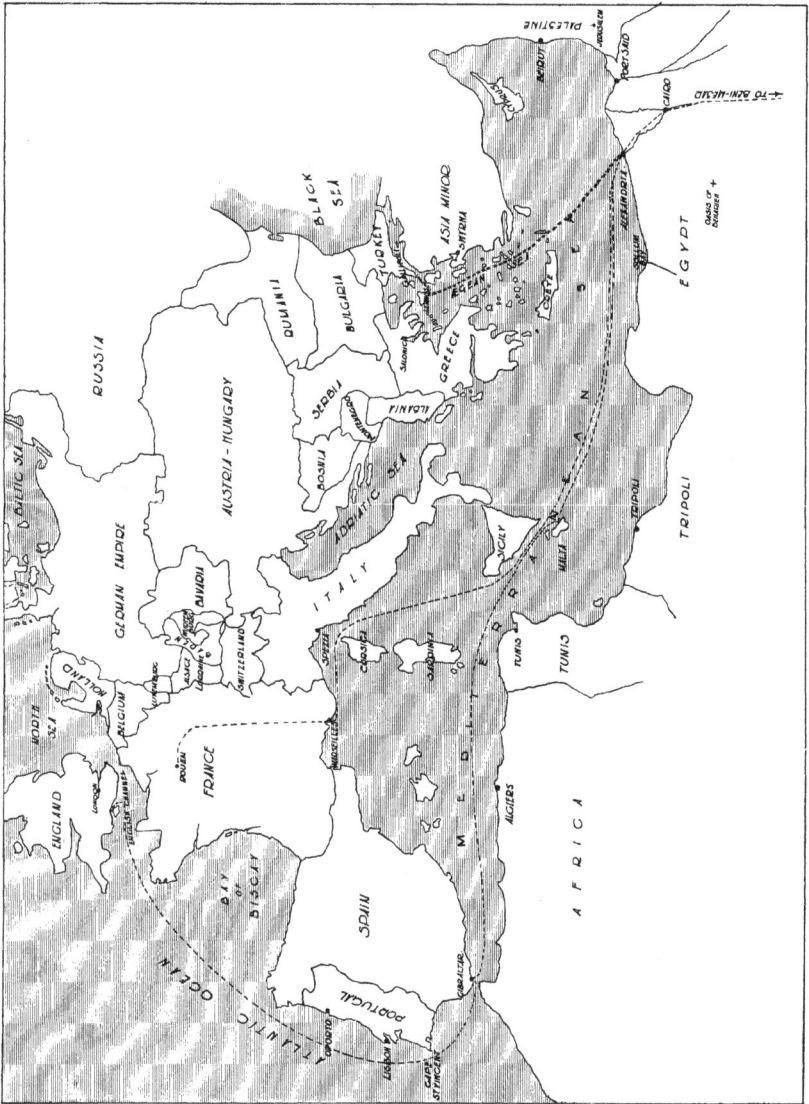

RUSSIA

GERMAN EMPIRE

BALTIC SEA

ENGLAND

HOLLAND

BELGIUM

FRANCE

SWITZERLAND

SPAIN

PORTUGAL

ATLANTIC OCEAN

BAY OF BISCAY

CAPE ST. VINCENT

GIBRALTAR

MEDITERRANEAN

AFRICA

ALGIERS

TUNIS

TRIPOLI

ITALY

AUSTRIA-HUNGARY

ROUMANIA

BULGARIA

SERBIA

ALBANIA

GREECE

TURKEY

ASIA MINOR

BLACK SEA

ADRIATIC SEA

AEGEAN

CRETE

EGYPT

PALESTINE

ALEXANDRIA

CAIRO

TO BENI-MEZAB

Oasis of + bouzes +

March 19th, 1915.

Colonel H. SPENCER was appointed Censor, and the Battalion received the greatest kindness and assistance from him during their stay at Malta.

In the evening the 2/3 Battalion gave a dinner at Imtarfa Barracks to H.E. the Governor and Commanding Officers of the three other Battalions of the London Regiment.

March 20th, 1915.

H.E. the Governor inspected Floriana Barracks.

A railway runs from Valetta inland to Citta Vecchia, and on Thursday and Saturday afternoons this railway was much used by all ranks for visiting the ancient capital of Malta, etc.

March 25th, 1915.

A course of instruction in the use of the Marindin Range-finding instrument was commenced under Sergt.-Instructor PRISCOTT, R.M.L.I.

A transport with the South Wales Borderers came into harbour on their way to the East, and Capt. TIPPITTS dined in the Officers' Mess.

March 26th, 1915.

H.E. the Governor moved from the Palace in Valetta to the Palace of St. Antonio ; the Palace guard was now mounted with a Sergeant in charge instead of an Officer as heretofore.

A parcel of 500 books from the Camps Library was received by the Battalion. These books were made good use of, and 250 were ultimately taken to Gallipoli, and the remaining 250 were left in Malta for the Convalescent Camps.

March 31st, 1915.

Army Schoolmaster BAKER died suddenly, to the great regret of all ranks, and especially of his pupils, with whom he was most popular. A military funeral was accorded him, and the Battalion provided a firing party of 1 Sergeant and 25 men. His coffin was taken to the cemetery on a gun carriage drawn by four mules, and the Regimental Brass Band headed the procession.

Colonel VICKERS DUNFEE and Lieut. L. C. COATES were present at the internment at Rinella Cemetery.

Capt. W. G. HAYWARD was invalided to England on the hospital ship " Plessey," and Lieut. L. C. COATES took over the duties of Adjutant to the Battalion.

April 2nd, 1915—GOOD FRIDAY.

The Battalion attended Divine Service at Barracca Garrison Church ; H.E. the Governor and Staff were present.

There was a religious procession through Valetta.

April 5th, 1915—EASTER MONDAY.

There was no holiday for the troops. The usual routine Company training, etc., was carried out.

A tablet was placed in the courtyard of the Officers' Mess to commemorate the stay of the Battalion in Floriana Barracks.

April 8th, 1915.

The 2/3 Battalion left Malta for Egypt *en route* for Khartoum. Colonel BENDALL and the Battalion had a very enthusiastic send-off on embarking at Valetta.

Colonel VICKERS DUNFEE, Major J. F. PARR and Capt. H. MORRIS were installed Knights Templar and Priory Knights of Malta in the Hall of the Order, 6, Strada Marsamuscetto, Valetta.

In the evening a concert was held at Valetta Gymnasium, under the presidency of Major V. H. SEYD.

April 10th, 1915.

The long-deferred picnic to the children of the Garrison Schools took place at Pembroke. Mrs. Hartmann and Mrs. Morris kindly provided the tea, and the children were conveyed out and home again on A.S.C. wagons.

Lieut. & Qr.-Master LAMBLEY made all arrangements for the tea, and Major V. H. SEYD organised the games for the children.

April 12th, 1915.

A medical examination took place of all officers and men of the Battalion with a view to their suitability for further service.

Half Battalion of Maoris arrived from Egypt. These Maoris were fine, tall and well set up fellows, but they were said to be some of the smallest species of this famous New Zealand tribe. They marched from Valetta to Ghain Tuffieha, where they encamped.

The Masonic Lodge of St. John and St. Paul, No. 349 E.C., under the Worshipful Brother J. M. ARNAUD, celebrated its centenary, and several officers of the Battalion were present.

The Worshipful Brother read a history of the Lodge, relating the early difficulties and important episodes which occurred since its consecration in 1815.

April 15th and 16th, 1915.

The Battalion carried out an all-night outpost scheme.

In the evening of the 16th the Battalion gave a concert at the Valetta Gymnasium in aid of the widow and family of the late Schoolmaster Baker. The concert was most successful, and realised £50.

April 18th, 1915.

His Grace the new CARDINAL ARCHBISHOP made his solemn entry into Notabile and drove from Valetta, accompanied by his suite.

At the entrance to the City he was met by the local band, and proceeded to the Piazza Sakkaja, where he received an address. Preceded by another band His Grace went to the Convent of the Rev. Fathers of the Order of Preachers, where, from the most remote times, Bishops have stayed on the night before making their entry to the Church.

In the evening the Cathedral and City were illuminated.

April 19th, 1915.

In the morning His Grace the ARCHBISHOP rode from the Convent, preceded by his Cross-bearer on horseback, clad in his pontifical robes, to the Cathedral ; His Grace was mounted on a white mare, under a canopy borne by eight members of the Maltese nobility. On entering the Cathedral the Archbishop celebrated Pontifical Mass.

The festivities concluded with horse races.

Colonel Driscoll, with the 25th Service Battalion R.F. (Legion of Frontiersmen), came into Valetta Harbour on their way to East Africa.

April 20th and 21st, 1915.

The Battalion carried out an all-night march and out-post scheme, under the orders of Major V. H. SEYD.

Colonel VICKERS DUNFEE and other brethren attended the Installation of W.M.E. Brother E. H. MORRIS in the Chair of the Waller Rodwell Wright Lodge, No. 2755 E.C.

In the evening of the 21st, H.E. the Governor, with his A.D.C., Lord WINDSOR, dined at the Officers' Mess, Floriana Barracks.

April 24th, 1915.

The final football match (Inter-Company) took place between the old " E " and " H " Companies ; " E " Company won by 1 goal to nil.

After the match each member of the winning team was presented with a specially fitted knife by the Command-ing Officer.

In the evening a Whist Drive was held for the Battalion in the Recreation Room.

Capt. F. C. J. READ designed and painted a copy of the Regimental Badge in the officers' quarters of the Main Guard at Valetta.

April 27th, 1915.

Night operations were carried out by the Battalion.

A detachment of the Battalion, consisting of three officers and 100 other ranks, under Capt. H. G. STANHAM, proceeded to the 9th Mile Stone for guard duties.

April 30th, 1915.

The following is an extract from Battalion Orders :

" The G.O.C. wishes to place on record his appreci-ation of the prompt and courageous act of Pte. V. W. ALLEN, " C " Company, in stopping a runaway horse on the 27th April, 1915."

The W.O's. and Sergeants of the Battalion gave a supper and concert in the Sergeants' Mess.

May 2nd, 1915.

Bathing was commenced at Malta, and swimming classes were started in the Battalion.

Six officers from the Royal Engineers were attached to the Battalion for two weeks' infantry training.

May 5th, 1915.

Wounded troops from Gallipoli were now being sent to Malta, and the Regimental Band, which had been specially trained in stretcher work, was occupied daily in unloading them in the harbour.

The Battalion carried out a long night march with tactical scheme from 4 p.m. to 7 a.m. the following morning. The scheme was set by Lord LUCAN, and all Battalions of the Brigade took part in it.

May 8th, 1915.

The Battalion paid a last token of respect to the remains of the late Capt. E. S. STEPHENSON, D.S.O., Gloucester Regiment, and provided a firing party of 100 men. Most of the officers of the Battalion attended the funeral.

May 11th, 1915.

The Battalion carried out a tactical march and outpost scheme at MALLEA BAY. The Battalion left Valetta at 7 a.m. and reached MALLEA HEIGHTS, 17 miles distant, at 1.30 p.m.

The Battalion returned to Floriana Barracks by 12 noon the following day.

May 14th, 1915.

A Brigade Field Day took place, and the Battalion covered 27 miles in full marching order.

The S.Y. " Erin," with Sir Thomas Lipton on board, came into Malta Harbour.

May 17th, 1915.

Major J. F. PARR, R.A.M.C., who had been Medical Officer to the Battalion since its arrival in Malta, left for England ; he took with him the best wishes of all ranks.

May 18th, 1915.

The Battalion carried out a tactical scheme, under orders issued by Major V. H. SEYD.

A Bayonet Fighting Class was commenced for officers.

Lieut. L. H. W. WILLIAMS, R.A.M.C., acted as Medical Officer to the Battalion.

May 22nd, 1915.

The Regimental Band commenced playing at the different hospitals in Malta.

Battalion Sports were held on the Marsa, and proved very successful. Officers and Sergeants entertained parties at tea, which was served on the Sports Ground.

May 23rd, 1915.

The news of the declaration of war by ITALY was received, and an Italian torpedo-boat, with despatches, arrived in the harbour.

The chief Town Band paraded the streets of Valetta carrying the flags of Italy and the Allies. Opposite the Grand Master's Palace, the residence of Lord METHUEN, the National Anthems were played, and Commendatore CARRARA, the Italian Consul-General, made a patriotic speech.

May 25th, 1915.

Owing to a great number of wounded arriving from Gallipoli, and there being only a very limited amount of accommodation on the Island for them, the Battalion evacuated Floriana Barracks and pitched a camp on the Parade Ground.

May 28th, 1915.

A Brigade Staff Tour was held for officers of all the Battalions ; the mode of conveyance was varied : 15 officers rode bicycles, 20 officers were on horseback, whilst 4 cabs and 3 motor cars were also used. Lunch was served at Pretty Bay.

May 29th, 1915.

A Concert was held in the Opera House, Valetta, under the patronage of H.E. the GOVERNOR and COMMANDER-IN-CHIEF.Lieut. S. N. DAVIES, 2/4 Battalion, contributed to the programme, and the concert proved a big success. The proceeds went to the wounded in Malta.

May 31st, 1915.

A Class of Instruction for N.C.O.'s. was commenced under the Brigade Major. The following were noted by the Brigade as having done good work on this course and having sent in good papers :

No. 1164 Sgt. Clark.
No. 3364 Lce.-Sgt. Gatford.
No. 3064 Lce.-Sgt. Russell.
No. 2833 Lce.-Cpl. Pippett.
No. 3407 Lce.-Cpl. May.
No. 2785 Lce.-Cpl. Tedder.

June 1st, 1915.

The drums and fifes of the Battalion played, sounded and beat Retreat on Mondays and Wednesdays on the Battalion Parade Ground, and on Fridays in the Palace Square.

June 5th, 1915.

The Battalion struck camp on Floriana Parade Ground and marched to Ghain Tuffieha, where it encamped. As most of the baggage of the Battalion was conveyed in one-horse native carts, the transport column was a very long one.

At Ghain Tuffieha the Navy kindly placed their camping ground and buildings at the disposal of the officers.

A tropical thunderstorm, with heavy rain, made the first night in the new camp somewhat uncomfortable.

Dr. NOBBS was appointed Medical Officer to the Battalion.

June 8th, 1915.

A lecture was given to the Battalion by Major H. A. CARR, 4th Battalion Worcester Regiment on " The Dardanelles."

June 10th, 1915.

A detachment of the Battalion, consisting of 3 officers and 85 other ranks was sent to Imtarfa Hospital for guard and fatigue purposes.

The Battalion played a cricket match against the Eastern Telegraph Company on the Marsa, with the following result :

Eastern Telegraph Company 100.
2/4 Battalion   200 for 7 wkts.

June 13th, 1915.

The Battalion attended Divine Service with the 2/1 Battalion on the Battalion Parade Ground.

In the afternoon a cricket match was played against a team from the Maori Contingent.

Patrols, under an officer, were detailed from the Battalion daily for duty on the coast at night, as suspicious lights were seen showing seaward, and natives were suspected of supplying enemy submarines with information, stores, etc.

June 15th, 1915.

In the evening an open-air Concert was held in camp. Large parties of the Maoris attended, and were highly delighted with the entertainment; they were greatly impressed by the friendship and cordial welcome that were extended to them.

June 16th, 1915.

A Special Fortress Order was issued as under :

" His Excellency the Governor and Commander-in-Chief cannot express his gratitude too warmly to all serving under his command who have given him such splendid support in helping to arrange accommodation for their comrades who are returning wounded from the Dardanelles. He knows the strain has been excessive, but the result has been beyond all expectations. So far all demands from the front have been met ; there has not been a hitch, nor has there been the slightest friction. It has been a labour of love, and all may rest assured their efforts will never be forgotten by those for whom they have given of their best."

June 18th, 1915.

The Battalion went for a route march to Citta Vecchia.

The Commanding Officer offered money prizes for the best kept and decorated tents in the Battalion.

" C " Company won 1st and 2nd prizes, and other prizes were given to " B " Company, " D " Company, and the Machine Gun Section.

June 20th, 1915.

The Battalion attended Divine Service with 2/1 Battalion.

Leaving for Malta, H.T. "Avon," escorted by H.M.S. "Eclipse"

The Regiment Transport under Lieut. Dennis, Chain Tuffieha

Commanding Officer and Major V. Seyd

Issuing Rations.   St. George's Barracks, Malta

Group of Officers, Malta

Barrack Room, St. George's Barracks, Malta

2nd Lieut. L. R. CHAPMAN was invalided to England.

A cricket match was played against the Australian Convalescents, with the following result :

Australian Convalescents, 194

2/4 Battalion   200 for 4 (Lce.-Cpl. Powell 124).

June 22nd, 1915.

The Maori Contingent left Malta for Egypt and the Dardanelles.

A Brigade Staff Tour for officers was carried out.

June 25th, 1915.

Major R. F. LEGGE, the Brigade Major, left Malta for England.

Lieut. W. R. BOTTERILL took charge of No. 2 Section 1st London Divisional Signal Company for a week.

June 27th, 1915.

Capt. F. C. J. READ, with " D " Company, marched to St. Andrew's Barracks and built wooden huts for hospital work, and erected marquees for convalescents.

No. 2867 Sgt. LANGLEY and No. 3343 Cpl. HILL left the Battalion to proceed to England to take up commissions.

June 28th, 1915.

A Reserve Machine Gun Section was formed in the Battalion, and all N.C.O.'s and men detailed for duty with this Section underwent a special course of instruction in machine gun work under Lieut. L. A. DICKINS.

July 2nd, 1915.

Four officers from the Royal Engineers were attached to the Battalion to give instruction in field engineering, etc. Platoons were practised in building barrel rafts and in erecting barbed wire entanglements.

The Rev. Mr. WEBB, Chaplain to the Forces, was attached to the Battalion ; he speedily won the hearts of all ranks.

July 6th, 1915.

The following letter was received by the Commanding Officer from Mr. A. BRIGG, Church Army, at St. George's Barracks.

" Please allow me to express my warmest thanks to you for the great interest and sympathy you so kindly showed in my work in Camp. I assure you I shall long remember your kindnesses and the way in which you gave me every facility.

" It is a matter of regret to me that I was unable to render more adequate service, but I am very proud indeed to have had the privilege of being so closely associated with the Battalion, and shall watch with a keen interest its future movements."

July 7th, 1915.

Information was received that, at a meeting of Past and Present Officers of the Regiment, held at Headquarters on the 25th June, 1915, with Col. RODNEY WILDE in the chair, a resolution was passed forwarding best wishes and kind remembrances to the Battalion at Malta.

July 9th, 1915.

Lieut. A. H. SIMPSON left the Battalion and proceeded to Gallipoli for duty with the 2nd Royal Fusiliers.

Capt. H. MORRIS was granted 28 days' leave to England on urgent business.

July 14th, 1915.

An open-air Concert was held in Camp in the evening.

July 17th, 1915.

H.E. the GOVERNOR and Lord LUCAN breakfasted at the Officers' Mess at 7.30 a.m. After breakfast these officers inspected the Camp.

July 18th, 1915.

The Battalion attended Divine Service on the Battalion Parade Ground. As the weather was now very hot this parade was held at 7.45 a.m., and breakfast was served afterwards.

July 19th, 1915.

The Battalion held a test for Scouts. Full marching order was worn, and the test, which was commenced at 5 a.m., consisted of :

Riding a mile on horseback.
Riding a mile on bicycle.
Making a sketch of enemy's position.
Marching a mile.
Cooking a meal.
Undressing and swimming 100 yards with rifle.
Firing 5 rounds blank ammunition.
Dressing and marching a quarter-mile to range.
Firing 10 rounds ball cartridge.

The Scouts worked in pairs and 16 pairs entered for the test.

July 20th, 1915.
Princess Mary's Christmas, 1914, Gifts arrived for the Battalion, and were very much appreciated by all ranks.

July 24th to 26th, 1915.
Colonel VICKERS DUNFEE was the guest of H.E. the GOVERNOR at his summer palace of VADALLA.

On the 26th of July the Battalion received orders to prepare a draft of 400 men for service in France.

No. 3133 Lce.-Corpl. A. J. COOK and No. 3343 Pte. L. C. ROGERS left the Battalion to proceed to England to take up commissions.

July 28th, 1915.
The Battalion commenced to pitch a camp for 1000 convalescents at Ghain Tuffieha.

2nd Lieut. N. L. THOMAS was invalided to England.

The Regimental Band commenced a fortnight's musical tour of all the Convalescent Camps and Hospitals on the Island ; officers and men of the Battalion also gave their help and support in arranging concerts for the wounded.

A cricket match was played against All Saints Convalescent Camp, with the following result :

All Saints Convalescent Camp   104.
2/4 Battalion   93.

July 30th, 1915.
H.E. the GOVERNOR and Staff came to Ghain Tuffieha to make arrangements for pitching a camp for 3000 convalescents.

The 2/1 Battalion entertained a party of our officers at dinner.

At this period the following detachments were being found by the Battalion :

Capt. F. C. J. READ with " D " Company at St. Andrew's Camps.

Capt. H. G. STANHAM with half of " B " Company at the Camp Hospital.

Lieut. J. R. WEBSTER with half " A " Company at Imtarfa Hospital.

Lieut. L. A. DICKINS with 50 men at St. Patrick's Camp.

July 31st, 1915.

The trip of the Regimental Band to the various hospitals, etc., was somewhat unfortunate ; on leaving the Camp the cart containing the band instruments was accidentally overturned. Three days later the marquee allotted to the band at St. Andrew's Camp caught fire and all the music was destroyed ; fortunately most of the instruments were saved.

August 1st, 1915.

The orders for the draft for France were cancelled and a draft of 400 men from England to reinforce the Battalion did not sail, although they had actually embarked at Southampton.

Capt. H. MORRIS returned to the Battalion from leave.

August 4th, 1915.

Lord Brassey's yacht, " The Sunbeam," arrived in the Grand Harbour ; on board were Lord Bingham, the Earl of Lucan's son, and the Hon Freeman Thomas, Lord Brassey's grandson. These gentlemen came to Ghain Tuffieha and visited the Battalion.

The officers of the Battalion were practised in revolver shooting.

August 11th, 1915.

Lord and Lady Lucan, with Lord Bingham, came out to Ghain Tuffieha and took tea with the officers of the Battalion in the Naval Officers' Ante-room.

A Competition for the best shot in the Battalion was held on the Naval Ranges, with the following result :

No. 1	2978 C. S. M. Emes	....	50 points.
No. 2	3438 Lce.-Cpl. Plaster	....	48 points.
Tie	{ 3448 Pte. Bearman	......	43 points.
	{ 3064 Pte. Hodges	....	43 points.

August 12th, 1915.

Officers' Revolver Competition was held, and won by Lieut. R. N. KEEN.

Three signallers from the Battalion left Malta with Capt. S. WALLIS for the Dardanelles ; they were attached to H.M.S. " Euryalus " for duty.

August 13th, 1915.

The following officers arrived from England and were attached to the Battalion :

2nd Lieut. B. F. L. YEOMAN.
2nd Lieut. N. W. WILLIAMS.
2nd Lieut. H. G. HICKLENTON.
2nd Lieut. C. P. DARRINGTON.

August 14th, 1915.

Orders were received for the Battalion to be prepared to embark for Egypt.

Lieut. A. McDONNELL, R.A.M.C., was attached to the Battalion as Medical Officer.

The Battalion was inspected by H.E. the GOVERNOR, who, in a very kind speech, said good-bye to the troops.

August 17th, 1915.

Annual horse and mule races took place at SLIEMA, and officers of the Battalion were invited as guests of the 2/2 Battalion.

Thousands of people lined the route, and, although the course was kept by the police, it was impossible to keep the natives back. Jockeys rode without saddles and bridles.

After the race, banners were presented to the winning jockeys.

August 19th, 1915.

The Battalion struck camp at Ghain Tuffieha and marched to the Marsa, just outside Valetta, during the night.

H.M. transport "Southlands," commanded by Capt. Kirk, arrived in the Grand Harbour from Gallipoli with General Stopford and Staff on board.

August 20th, 1915.
The Battalion—strength 30 officers and 750 other ranks—embarked on H.M.T. "Southlands." The transport also carried 50 naval ratings and 400 Colonials. Ten horses of the Battalion also embarked.

A little white dog belonging to one of the men was sold to a Maltese just before the Battalion embarked on the lighters ; but, not to be outdone, the little dog jumped into the water after the lighter, and was ultimately allowed to sail with the Battalion.

Life belts were issued to all ranks, and guards with machine guns were posted fore and aft, and all precautions against submarines were taken.

The weather was very hot, the temperature in the cabins being 95 degrees.

August 21st, 1915.
H.M.T. "Southlands" steamed out of the Grand Harbour at 7 a.m. with bands playing. Troops on board French battleships in the harbour gave us a very hearty send-off.

Officers and men of the Battalion were vaccinated.

August 23rd, 1915.
The following extract from Special Fortress Orders by F.-M. Lord METHUEN, G.C.B., G.C.V.O., C.M.G., Colonel Scots Guards, Governor and C.-in-C. Malta, is published for information :

" It is a pleasure for His Excellency to say with truth that it has been a source of satisfaction to him to have had the four Territorial Battalions of the City of London Regiment under his command. Their conduct has been excellent, under trying conditions lately, on account of the heavy and unceasing fatigue work they have had to perform. Their appearance in Valetta, the smart way in which the men salute, the alacrity of the Main Guard in turning out, all show the efficiency of the Battalions.

" His Excellency wishes officers, N.C.O's. and men

' God-speed,' and if from Egypt they go to the front, he looks to them with confidence to uphold the high reputation of the City of London Regiment."

August 25th, 1915.
H.M.T. " Southlands " arrived in Alexandria Harbour at 10 a.m., but it was mid-day before the ship was berthed.

The Battalion disembarked, and fatigue parties were detailed to off-load the baggage, etc. The Battalion marched through Alexandria to a camp on the seashore near the Sporting Club.

Lady Cardigan most kindly brought comforts for the men of the Battalion.

Now that the Battalion was in Egypt, great satisfaction was expressed that all postage to England was free, though still subject to Censor.

August 26th, 1915.
The Battalion provided all the guards necessary in Alexandria, which included the Main Guard, Ras-el-tin Guard, Cable Guards, Town Picquets, etc.

As in Malta, the Regimental Band was kept busy entertaining the wounded and convalescents in the various camps and hospitals.

Capt. R.N. ARTHUR, with two officers and 100 other ranks from " A " company, formed a detachment at Kom-il-Dick Fort.

Owing to the hot weather troops were allowed to drill and do camp fatigues in shirt sleeves ; shorts were also allowed to be worn.

Troops were allowed to travel half fare on the tramways.

August 27th, 1915.
The following is an extract from a letter received by the Commanding Officer from the Rev. S. Llewellyn Webb, who was attached as Chaplain to the Battalion while in Malta :

" I feel I must just send you a few lines to try and express my gratitude to you, not only for the hearty welcome you gave me to your Battalion and the considerate way you helped me in my work, but also for all your kindness in the matter of trying to get me off to go with you.

" I was, and still am, very disappointed, although one could not say much, yet I felt a great deal when the time came to say ' good-bye.' All the officers and men were so friendly and nice that it made it additionally hard to leave them."

August 28th, 1915.

Lieut. J. R. WEBSTER was detailed to convey important prisoners from Alexandria to Cairo.

Lieut. A. H. SIMPSON was in the 21st General Hospital, Alexandria, suffering from a wound received on August 9th while working his machine gun at Cape Helles. He was eventually invalided to England on the 8th Sept.

August 29th, 1915.

The Battalion attended Divine Service at 8.30 a.m. on the Battalion Parade Ground.

Another Scout Class was formed under 2nd Lieut. E. G. LOVELL.

August 31st, 1915.

The 2/1 Battalion and the 2/2 Battalion London Regiment arrived at Alexandria from Malta, and proceeded by train to Cairo.

The Commanding Officer inspected all guards found by the Battalion on the Parade Ground before they marched off to their various duties.

There was a meeting of the Staff at Command Headquarters.

The Commanding Officer called on the Municipal Council and obtained the loan of a large map of Alexandria for police purposes.

September 1st, 1915.

All tents in the camp were struck for the day at 9 a.m. to allow the ground inside the tents to be exposed to the sun. Camp was re-erected at 4 p.m.

An inspection of clothing, etc., by Companies was held before a Clothing Board, under the presidency of Major V. H. SEYD.

September 4th, 1915.

At 6.30 a.m. Major-General Sir A. WALLACE, C.B., and Staff inspected the Battalion.

8TH ARMY CORPS. MAP SHOWING BRITISH & FRENCH TRENCHES.

GALLIPOLI PENINSULA.

SOUTHERN ZONE. 7TH JULY 1915.

AEGEAN SEA

THE DARDANELLES

MORTO BAY

GULLY BEACH

X. BEACH

REFERENCE

Reserved Trenches
Main Communication Trenches
Other Trenches
Roads
Tracks
Wells
Survey Stations
Advanced Dressing Stations
Regimental Aid Posts
(NOTE—Right of Ravines and Nullahs only Approx.)

Surveyed by Div Eng R.N Div. (except right, of which
plan was supplied by French H.Q.)
Base measured by Range Finder.
Triangulation fixed by box sextant.
Detail filled in by prismatic and photographs

In the afternoon a Race Meeting was held at the Sporting Club, and was attended by many members of the Battalion.

Capt. H. MORRIS rode in one of the races.

September 6th, 1915.

Lieut. R. N. KEEN was bitten by a dog in Alexandria, and was sent to Cairo for Pasteur treatment.

An N.C.O's. Class of Instruction was commenced under Regimental Sergt.-Major HAIGH.

The rifles of the Battalion were inspected and overhauled by the Armourer Sergeant.

September 8th, 1915.

Permission was given for officers of the Battalion to have two days' leave in Cairo ; rank and file were allowed one day.

Tents in camp were struck at 9 a.m., and were re-pitched at 4 p.m.

September 10th, 1915.

A Military Court was convened by order of Lieut.-General Sir J. G. MAXWELL, K.C.B., K.C.M.G., with Colonel VICKERS DUNFEE as President, and assembled at the CARACOL ATTARINE, Alexandria.

The Regimental Band played at Lady Howard de Walden's Convalescent Home at 4 p.m.

September 14th, 1915.

The 2/3 Battalion London Regiment from Khartoum left Alexandria for MUDROS.

The Regimental Band played at the Greek Hospital at 4 p.m.

September 15th, 1915.

Corpl. S. A. EDWARDS, with three other N.C.O's., took advantage of the one day's leave which had been granted to the Battalion, and the following is an extract from a Press cutting relating his experiences :

" After leaving the camp we made for Sidi-Gaber Station, the first stop on the Alexandria-Cairo line. After a bit of a struggle round the ticket office, we got into the 7.10 a.m. Cairo express, the first real train we had been in since December 23rd, 1914. Only those who have been deprived of a train journey for such a long time can realise the delight of being in one again. We travelled second class at half fare, being in uniform, as we were told it was *infra dig* to travel third, these being used by the natives ; the second class carriages were very comfortable, each carriage being open entirely to the corridor.

" Cairo was reached at about 10.20 a.m. I was surprised to find that all the country I passed through was under cultivation, every inch of it, and it was delightful to see the miles of refreshing green after months of bare rock in Malta. The crops consist principally of maize, sugar cane, cotton, and date palms. If one could take away the mud huts, Arab people and date palms, and substitute little cottages, Flemish people and poplars, I should have imagined I was travelling between Ostend and Brussels, for the land is as flat as a billiard table all the way. All the cultivation is done by irrigation apparently ; the Nile overflows at certain periods, and brings with it a rich slime, which is left on the land when the waters subside, and I understand the crops are planted in this mud as soon as possible after the water has gone. All the fields have canals and channels cut through them. We passed many mud villages, just hovels formed out of dried mud, very picturesque, but I should not care for a stay in one in spite of all the roughing we have done this year. On the road by the railway line we saw small camels, donkeys, natives, and many interesting sights of Eastern life. It looks funny to see a gaily dressed native on a little donkey, the former holding an umbrella over his head to keep off the sun's rays.

" The stations on the line reminded me more of Continental stations than English ones ; Cairo station is quite a fine building. A native guide pounced on us as soon as we got into the station, and we allowed ourselves to be unprotestingly rushed off. We caught a tram at 11.30 a.m. for the Pyramids. It was a three-quarters of an hour ride through delightful avenues of trees, and over a fine bridge which spans the Nile. We passed the Gezirah Gardens, also the Zoological Gardens, but time would not allow us to visit them. At last the Pyramids came in sight, and we beheld what not one of us ever dreamt we would set eyes on.

" The Pyramids we visited are the principal ones in Egypt, but there are many others in the land, some of which we could see in the distance. On leaving the tram we chartered a donkey apiece, and first visited the tomb of Rameses the First, with Egyptian carvings round the walls. Next we saw the Sphinx, looking stolidly away at the Nile as he has been doing for thousands of years. I imagined he was a bigger affair than he turned out to be, but the monument is very wonderfully carved, as it is out of one big piece of rock. We then turned our mokes' heads to the largest Pyramid in Egypt, that built by King Cheops some 6000 years ago.

" The Pyramids are wonderful, and we were informed that it took 100,000 men, working in shifts of three months at a time, 30 years to build the biggest one. The appearance of the outside of the Pyramids is as of a flight of exceedingly steep steps ; at one time the Pyramids were quite smooth, and were covered with alabaster, but now only the top of the second largest Pyramid has alabaster on it. We did not know whether to climb to the top of old Cheops' tomb or go inside it, but not having time for both, we eventually decided to climb, and in about 15 or 20 minutes we were at the top. We had a very fine view of the surrounding country. We could see away into the Libyan Desert, a vast ocean of sand hillocks disappearing at the horizon, then a good view of Cairo and the other Pyramids in the distance. We then came down and made our way to the tram terminus café, where we partook of much-needed refreshment before catching the 3 p.m. tram to Cairo.

" Cairo is a fine city, but we could not hope to see anything of it in the time, so we had some tea and bought a few p.c.'s. Our train left Cairo at 6.35 p.m., and we eventually arrived back in camp shortly after 10 o'clock, after a splendid and interesting day."

September 18th, 1915.

The Battalion drew khaki clothing out of store and returned their drill uniforms ; all ranks were supplied with new underclothing and cholera belts, etc., were also issued.

2nd Lieut. H. W. VERNON was admitted to No. 19 General Hospital, Alexandria ; this hospital was originally the German Civil Hospital.

43

September 21st, 1915.

The Machine Gun Section, with four guns under Lieut. L. A. DICKINS, was inspected complete with mules and equipment.

The Regimental Band played at the Government Hospital.

September 24th, 1915.

Major-General Sir A. WALLACE, C.B., inspected the whole Battalion at drill.

The Regimental Band played in Camp from 5.30 to 7 p.m.

September 25th, 1915.

Major-General Sir A. WALLACE, C.B., gave a dinner to the Staff at the Savoy Hotel, Alexandria, and after dinner entertained them at a gala performance at the theatre. The following were present :

> D. A. Cameron, Esq., British Consul.
> O.C. Royal Artillery.
> Colonel Beach, R.A.M.C.
> Colonel Vickers Dunfee, V.D.
> Capt. Long, A.D.C.

September 29th, 1915.

No. 3311 Sgt. SYME and No. 3340 Pte. PEACOCK left the Battalion to proceed to England to take up commissions.

The Regimental Band played at Lady Howard de Walden's Convalescent Home.

October 1st, 1915.

The Greek Reservists were called up, and amidst great enthusiasm they marched to the Docks at Alexandria ; each carried a Greek flag and a Union Jack in his cap.

The Boy Scout movement has been well supported in Alexandria, and every Sunday numbers of Boy Scouts are seen in the parks training.

In addition to the engagements previously stated, the Regimental Band performed as follows :

> Sept. 13th, Victoria College Hospital.
> Sept. 17th, Glymonopoulo Camp.
> Sept. 19th, No. 21, Ras-el-Tin Hospital.
> Sept. 27th, No. 15, General Hospital.
> Sept. 30th, Victoria College Hospital.

44

October 6th, 1915.

Brigadier-General the Earl of LUCAN inspected the Battalion on the Battalion Parade Ground in the morning and addressed the Battalion.

The following is an extract from his speech :

" I wish you all every success, good luck and a safe return to England. I trust we shall all meet again. I am proud that I have been in command of the 1st London Infantry Brigade, and am exceedingly sorry that I am not coming with you ; I had hoped that the four Battalions of the London Regiment would 'have gone to the front as a Brigade. I much appreciate the very hard work you all did at Malta, and I send you from here with every confidence that you will acquit yourselves in the future as I know you have done in the past, and you will uphold the great reputation which you have gained. I feel sure you will do great credit to yourselves and to the City of London Regiment wherever you go."

" C " and " D " Companies left Sporting Club Camp and marched to the Docks, Alexandria, where they embarked on H.M.T. " Karroo."

The Commanding Officer received the following letter from Major-Gen. Sir A. WALLACE, C.B., O.C. Troops, Alexandria :

" Now that your Regiment is leaving, I should like to let you all know how much I have appreciated the good discipline and bearing all have shown. It has made it a pleasure to have you in my command.

" Not only has your Battalion been well conducted, but the A.P.M. has brought to my notice the great assistance he has received from your Regiment in the maintenance of discipline in the garrison.

" Sorry to lose you ; I congratulate you on going to the front ; you have done your duty here. You will meet with hardships and trials, but I feel you will always fulfil your duty.

" Good-bye and Good luck to all."

October 7th, 1915.

Major-General Sir A. WALLACE, C.B., Capt. HAY, Capt. SAUNDERSON, A.D.C., and Major V. H. SEYD dined with the Commanding Officer at the Union Club, Alexandria.

A dance was given at Hotel Regina as a farewell to the officers of the Battalion.

2nd Lieut. N. W. WILLIAMS, with escort, conveyed Turkish prisoners from Alexandria to Cairo.

October 8th, 1915.

Réveillé was sounded at 5 a.m. ; camp was cleared and handed over to the 2/8 Middlesex Regiment.

" A " and " B " Companies, with the Regimental Bands, pack animals and machine guns, marched through Alexandria to the Docks. At the Main Guard, Major-General A. WALLACE, C.B., and his Staff watched the column march past.

On arrival at the Docks these troops, after loading the Battalion luggage, etc., embarked on H.M.T. " Karroo."

Capt. G. H. MOORE and Capt. H. PARKHOUSE did not embark with the Battalion, but remained on duty in Egypt as they were medically unfit for active service.

Lieut. H. W. DENNIS was granted leave to England on account of urgent private affairs, and did not sail with the Battalion.

2nd Lieut. F. R. C. BRADFORD was left behind in hospital.

October 9th, 1915.

The " Karroo " left Alexandria at 7.30 a.m. in a very calm sea. When the ship was well out of the harbour, one was able to see quite clearly where the waters of the Nile entered the sea, the difference in colour of the water being particularly noticeable.

In addition to the 2/4 Battalion on board, the transport carried a large number of native workmen proceeding to Mudros.

Every man on board was served out with a life-belt, which had to be worn all day. An armed submarine guard consisting of 1 officer and 25 other ranks, with machine guns, was found daily for duty during the voyage.

At 4 p.m. a submarine alarm practice took place.

October 10th, 1915.

The Battalion attended Divine Service on deck at 9.30 a.m. ; the hymns, " Rock of Ages " and " For those in Peril " were sung by the troops.

After the service the usual inspection of the ship took place, and at 11.45 a.m. another submarine alarm was practised, the troops falling in very quickly at their respective stations.

At night guards were doubled as we were in the dangerous island zone, and all troops slept with life-belts on.

All officers and men were inoculated against cholera.

A French destroyer picked us up and acted as our escort.

The Commanding Officer observed how quickly the troops settled down to their duties at sea ; whether it was a submarine guard, washing decks or scrubbing mess tables, there was always the same happy readiness to cheerfully obey orders.

October 11th, 1915.

Capt. E. R. LARGE, R.N.R., commanding H.M.T. " Karroo," expressed his entire satisfaction with the way in which both the troops on board and the crew of the ship took up their stations on the alarm being sounded ; every man was at his post within three minutes from the sounding of the alarm signal.

Our escort was now increased to two destroyers, and these ships signalled to us the latest wireless news.

The following is an extract from Battalion orders :

" No. 3127 Sgt. ROBINSON was appointed N.C.O. in charge of the Regimental Records at the Base, and remained in Alexandria.

" The Commanding Officer desires to place on record his appreciation of the conscientious and capable manner in which Sgt. Robinson has always carried out his duties."

October 12th, 1915.

The transport arrived at dusk outside Mudros Harbour, and, after waiting for a hospital ship to come out, we entered the harbour and anchored in mid-stream.

A Regimental Concert was held on deck in the evening, and was attended by the Captain, officers and crew of the transport, in addition to all members of the Battalion.

October 13th, 1915.

The Battalion remained on board H.M.T. " Karroo " in Mudros Harbour.

H.M.T. " Southlands " was also in the harbour with a large hole in her as a result of a torpedo from a submarine she had encountered after disembarking us at Alexandria in August.

October 14th, 1915.

The Battalion was still on board H.M.T. " Karroo " in Mudros Harbour. Two days' rations were issued to all ranks as follows :

2 lbs. biscuits.
2 lbs. corned beef.
2 days' tea and sugar.
2 portions of Oxo.

The cases containing the above were broken up, and the wood was distributed to the troops for lighting fires.

October 15th, 1915.

The Battalion was transhipped to H.M.T. " Sarnia " during the morning, and left Mudros Harbour about 3 p.m. The Captain and crew of the " Karroo " gave us a splendid send-off, and our Regimental Band played as we left the harbour.

The voyage from Mudros to the Peninsula did not take long, as at about midnight our transport arrived off Cape Helles. After a wait of about an hour, we disembarked, and marched in single file along a pier made of sunken ships to " W " beach ; here the first sound of firing and exploding of shells reached our ears.

October 16th, 1915.

On arrival on the Peninsula the Battalion was attached to the 1st Royal Naval Brigade.

In the early hours of the morning the Battalion had all disembarked at " W " beach, and a march of one and a half miles brought us to our bivouac of dug-outs. On arrival here it was found that the " Drake " Battalion, under Colonel KING, had provided a supper for both officers and men, and everything was done to make us as comfortable as possible.

The kind consideration so generously extended to us on our arrival was accorded to us throughout our stay on the Peninsula.

48

Capt. McDonald, R.A.M.C., inoculating against enteric, Dardanelles

On H.T. " Karroo," men watching the Maxim Section at practice

Captured Turkish Gun, " Sedd-el-Banr," Cape Helles, Gallipoli

BIRD'S-EYE MAP OF THE DARDANELLES

The Battalion baggage was brought ashore in lighters during the morning.

On the Peninsula the 24-hour day was used, and all times were indicated by a group of 4 figures, the letters a.m. and p.m. being omitted. The following is an example :

> 10.5 a.m. was written as 1005.
> 2.10 p.m. was written as 1410.
> 7.35 p.m. was written as 1935.

October 17th, 1915.

The following comprised the Royal Naval Division Staff :

G.O.C.	Maj.-Gen. A. Parris, C.B.
G.S.O.1	Lt.-Col. A. H. Olivant, R.A.
G.S.O.2	Maj. E. F. P. Sketchley, R.M.L.I.
G.S.O.3	Capt. Parris.
A.A. & Q.M.G.	Lt.-Col. G. S. Richardson.
D.A.Q.M.G.	Capt. Walmesley.
A.P.M.	Major the Hon. A. G. V. Peel.
A.D.M.S.	Flt.-Surg. A. Gashell, R.N.
D.A.D.O.S.	Major Taylor.
C.R.E.	Col. Carey.

The following comprised the Staff of the 1st Naval Brigade :

G.O.C.	Brig.-Gen. D. Mercer, R.M.L.I.
B.Major	Lieut.-Col. J. A. Tupman, R.M.L.I.
Staff C.	Major W. Wilberforce.

The Commanding Officer, Major V. H. SEYD, and a portion of the officers of the Battalion visited a sector of the trenches.

The Brigade-Major gave a lecture on the position on the Peninsula.

Col. VICKERS DUNFEE dined with Major-General 'A PARRIS and Staff.

October 18th, 1915.

Working parties from the Battalion were employed on the beaches unloading stores, etc.

Large flocks of wild geese passed over the Peninsula going South.

In the afternoon the Commanding Officer, Major V.

49   E

H. Seyd, Capt. R. N. Arthur, and Capt. H. G. Stanham paid a second visit to the trenches.

The Turkish Feast of Barram commenced, and orders were received that all troops were to exercise special vigilance and to be in instant readiness by day and night in case of attack.

Every opportunity was to be taken of worrying the enemy all along the line by day and night whilst this Feast was on.

October 19th, 1915.

No. 3320 Pte. J. B. Evans left the Battalion to proceed to England to take up a commission ; he was the first man of the Battalion to leave the Peninsula.

Working parties were again supplied by the Battalion.

Capt. L. C. Coates, Adjutant to the Battalion, was admitted to hospital suffering from pleurisy ; his duties were taken over by Lieut. J. R. Webster.

October 20th, 1915.

At 7.30 a.m. the Battalion moved out from its rest bivouac and proceeded by small parties to the Eski Lines, a reserve line of trenches.

On the march up to the trenches the following casualties took place :

Capt. H. Morris	.. ..	Wounded.
3028 Pte. Housden	.. ..	do.
2893 Pte. Maunder	.. ..	do.

The food on the Peninsula was quite good ; the drinking water came from Alexandria and always had to be treated with chlorine.

Rum, unsweetened lime juice, candles, matches, tobacco, and cigarettes were regular free issues to all ranks.

October 22nd, 1915.

The weather turned very wet.

This evening finished the Turkish Feast of Barram, and it was thought that the Turks might possibly make a demonstration ; nothing unusual, however, developed, although the Turks received a very hot time from our guns on land and from ships at sea.

October 23rd, 1915.

Half the officers and N.C.O's. of the Battalion were attached to Battalions in the front line for forty-eight hours' instruction, after which time they were relieved by the remaining officers and N.C.O's., who went to the front line for a similar period.

A Bombing Class for officers and other ranks was commenced at the Divisional Bomb Schools.

A working party from the Battalion was out repairing a trench when three Turkish shells fell close to them, and the party was ordered down to take cover. About 15 minutes afterwards No. 2632 Pte. J. MOLES, who was one of the party, said : " I will jump up and finish the work," but as he was scaling the parapet he was wounded. He was at once put on a stretcher and taken down the line.

October 24th, 1915.

Work of repair, etc., to the Eski Lines was carried out daily whilst the Battalion was in the trenches.

A telescopic rifle was issued to the Battalion for experimental purposes. Sergt. RAYMOND was detailed to try this rifle, and he made some good practice on Turks at 1000 yards.

A summary of the latest official wireless news from all fronts was printed on the Peninsula and issued daily to all units. This summary was known as the Peninsula Press, and these news sheets were hung up in conspicuous places and were read and appreciated by all the troops.

October 27th, 1915.

At 9 a.m. the Battalion was relieved in the Eski Lines by the 2/2 Battalion, and proceeded to Rest Camp.

In the afternoon a gale sprang up and the sea was very rough. No proper mail had arrived on the Peninsula for the last two weeks.

The Battalion was inoculated again, and out of all the officers and men only 12 men refused this protective measure.

October 28th, 1915.

To-day was a rest day for all troops coming out of the trenches ; only inspections under Company arrangements took place.

Full mail with newspapers to October 5th arrived from England.

October 29th, 1915.
Parties from the Battalion were at work on the new winter quarters.

Heavy firing took place between " Asiatic Annie " and the big French guns near our Rest Camp ; shells from Asia dropped far too close to our camp to be pleasant.

October 30th, 1915.
The following is a copy of Special Brigade Order by Brig.-General the EARL OF LUCAN, Commanding 1st London Infantry Brigade :

" On the occasion of the 2/4 London Regiment leaving the 1st London Infantry Brigade, the Brig.-General wishes to place on record his appreciation of the work and conduct of the Battalion during the nine months in which they formed part of his Brigade.

" All ranks have shown the greatest keenness in their training at Malta. Their conduct has been excellent, and they have readily adapted themselves to military life.

" In wishing success and good luck to all ranks, the Brig.-General is confident that the Battalion will render a good account of itself and maintain the reputation of the 1st London Infantry Brigade."

October 31st, 1915.
No. 3407 Lce.-Cpl. R. MAY left the Battalion to proceed to England to take up a commission.

Major V. H. SEYD, President of the Regimental Institutes, bought all cigarettes, chocolates, etc., that could be obtained from the Divisional Canteen and distributed same to all Companies. Unfortunately, supplies of such luxuries were very small on the Peninsula, but perhaps the parcels received from home were more appreciated on this account.

The Regimental Band played at Divisional Headquarters ; the drums of the Battalion beat Retreat in the Battalion Rest Camp.

November 1st, 1915.
The new month was heralded in with cold winds and rain.

Seven thousand sandbags were issued to the Battalion for work on the new winter quarters.

In the afternoon a Brigade Conference took place at Brigade Headquarters.

The transport and chargers of the 2nd Battalion Royal Fusiliers having been placed at the disposal of the Battalion, officers were able to obtain a fair amount of horse-exercise.

The Rest bivouacs were heavily shelled from 3 p.m. to 5 p.m. from Asia, and the big French guns thundered away in reply.

November 3rd, 1915.

The Battalion proceeded up the line for another tour in the trenches. " A " and " B " Companies relieved two Companies of the 2/2 Battalion in the Eski Line. " C " Company was attached as a Company to the " Hawke " Battalion, and the four platoons of " D " Company were attached to " Drake," " Nelson," " Hood " and " Hawke" Battalions respectively in the front line.

A case of comforts was received from Lady Ian Hamilton's Fund ; the case included eight packages of pickles, which were very much appreciated by the troops.

November 4th, 1915.

Work in repairing and rebuilding trenches was carried out regularly.

Whilst a party from " A" Company was at work the body of a man from the Worcester Regiment was found ; his private effects and identification disc were removed and the body was reverently and quietly re-buried.

The Commanding Officer, with Major Seyd, made a tour of all the front line trenches in our sector.

No. 3433 Pte. J. B. BATT was wounded in the head.

November 5th, 1915.

The 52nd Division carried out a very successful attack. At 3 p.m. mines were fired from three different points, and assaulting parties dashed forward, and Turkish trenches were captured east and west of Krithia Nullah.

The units taking part in the attack were the Royal Scots, the Scottish Rifles and the Ayrshire Yeomanry ; about 70 dead Turks were found in the captured trenches.

The Battalion carried out work of repairing trenches, and also built a strong point in the Eski Lines ; in the course of this work several dead bodies of Turks had to be removed.

November 7th, 1915.

Days were now drawing in ; dawn was at 6.30 a.m., and sunset at 5.30 p.m.

A small party of officers from the Battalion visited Gully Ravine and Gully Beach.

No. 3173 Pte. F. C. PFEIFFER was shot through the head, and died on his way to the hospital at 11 p.m. His body was wrapped in his blanket, and was laid in a grave at PINK FARM CEMETERY. The Roman Catholic Chaplain officiated, and the Commanding Officer, with Major V. H. Seyd and Lieut. McDonnell, R.A.M.C., attended the burial, which took place the following day, the 8th November, 1915.

November 9th, 1915.

A favourite occupation when off duty was to go down to the pier off Gully Beach and throw bread into the sea. Fish of the whiting type came after the bread, and then a Mills' grenade was thrown in. The fish were stunned by the explosion, and two or three men, with the help of a net, were sure of getting a good haul. The fish seemed to recover after a few minutes, unless they had been actually hit by a piece of the bomb.

November 10th, 1915.

The Battalion was relieved in the trenches, and returned to the Rest Camp.

A heavy rainstorm came on about 7.30 p.m., and flooded out all the dug-outs and shelters.

Mails and newspapers up to the 18th October arrived from England.

November 11th, 1915.

The following is an extract from the R.N. Divisional Orders :

" The G.O.C. R.N. Division congratulates the 1st R.N.D. Brigade on the good work done by them in the trenches during the past week."

The G.O.C. R.N.D. held a Conference at Divisional Headquarters, at which C.O.'s. and Adjutants from all Battalions in the Division attended.

A snake over five feet long was captured near the Quartermaster's Stores ; a large pickle jar and some spirits of wine were obtained from the R.A.M.C. and the snake was safely bottled.

November 12th, 1915.

After a very stormy night the weather turned rather cold.

Large working parties from the Battalion were again employed on digging on the new winter quarters.

The Secretary of State for War, EARL KITCHENER OF KHARTOUM, landed at Cape Helles for a short time.

The Regimental Band played at Brigade Headquarters in the evening.

November 13th, 1915.

The Battalion supplied more digging parties for work on the new winter quarters.

The Commanding Officer, Major V. H. Seyd, Lieut. J. R. Webster, and Lieut. and Q.M. J. W. Lambley rode over to the French Sector.

The Regimental Band played in the " Drake " Battalion Rest Camp in the evening.

November 14th, 1915.

Divine Service was held at 7.30 a.m. in the Mess dug-out.

Working parties were supplied as usual.

No. 3304 Lce.-Cpl. S. GARDINER and No. 2965 Pte. H. WALLER were accidentally killed at bombing practice at Divisional Bomb School.

Lce.-Cpl. GARDINER was a qualified instructor, and was superintending the throwing of live bombs when the accident occurred. A formal Court of Enquiry was held, but it was never ascertained exactly how the accident happened, as only Lce.-Cpl. Gardiner and Pte. Waller were in a trench together at the time.

The bodies were buried in PINK FARM CEMETERY at 5 p.m., and the burial was attended by the Commanding Officer, Major Seyd and Company Officers, in addition to the Commandant and all the class of the Bomb School.

The Regimental Band played in the "Nelson" Battalion area in the evening.

November 15th, 1915.

A heavy rainstorm occurred during the night and flooded the bivouacs ; in the morning the sea turned very rough.

The Battalion supplied working parties as usual.

A football match was played against the R.A.M.C. in the afternoon, with the following result :

R.A.M.C. .... 2 goals
2/4 Battalion .... 1 goal.

November 16th, 1915.

Heavy rain again occurred during the night.

Battalion working parties were again employed on the new winter quarters.

The Turks made a local attack on the right of our Divisional front, but were repulsed with heavy losses ; many prisoners remained in our hands.

Newspapers up to the 22nd October arrived from England.

November 17th, 1915.

The Battalion moved up for another tour in the trenches and occupied the Eski Lines.

" B " Company was attached to " Hawke " Battalion, and " A " Company was attached to " Hood " Battalion in the front line for a period of three days each.

There was a heavy thunderstorm from 7 p.m. to 9 p.m., and many of the trenches were flooded out.

November 20th, 1915.

Small parties of the Battalion received their first lecture on Gas. Gas protectors, helmets and respirators were issued to all ranks and had to be always carried ; no gas, however, was ever used so far as we knew on the Peninsula.

No. 3057 Pte. R. E. GATE was killed whilst looking through a periscope in a front line trench. A bullet came through a sandbag, passed through his head and killed him instantaneously. His body was buried in the evening in a little corner behind the front line, and a cross and a few stones marked his resting-place. Major V. H. Seyd and Company Officers attended the burial.

Mail with letters up to the 3rd November arrived from England.

November 21st, 1915.

At 3.30 p.m. the Turks opened heavy rifle and machine gun fire on our front line positions. All working parties from the Battalion were instantly recalled, and all troops stood to arms in their battle positions.

A strong Turkish attack developed on the right of our Brigade Sector, but the enemy never reached our trenches. Everything was normal by 6 p.m.

November 22nd, 1915.

At about 12 noon a working party from the Battalion, repairing a main communication trench, had shrapnel fire opened on them, and unfortunately the following casualties occurred :

No. 2738 Pte. A. CHICK, killed.

No. 2652 Pte. W. WHITFIELD, wounded.

No. 2595 Sergt. J. C. ROY, wounded.

The body of Pte. CHICK was buried in the evening in PINK FARM CEMETERY, the Commanding Officer, Major V. H. Seyd, Capt. H. G. Stanham, and Lieut. Giannacopulo being present at the burial.

A statement appeared in Battalion Orders referring to the above casualties, that Sergt. ROY, although wounded himself, behaved very gallantly ; he attended and dressed the other wounded before reporting his own wounds.

November 24th, 1915.

No. 1787 Lce.-Sergt. NICHOLSON was wounded in the head while in the front line trenches ; he was firing at a party of Turks and had got off five rounds before he was hit.

The Battalion was relieved and returned to the Rest Camp. Unfortunately the camp had suffered considerably from the heavy storms and bad weather whilst the Battalion was in the trenches.

Newspapers up to October 28th arrived from England.

The Signal Section of the Battalion commenced a course of training in field telephone work.

November 26th, 1915.

A storm, which had been threatening for some days, broke over the Peninsula and the wind increased considerably during the afternoon. At dusk rain came down in torrents, and many of the dug-outs were soon filled with water.

The troops spent a very unpleasant night in the Rest Camp, but with the help of Quartermaster Lieut. Lambley, and a good tot of rum each they kept up their spirits by singing. At daybreak hot tea was served before the digging parties left the camp for their work at 7 a.m.

November 27th, 1915.

To-day was the 43rd day the Battalion had spent on the Peninsula, and a dinner was given in the evening to Brig.-General D. Mercer and his Staff.

In the afternoon the wind shifted suddenly to the north, and a bitter, biting, piercing frost set in. Drenched great coats grew so stiff that they would stand up by themselves ; the water froze round the men's feet as they lay snatching the wretched sleep of utter exhaustion. Some of them were only kept alive by being made to work hard all day with pick and shovel.

November 26th, 1915.

The ground was covered with snow this morning, and the fierce north wind was so strong that you could not stand against it ; it lashed the face and inflamed the eyes.

This weather continued all day, but working parties from the Battalion carried out their work on the new winter quarters with the best of spirits. The thermometer kept well below freezing point.

November 29th, 1915.

The blizzard continued, and it was with difficulty that the troops kept the circulation of the blood going.

The breakwaters and piers made on the beaches by sinking old ships filled with sand were damaged to a considerable extent, and the landing of fresh supplies, stores, etc., on the Peninsula was quite out of the question.

The elements were indeed a supreme test of the endurance of British troops, but they came through it magnificently.

A famous war correspondent, who was at Cape Helles at the time of this storm, etc., wrote :

" Never probably since Crimean days have British Forces in the field had to endure such cold as the last days of November brought to our men at the Dardanelles."

2nd Lieut. C. P. DARRINGTON was admitted to hospital.

November 30th, 1915.

Fortunately the blizzard had beaten itself out by this time, and a spell of warmer weather set in, which enabled the damage done to be repaired, the flooded trenches drained, the washed-away parapets rebuilt, and the smashed jetties mended again.

Letters up to the 27th October arrived from England.

December 1st, 1915.

The Battalion moved up and took over the front line trenches.

Companies were distributed as follows :

" A " Company in front line from sap B to sap H.

" C " Company in front line from sap H to sap N.

" D " Company in support line Worcester Flats.

" B " Company in support line Munster Terrace.

The four machine guns of the Battalion occupied positions in the front line.

December 3rd, 1915.

From 3 p.m. to 6 p.m. a very heavy fire was opened on both our front line and reserve trenches from Achi Baba ; an attack was expected, but the Turks did not leave their trenches.

The following casualties occurred :

No. 2417 Pte. A. LONERAGAN   .... killed.
No. 3459 Pte. CRACKNELL .... killed.
No. 2478 Pte. J. CAVALIER .... wounded.

The bodies of Pte. Loneragan and Pte. Cracknell were buried at 1st. R.N. BRIGADE DUMP CEMETERY ; the Company Officers attended the burials.

December 4th, 1915.

An Inter-Company relief was carried out.

" D " Company relieved " C " Company in the front line.

" B " Company relieved " A " Company in the front line.

On being relieved, " A " and " C " Companies went into support trenches at Munster Terrace and Worcester Flats respectively.

2nd Lieut. N. L. THOMAS and 2nd Lieut. F. R. C. BRADFORD rejoined the Battalion.

December 5th, 1915.

Colonel VICKERS DUNFEE was granted a month's leave to proceed to England in connection with his business, which required immediate attention.

He embarked at midnight from the River Clyde and proceeded to Mudros and returned to England as O.C. Troops on H.M.T. " Olympic."

Before leaving the Battalion, Colonel VICKERS DUNFEE desired that all ranks be notified that he would be pleased to see their relatives in England if they would communicate with him at his home address. He also wished to take the opportunity of assuring them how thoroughly he appreciated the unswerving fidelity and devotion they had at all times shown him and how readily and willingly they had followed his leadership. He desired them to extend to Major V. H. SEYD the same loyal support which they had extended to him.

During the Commanding Officer's absence, Major Seyd took command of the Battalion, and he expressed great regret at losing the Commanding Officer even for a short time, and he felt that his regret would be shared by one and all, as all ranks knew that the happiness and efficiency of the Battalion ever since it was raised had been due to his unfailing energy and his care for those under him.

The following is an extract from a letter from the Regimental Medical Officer to Colonel Vickers Dunfee after he had left the Battalion on leave :

" Only just a few lines to wish you a pleasant journey and a complete rest, so that you will reach home in good form and feel your good old self again.

" How you would have loved to have heard what each and every one of your officers said on hearing that you had gone. They were all unanimous in expressing regret at losing the most popular C.O. a battalion could possibly have, and all sincerely wish you God-speed."

December 6th, 1915.
The following casualty occurred :
No. 2730 Pte. G. JOHNSTONE ....wounded.

Twenty-four cases containing Christmas presents from the ladies of the Battalion arrived for the troops ; also two cases for the officers.

December 7th, 1915.
An Inter-Company relief was carried out.
" C " Company relieved " D " Company, who returned to a support position in Worcester Flats.
" A " Company relieved " B " Company, who returned to Munster Terrace.
The following casualties occurred :
No. 3176 Pte. W. COPE .... killed.
No. 3197 Pte. W. J. JEFFERIES .... killed.
No. 2551 Sergt. A. HERRIDGE ...... wounded.

Pte. Cope was batman to Capt. Stevens, and was cleaning up the officers' dug-out when a piece of shrapnel struck him in the neck and severed an artery.
Pte. Jefferies was shot through the head about 11 p.m.
The bodies of Pte. Cope and Pte. Jefferies were buried in the 1st R.N. BRIGADE DUMP CEMETERY, and the Company Officers attended the burials.
Sergt. Herridge was only slightly wounded, and did not go off duty.

December 8th, 1915.
The following casualties occurred :
No. 3103 Pte. W. L. GILBERT .... killed.
No. 2997 Sergt. A. HEED .... wounded.
No. 2695 Sergt. T. MOSELEY ...... wounded.
No. 3164 Pte. MALES .... wounded.

Pte. Gilbert was sitting on a fire-step writing home to his mother when a shell struck him. His body was buried in the 1st R.N. BRIGADE DUMP CEMETERY, and his burial was attended by all the Company Officers.

Sergt. Moseley was only slightly wounded, and did not leave the Battalion.

2nd Lieut. H. W. VERNON was completely buried by a shell, but fortunately was dug out without being hurt.

December 9th, 1915.

An Inter-Company relief took place.

" B " Company relieved " C " Company, and " D " Company relieved " A " Company.

The following casualty occurred :

No. 3060 Pte. PEARSE .... killed.

His body was buried at the 1st R.N. BRIGADE DUMP CEMETERY, and the Company Officers attended the funeral.

2nd Lieut. J. W. PRICE and 2nd Lieut. S. DAVIS, with 49 other ranks from the 4th Reserve Battalion, arrived from England and were taken on the strength of the Battalion.

December 10th, 1915.

" A," " B " and " C " Companies of the Battalion were relieved in the trenches and returned to the Rest Camp.

" D " Company and the four machine guns of the Battalion were attached to the " Drake " Battalion, and did not return to camp until the following day.

The following casualties occurred through a Turkish bomb being thrown into the Worcester Barricade :

No. 2654 Pte. F. C. WISE .... wounded.
No. 2665 Pte. D. OSBORNE .... wounded.

December 11th, 1915.

Lieut. L. A. DICKINS was appointed Machine Gun Officer to the Brigade.

Capt. R. N. ARTHUR took over the duties of Second in Command of the Battalion vice Major V. H. SEYD, who was acting as Commanding Officer.

December 12th, 1915.

The first Church Service was held at which any large number was allowed to assemble ; at this Service a large number of officers and 125 other ranks attended, and the Regimental Band played two hymns.

The following is an extract from Battalion Orders, issued 12th December, 1915 :

" The Commanding Officer would like to place on record that whilst with the Grenade Section in the trenches last week, No. 2827 Pte. HEDGER threw back a live grenade which had fallen in the trench, thereby saving his comrades and himself from injury."

December 14th, 1915.

The Battalion moved up for another tour in the trenches and Companies were distributed as follows :

" A " and " B " Companies in the front line, " C " and " D " Companies, with Battalion Headquarters in the French Eski Lines, Tranchee d'Amade.

2nd Lieut. SIMON and 42 other ranks of the 2/3 Battalion were attached temporarily to the Battalion for duty.

December 16th, 1915.

The following notice was kindly sent by Mrs. DUNFEE to the next-of-kin of all the members of the Battalion :

" My husband has arrived home on short leave from the front. Should the parents or other relatives of the members of the Battalion wish to see him, he will gladly arrange an appointment on receipt of letter to that effect.

" He states that the conduct of all ranks has been simply ' Grand.'
December 16th, 1915.   LILLA DUNFEE."

Needless to say many of the parents and relatives of members of the Battalion availed themselves of this opportunity of hearing the latest news of their dear ones.

December 17th, 1915.

" B " Company relieved " A " Company in the firing line, whilst two platoons of " C " Company took up a position in local reserve.

Capt. F. C. J. READ was evacuated to Mudros suffering from jaundice.

December 18th, 1915.

Lieut. R. C. L. DICKINS left the Battalion and was evacuated from the Peninsula suffering from jaundice.

The following casualties occurred :

No. 3294 Pte. S. E. CHIPPS ...... wounded.
No. 3496 Pte. L. B. MOTT .... wounded.

Two platoons of " D " Company relieved the two platoons of " C " Company in local reserve.

December 20th, 1915.

Lieut.-General Sir FRANCIS DAVIES, K.C.B., Commanding the 8th Army Corps, issued an order announcing the safe withdrawal of our troops from Suvla and Anzac, and stated that the position at Cape Helles would not be abandoned.

" A " Company relieved " B " Company in the front line.

The following casualties occurred in the Battalion :

No. 4417 Pte. T. MALLINDINE .... killed.
No. 1872 Drmr. G. BLAKE .... killed.
No. 4743 Pte. T. W. BEESLEY ...... wounded.
No. 3346 Pte. S. O'HANLON ...... wounded.
No. 2976 Pte. WHITER .... wounded.
No. 3048 Pte. S. BRIGNELL ...... wounded.
No. 3295 Pte. BROOKS .... wounded.
No. 1732 Pte. A. E. GURR ...... wounded.

The body of Pte. Mallindine was buried at ZIMMER-MAN'S FARM CEMETERY on the 21st December, and the body of Drmr. Blake was buried in POINT D'EAU CEMETERY on the 22nd December. The Rev. B. CLOSE officiated on each occasion, and the Company Officers attended the burials.

December 21st, 1915.

Lieut. L. A. DICKINS was seriously wounded, and was succeeded by 2nd Lieut. H. G. HICKLENTON as Machine Gun Officer. Lieut. Dickins was in the trenches with Lieut.-Col. Tupman, the Brigade-Major, when shrapnel burst over them. Lieut. Dickins was severely wounded in the head, and was evacuated off the Peninsula, but Lieut.-Colonel Tupman was only slightly wounded, and he did not go off duty.

The night was very stormy, and lightning struck one of the machine guns of the Battalion.

Communication Trench, Eski Lines

Working Party under Lieut. V. Bowater

Lancashire Landing, Cape Helles, Dardanelles

Rest Bivouac, Cape Helles

In an Advance Gap of the Front Line Trenches, Dardanelles, showing Trench Mortar Catapult

River Clyde Landing Stage, Cape Helles

Parading for the Trenches, Cape Helles

Malta. After the March to Melleha

Rest Bivouac, Dardanelles

December 22nd, 1915.

Two platoons from the " Hood " Battalion relieved the two platoons of the 2/4 Battalion in local reserve ; after relief these platoons returned to Tranchee d'Amade.

" A " and " B " Companies were also relieved, and returned to a new Rest Camp called Cæsar's Camp. The Battalion machine guns were taken out of the front line, and half the Section returned to Cæsar's Camp and the other half went into Tranchee d'Amade.

December 23rd, 1915.

2nd Lieut. S. C. G. BLOWS joined the Battalion from England.

A big Turkish shell struck a dug-out occupied by men of the Battalion in the Rest Camp, and unfortunately the following casualties occurred :

No. 3319 Pte. S. R. GRIFFIN	killed.
No. 3332 Pte. D. HALDANE	wounded (since died of wounds).
No. 3328 Pte. A. G. BONNETT	wounded.
No. 1740 Pte. T. H. BROWN	wounded.
No. 2221 Pte. E. H. TUCK	wounded.
No. 3366 Lce.-Cpl. STOTTER	wounded.
No. 2439 Cpl. HAYNES	wounded (slight).

The body of Pte. Griffin was buried in ORCHARD GULLY CEMETERY, and Company Officers attended the burial.

December 24th, 1915.

Major V. H. SEYD issued the following Order :

" The Commanding Officer extends to all ranks the heartiest Christmas greeting. He is fully alive to the discomforts and hard work which are inevitable under present circumstances, but having noted with the greatest pride the splendid bearing and cheerfulness of all ranks, he feels absolutely confident that the 2/4 Battalion London Regiment R.F. will have no difficulty in making its Christmas as merry as possible, and in carrying on in the same way in the New Year.

" The Commanding Officer feels sure that all ranks desire to express their hearty thanks to Mrs. Vickers Dunfee and friends for the handsome and useful presents provided and packed by them."

F

December 25th, 1915.—CHRISTMAS DAY.

" B " Company, with two platoons of " A " Company, left Cæsar's Camp and proceeded up the line and joined " C " and " D " Companies in Tranchee d'Amade.

2nd Lieut. H. G. HICKLENTON, with the three machine guns in Tranchee d'Amade, took up positions in the front trenches ; one gun was in the firing line and the other two guns were placed in the support trenches for anti-aircraft work.

The friends of the 2/4 Battalion in England sent every man in the Battalion a Christmas card with the following lines :

> God bless your arms,
> God speed your victory,
> God grant your safe return.

December 29th, 1915.

Lieut. A. MCDONNELL, R.A.M.C., was admitted to hospital.

During the time this officer was Medical Officer to the Battalion he earned the regard and esteem of all ranks by his unfailing care and attention to both sick and wounded. Though he had been in poor health for some time, he refused to go to hospital, but stuck to his post to the very last.

Both officers and men owe Lieut. McDonnell a deep debt of gratitude.

Surgeon A. E. GOW, R.N., was posted to the Battalion as Medical Officer.

December 31st, 1915.

Lieut. S. N. DAVIES and 63 other ranks left the Battalion and were evacuated to Mudros. Later in the day, 2nd Lieut. S. DAVIS, with 50 other ranks of " B " Company, also left the Peninsula.

2nd Lieut. SIMON and the detachment of the 2/3 Battalion were transferred to the 29th Division.

The following casualties occurred :

No. 3118 Pte. L. L. THOMPSON .... killed.
No. 3074 Lce.-Sergt. A. HOLDS-
    WORTH .... wounded.
No. 3174 Cpl. W. PRIOR .... wounded.
No. 3123 Pte. J. WOOD............ wounded.

No. 3488 Pte. F. W. RICHARDSON .. wounded.
No. 3046 Sergt. RUSSELL .... wounded.
No. 3487 Sergt. MORPHEW ...... wounded.

Sergeants Russell and Morphew were only slightly wounded, and did not leave the Battalion.

The body of Pte. Thompson was buried on 1st January, 1916, at ORCHARD GULLY CEMETERY. Officers from his Company attended the funeral.

January 1st, 1916.

The Companies in Tranchee d'Amade and the half Machine Gun Section in the front trenches returned to Rest Camp.

Capt. R. N. KEEN, 2nd Lieut. W. A. STARK, 2nd Lieut. H. W. VERNON, 2nd Lieut. D. GIANNACOPULO, 2nd Lieut. H. G. HICKLENTON, and 2nd Lieut. J. W. PRICE, with 147 other ranks, left the Battalion and embarked from Cape Helles.

January 3rd, 1916.

No. 2984 Lce.-Cpl. DAVIES, No. 2970 Pte. ROBINSON, and No. 1784 Pte. WRIGHT, of the Machine Gun Section, embarked from Cape Helles with the six machine guns of the Battalion.

January 4th, 1916.

Lieut. S. N. DAVIES was admitted to hospital after he and his party had safely landed at Mudros.

The following were slightly wounded in the Rest Camp at Cape Helles :

No. 3024 Pte. A. LEWIN.
No. 3251 Pte. A. F. LEVY.
No. 2650 Pte. H. W. WALDER.

January 6th, 1916.

Capt. R. N. ARTHUR, Capt. H. G. STANHAM, Lieut. V. S. BOWATER, Lieut. W. R. BOTTERILL, 2nd Lieut. F. R. C. BRADFORD, and 2nd Lieut. S. C. G. BLOWS, with 118 other ranks left the Battalion and embarked from Cape Helles.

January 7th, 1916.

Major V. H. SEYD, Capt. W. N. TOWSE, Lieut. W. H. STEVENS, Lieut. J. R. WEBSTER, 2nd Lieut. N. L. THOMAS,

2nd Lieut. E. G. Lovell, 2nd Lieut. N. W. Williams, Surgeon A. E. Gow, and Lieut. and Quartermaster J. E. W. Lambley, with 155 other ranks, being the remainder of the Battalion on the Peninsula, embarked from Cape Helles.

This party left "V" Beach at night and embarked on to a steam trawler from the River Clyde; troops were eventually transhipped to a big transport which disembarked them in Mudros Harbour on the morning of the 8th.

The following men of the Battalion were attached to a Dumezyl Battery, and volunteered to remain behind on the Peninsula after the Battalion had left to assist connecting up mines for the evacuation of Cape Helles :

No. 3667 Pte. Lingwood.
No. 3143 Pte. Cottrell.
No. 3226 Pte. Turner.
No. 3361 Pte. Trayner.

January 8th, 1916.

The Battalion was accommodated under canvas at South Camp, West Mudros.

The Camp presented a very pleasant spectacle at night after the bivouacs, etc., the Battalion was used to on the Peninsula; and lights were allowed in the tents. Mudros Harbour, where several illuminated hospital ships were lying, made a fine background to the Camp.

The evacuation of the Gallipoli Peninsula will always figure in history as one of the most remarkable achievements of combined naval and military strategy, and the reader may therefore find some interest in the following accounts of experiences on the night of January 8/9th, 1916, the last night of the Allied occupation :—

" A few weeks prior to the evacuation I was detailed from the 2/4th London for a course with the ' Dumezyl ' Battery, under the command of the late Commander Alan Campbell, R.N.D. The ' Dumezyl ' is what is commonly known as an aerial torpedo, and is really a terrible type of trench mortar. Our Battery, which was the first of its kind ever used by the British Army, had just been taken over from the French, and it was used with such good effects against the Turks, that I believe it led to the formation of heavy trench mortars in our own Army.

" The mines referred to were composed of a number of these torpedoes buried in the trenches, together with enormous quantities of ammonal and other surplus high explosives which could not be evacuated. The mines were laid at frequent intervals, and in contact with almost invisible trip wires. These efforts, planned with the purpose of covering the withdrawal of our troops, were not futile, as is evidenced by the report of the German General Liman von Sanders, who states that the Turkish troops met with disaster when, finding that our forces were leaving, they incautiously came in contact with our traps, and suffered severe losses.

" BLANDFORD,
    "*January 8th*, 1919.   ROBERT J. LINGWOOD."

January 8th, 1916.
    " We understand that to-night is to be *the* night. What a relief it is to know that after all the excitement of the rehearsals of the past few nights, the evacuation of the Peninsula is imminent—every man feels the responsibility of the whole business, and that success hinges partly on our ability to bluff ' Johnny Turk ' right up to the last moment. We are told by Commander Campbell, R.N.D., that our destination is ' V ' Beach, and in a short lecture he advises every man to look after himself after he has performed his allotted duties, although, if possible, he wishes us to keep a certain rendezvous after the last man has passed the barricades and the mines have been connected with the electric batteries. He expects that we shall all leave the Peninsula about 1 a.m., but no man can be taken off after 2.30, as the last destroyer will leave the Beaches at that hour. Our party will consist of Commander Campbell, Lieut. Hobbs, Lieut. Borough Green (R.N.D.), and Lieut. Strange (2nd London), C.P.O. Mason, and 27 P.O.'s and men.
    " We leave our bivouac at 6.30 p.m. for our respective posts, which are situated close to each group of mines to wait there in silence until every man has left for the Beaches, and then close the barricades and connect up the mines. The night is very still, and it will be late before the moon rises. The firing lines and reserve trenches in our sector are now held by only a few companies of

69

men, a few machine guns, and not a single field gun—these have all been removed or destroyed. It is very quiet, except for an occasional burst of machine gun fire from the Turkish trenches. About 7.30 footsteps approach, the countersign is given, and 50 men of the ' Hood ' Battalion file silently past, their feet carefully padded with sandbags These are soon followed by the remaining machine gunners and another 50 men of the ' Drake ' Battalion. There are now only a few men left in the firing-line, and these continue to send up the ' Very ' lights and fire an occasional shot to hang the time out ; as a matter of fact, we could not make much show now if the enemy should become suspicious and attack. Just a glimpse of the moon, or a premature contact with one of our mines close at hand, and the game is up, but fortune smiles upon us and all goes well. That immense shaft of light sweeping the sky at intervals tells us that the Turk is as watchful as ever ; it is an extremely powerful search-light situated at the Turkish Fort of Chanak, and its glare throws that sinister monster Achi Baba into bold relief. At 11.30 the last men leave the firing line. Engineers and our bombers come through our sector promptly, but there is some delay in getting the line clear. However, just on the stroke of twelve, Lieut. Hobbs and his party approach our position at the last mine, and pass word that the other mines have been connected up and the barricades closed without mishap.

January 9th, 1916.

" The miners and bombers pass on to join Commander Campbell and the rest of the party, and, whilst Mr. Hobbs picks up the trip wire and places this in position, I connect the mine wires with the battery. The last mine is connected up, and we walk on to join the rest of the party. A hurried roll call, in whispered tones, to find that only two men are missing, and we walk away at a brisk pace for the Beach. The three-mile journey to the Beach is uneventful, and although we are all glad to get away from this detestable land of death and disease, yet one regrets to think of the vain sacrifices which have been made to hold this miserable stretch of territory. We arrive at our destination near the remains of the famous old transport, ' River Clyde.' It is 2.30, and there are about 300 men lined up along the Beach waiting for a destroyer to take them off, but a very heavy sea is running, and barges and drifters laden with mules are breaking away from their moorings to destruction. After some time has elapsed a destroyer, at great risk, manages to get to the leeward of the ' River Clyde,' and we lose no time in getting aboard. We crowd every inch of space, and at 3.30 H.M. destroyer ' Grasshopper ' shoots off into Gallipoli Straits, every man clinging to the nearest support to prevent being washed overboard. The seas get worse, and the destroyer rolls in an alarming manner, but the crew are splendid, and, in spite of great difficulties, they manage to get hot food and drink for some of the men who are badly injured or exhausted. We had hardly left the shore when our stores and dumps began to burn up, having already been saturated with petrol, and in a few minutes the coast for miles was one mass of flame. The Turks now realised that there was ' something doing,' and all their batteries, including those on the Asiatic shore, bombard the Beaches and our vacant lines. We clearly saw their shrapnel bursting all over the Peninsula, intermingled with alarm star shells of red and green lights. Presently we heard the din of numerous explosions, and knew that our mines have done their work. Dense smoke now covers the whole area, and the scene is hidden from view. Our destroyer was the last boat to leave Gallipoli, and on account of the heavy weather was unable to put into harbour.

" At dawn we found ourselves outside the harbour boom at Imbros, and entered the harbour to be transferred to H.M.S. ' Mars,' and thence to Mudros."

All towns and villages were placed out of bounds except Mudros West.

The Commanding Officer received a very gratifying communication from O.C. Dumezyl Battery, who stated that Ptes. COTTRELL, TURNER, TRAYNER, and LINGWOOD behaved with the utmost zeal and devotion to duty in connection with the final operations at Cape Helles ; he specially mentioned Pte. Cottrell's bravery on several occasions.

January 10*th*, 1916.
The Battalion ceased to be attached to the Royal Naval Division, and became part of the 29th Division.

Both officers and men of the Battalion will ever remember with the most cordial feeling of friendship their attachment to the Royal Naval Brigade. From the day the Battalion landed on the Peninsula to the day of the evacuation of Cape Helles, the 2/4 Battalion enjoyed the utmost friendship and good feeling from the Naval Brigade, and all ranks greatly regretted the inevitable parting.

The last number of the Peninsula Press, No. 96, was published.

January 11*th*, 1916.

Capt. R. N. KEEN was admitted to hospital at Mudros.

Large fatigue parties from the Battalion were detailed to sort letters, parcels and papers which had accumulated at Mudros. Owing to the evacuation of the Peninsula, no mails had been sent further than Mudros for some weeks previous to the withdrawal, so no Christmas parcels had been received by the Battalion.

When the mails and parcels for the Battalion had been brought into camp and duly distributed to the Companies, there was much jubilation and excitement in undoing the parcels and reading the letters from home.

January 12*th*, 1916.

Company training and route marching were carried out.

The following is an extract from R.N. Divisional Orders, No. 341 :

" EVACUATION—APPRECIATIVE MESSAGE.

" 1. The Corps Commander wishes to express to all ranks his deep appreciation of their conduct and discipline which enabled this difficult operation to be carried through so successfully.

" 2. The R.N.D. has been continuously engaged in operations on the Peninsula since the first landing in April. There is no doubt it has earned and gained a high reputation, of which all ranks must be proud.

" At the conclusion of this campaign the G.O.C. wishes to express his high appreciation of the services rendered, and looks forward with great confidence to its successful employment in another theatre of war.

" As regards the evacuation of Cape Helles, the G.O.C.

MAP SHOWING CEMETERIES
ON THE
GALLIPOLI PENINSULAR

REFERENCE.
1   V BEACH.
2   LANCASHIRE LANDING.
3   R.N.D
4   52ND. DIVISION.
5   SKEW BRIDGE.
6&7 ROMANOS WELLS.
8   KRITHIA NULLAM Nº1.
9   GEOHEGANS BLUFF
10 11&13 PINK FARM.
12   W BEACH.
14&15 GULLY RAVINE
16   Dº   INDIAN.
17   Y BEACH.
18   INNISKILLING
19   CHURCH FARM.
20   BROWN HOUSE.
23   KRITHIA NULLAM
26   REDOUBT.

thanks all ranks for their loyal co-operation and the excellent discipline displayed ; the success of the operation would not have been possible otherwise."

January 13th, 1916.
Company route marches took place.
The following rejoined the Battalion for duty :

No. 2606 Cpl. ALLUM.
No. 2516 Pte. PARSONS.
No. 2787 Pte. RUSSELL.
No. 2749 Pte. RODD.
No. 2596 Pte. TUTHILL.
No. 2806 Pte. TYLER.
No. 3221 Pte. TENTORI.
No. 3502 Pte. DAVIES.
No. 3240 Pte. REEVES.

In returning the above to the Battalion, O.C. Transport Depôt, Mudros West, wrote :

" They have been attached to this Depôt since the 14th December, 1915, for transport duties. During the time they have been attached to me they have performed their duties most willingly, and have been of great assistance to the working of the transport of this Depôt."

Cpl. Allum was specially mentioned as having done good work.

January 14th, 1916.
No. 3283 Sergt. F. W. WALKER left the Battalion to proceed to England to take up a commission.
The Commanding Officer expressed his great appreciation of the efficient and conscientious manner in which Sergt. Walker always carried out his duties.
Sergt. PARSLOW took over the duties in the Orderly Room.

January 16th, 1916.
Surgeon A. GOW, R.N., left the Battalion and rejoined the Royal Naval Division.
Lieut. J. E. LOUDEN, R.A.M.C., was attached to the Battalion as Medical Officer.

January 18th, 1916.
The Battalion embarked on H.M.T. " Ionian " and left Mudros for Egypt.

73

January 21*st*, 1916.

The Battalion arrived at Alexandria.

Capt. L. C. COATES and Lieut. A. McDONNELL, R.A.M.C., late Adjutant and Medical Officer respectively of the Battalion, were in hospital in Alexandria ; they left for England on the 22nd January.

January 22*nd*, 1916.

The Battalion entrained at Alexandria and left there at 3.30 p.m. for Wardan, which was reached at about 8 p.m.

The Battalion encamped in the desert about three-quarters of a mile from the station ; it provided its own tents, which had been brought from Mudros.

The Battalion became part of the 53rd Division.

Lieut. H. W. DENNIS rejoined from leave ; 2nd Lieut. G. F. BISHOP reported for duty from Alexandria.

January 23*rd*, 1916.

Mrs. VICKERS DUNFEE, as a result of a cable received from Major V. H. SEYD, sent the following message to the next of kin of all members of the Battalion :

"All well. In Egypt. Address all letters as before, Mediterranean Expeditionary Force."

January 25*th*, 1916.

Company training with preliminary musketry and physical training was carried out daily.

Permission was granted for parties of 15 other ranks to proceed to Cairo every day.

The Battalion received the bad news that No. 3375 Pte. F. C. LANNING had died in hospital on the 18th January from peritonitis.

January 29*th*, 1916.

The Battalion carried out a route march ; Capt. R. N. Arthur was in charge.

One hundred and seventy bags of mails arrived for the Battalion, which included belated Christmas presents and letters.

February 16*th*, 1916.

The Battalion, with two Companies of the 2/2 Battalion,

left Wardan by rail and detrained at Beni Mazar, where the troops encamped and became part of " The Force at Minia."

The troops were received at Beni Mazar by Mohamed Marzouk and Mamour Markaz.

Major V. H. SEYD assumed command of all troops at Beni Mazar, which included :

2/4 Battalion London Regiment.

Two Companies of the 2/2 London Regiment.

One Camel M.G. Section Lovat's Scouts, with a detached post at Saqula, which was composed of :

One Company of Infantry.

One Troop Australian L.H.

Engineers, etc.

An armoured train was attached to the force at Beni Mazar.

February 17*th*, 1916.

2nd Lieut. D. N. GIANNACOPULO was appointed temporary R.T.O. at Beni Mazar.

Three orderlies from the Battalion were always on duty and three signallers were stationed at the Mamour's office.

February 19*th*, 1916.

The following are extracts from letters which the Commanding Officer received from the Royal Naval Division :

" I must write a line to thank you and your Battalion for all the good work you did when with us on the Peninsula. . . . We all admired the cheerful spirit your men showed under very trying circumstances.

A. PARIS, Maj.-Gen.

G.O.C. Royal Naval Division."

" Very many thanks for all you have done to help us along in the past.

J. A. TUPMAN, Lieut.-Col.

Brigade-Major 1st R.N. Brigade."

February 21*st*, 1916.

Lieut.-Gen. Sir J. G. MAXWELL, K.C.B., K.C.M.G., C.V.O., D.S.O., and Brig.-Gen. A. STIRLING, G.O.C., Minia Forces, visited the troops at Beni Mazar, and were received by Major V. H. Seyd.

Mirza Mohed Ali F. Bey Abdul Gawad gave permission for the troops at Beni Mazar to visit his orange groves.

February 22nd, 1916.

The officers of the Battalion were entertained at lunch by the French Consul at Eshruba ; the Colonel and several other officers of the Australian Light Horse were also present.

After lunch a display of Bedouin and Arab riding was given.

February 25th, 1916.

Lieut. E. G. LOVELL left the Battalion and reported for duty at Staff Headquarters, Minia.

Telephone installation between Headquarters, Minia, Saqula and Beni Mazar was completed.

Mohammed K. Gold, of El Keis, sent the following present to the Battalion :

> 50 fowls.
> 2 turkeys.
> 1,000 eggs.
> 600 oranges.
> 2 boxes of pastry.

February 26th, 1916.

Colonel VICKERS DUNFEE rejoined the Battalion from England.

Capt. HUNTER, with two officers and 54 other ranks of the 2/2 Battalion with interpreter, left Beni Mazar to proceed to Nag Hamadi on detachment for guarding the bridge over the Nile there. A detachment of one officer and 10 other ranks from the 2/1 Cheshire Field Company R.E., were detailed to join Capt. Hunter and to be under his orders.

A football match between officers and sergeants took place in the afternoon, to which the officials and notables of Beni Mazar and surrounding villages were invited. The Battalion with bands paraded to receive these guests.

February 27th, 1916.

Colonel VICKERS DUNFEE proceeded to Minia to report to Brig.-General Stirling, G.O.C., Minia Forces.

The following is an extract from Minia Force Orders, February 27th, 1916 :

" Colonel Vickers Dunfee rejoined the 2/4 Battalion London Regiment, and assumed command of all troops at Beni Mazar on the 26th February, 1916."

MIRZA BEY, who, during the stay of the Battalion at Beni Mazar, proved such a loyal and devoted friend to both officers and men, sent the following presents to the troops :

    4 sheep.
    6 turkeys.
  200 fowls.
    3 baskets of eggs.

February 27th, 1916.

The following are extracts from an article written by Lieut. C. DEAMER, of the 2/2 Battalion, on the situation and life of the troops in Egypt, which appeared in the London Press :

" ' Are you happy, lads ? ' said a General to us on one occasion in the trenches at Cape Helles. ' Yes, thank you, sir,' we answered mournfully, knowing we should be moved that night to another sector. Indeed, as Pte. Snooks, our regimental pessimist, remarked : ' Them tin 'ats are allus the same. " Are yer 'appy ? " they ses. " Then yer can clear aht then. Is there anything yer want, lads ? Well, yer shan't 'ave it, then." '

" But here it is quite different. Generals do exist certainly, but they leave us more or less at peace among the sugar canes and palm trees, in a sleepy little Egyptian town 500 miles south of Cairo on the Nile. At first the ' Gippy ' natives watched our movements furtively from behind latticed windows, for they had never seen British soldiers before and trembled at the sight of fixed bayonets. But when they discovered that we were stationed there merely to ' drive away the enemies ' they came forth in their thousands and welcomed us as deliverers.

" All this accounts for our present prosperity. Turkeys larger than Cæsar ever knew strut about in our camp waiting for the day of judgment. Chickens in coops (one climbed the Colonel's tent this morning and crowed lustily from the top) and sheep in pens continue to arrive as presents from the admiring populace and from local celebrities. Several hundred eggs arrived yesterday, and to-day an orgy of oranges. The sugar harvest is now in full swing ; two or three towering canes may be bought for a penny. The troops buy quite a large quantity of sugar cane, which they chew solemnly or distinguish their tents by making green leafy portals out of the bent cane.

" Most of the sugar is packed on camels, and in the evening we often see hundreds of these beasts moving with their long, stately strides towards the Nile, to the spot where the sailing boats are laden. On each side of the river stretches cultivated ground for about five miles, cultivated land composed mostly of Nile mud, which forms the Nile valley. Thus the irrigated land clings to the water right down the backbone of Egypt, from Alexandria to Luxor, from Luxor to the Second Cataract, flanked on either side by illimitable tracts of desert.

" Our little town boasts two people of supreme importance—the Bey (an Arabic title corresponding to our Knighthood) and the Mamur, or native government official of the town. The Bey, a rich landowner, entertained a few of us at luncheon recently with true Oriental splendour, for, after devouring an excellent Nile fish, I suddenly noticed the startled face of my Company Commander as he tackled a sheep roasted whole, on a quite colossal dish. A Mahometan strongly dislikes dissecting any animal, and prefers to cook it whole. Pigeon came up next—the blue rock pigeon found in Upper Egypt—and then we devoured consecutively turkey, snipe and veal. Truly a feast for such Gallipolean appetites as ours. Unfortunately the comfort of the meal was marred by incessant toasts, during nearly every course. During the soup we drank the King's health ; the Sultan of Egypt's prosperity was confirmed in a fishy atmosphere ; the Prince of Wales, the Colonel, our host and others all had their place ; and, finally, speeches in English, French and Arabic completed the experience.

" We returned this gargantuan feast a day or two later, and invited the Bey, together with all the local celebrities, to tea, and a specially arranged gala football match. They came in their hundreds, and the ground was soon dotted with the local notables, in long white garments and scarlet fez. At half-time they began to go away, sorrowfully thinking the game over, but a police corporal explained the position to them, gesticulating wildly with an enormous piece of sugar cane in his hand.

" Naturally at the subsequent tea social mistakes were made. For instance, an enterprising cabdriver, together with a smartly dressed waiter, got placed among the seats of the mighty, and were seen graciously accepting buns from the Colonel's hands. Finally an interpreter read a patriotic speech expressing satisfaction and pleasure at our presence in Egypt."

February 28th, 1916.

A party of 400 all ranks from the Battalion carried out an experimental run on the armoured train from Beni Mazar to Maghagha.

The troops were in light marching order, and each man carried 120 rounds of ball ammunition.

Lieut. R. C. DICKINS reported back to the Battalion for duty.

February 29th, 1916.

Another experimental run on the armoured train took place, and the following is a report Colonel VICKERS DUNFEE, O.C. Troops Beni Mazar, sent to Headquarters, regarding the practice :

" Eleven officers and 236 other ranks of the Battalion together with a Machine Gun Section of Lovat's Scouts, entrained on the armoured train at Beni Mazar at 10.15 this morning for Maghagha. The permanent crew of the train, viz., Major Dobson in charge, with one officer and 25 native other ranks, were already on board. The train was armed with Krupp guns, in addition to the two machine guns of the Lovat's Scouts.

" The entraining took seven minutes ; 120 men were accommodated in front of the engine, and the remainder of the party were placed in rear of it. The construction of the carriages did not admit of rapid entraining or detraining. The journey to Maghagha took 35 minutes.

" The detachment marched through Maghagha to the River Nile, where arms were piled and the men allowed to fall out and eat the field rations they carried on them.

" At 1.30 p.m. the return march was made through the principal streets of the town to the station, where the

troops again entrained. The entraining was expeditiously
carried out, and the train left Maghagha at 2.15 p.m., and
the troops were back in camp at Beni Mazar about 3 o'clock.

" The demeanour of the people was satisfactory, and
every assistance was afforded by the local police."

The conduct of the troops and of the natives at Beni
Mazar was so good that the order forbidding parties of
men, less than six in number, to walk out together was
rescinded, but troops had to go about in pairs.

March 1st, 1916.

Camp was struck for two hours to air the ground.

Sun helmets were issued to all ranks, and the regimental flashes were sewn on both sides of the helmets.

Capt. H. G. STANHAM took over command of the
Saqula detachment.

2nd Lieut. H. B. TAYLOR, recently gazetted from the
2/4 Battalion to the 4/4 Battalion in England, left Beni
Mazar to report to D.A.G., 3rd Echelon, Alexandria, for
instructions.

March 2nd, 1916.

Colonel VICKERS DUNFEE visited the Saqula detachment, and the following is a report on his visit there :

" I visited this bridgehead and found that the scheme
of defence was nearing completion.

" Lieut. Moon appears to have utilised every point
suitable for defence, and has made the best use of the
engineering supplies available. The wire required has
not yet arrived, and its delivery should be expedited.

" Only two machine guns are on the ground, and I
think it would be an advantage if a further two could be
permanently kept there.

" I then proceeded to the Camp of the 1st Australian
L.H. and saw Colonel Meredith, who promised to give
every assistance to the Battalion in carrying out field
firing should such be approved.

" I have appointed Capt. H. G. Stanham, 2/4 Battalion,
to command the detachment."

March 3rd, 1916.

Officers as mentioned below assembled at the Orderly

Room of the 2/4 London Regiment, Beni Mazar, at 9.45
a.m. for the purpose of trying by Field General Court-
martial an accused person :

President.. Major V. H. Seyd .. 2/4 Battalion.
Members Capt. R. N. Arthur .. 2/4 Battalion.
Lieut. R. H. Wagner 2/2 Battalion.

As the result of an accident whilst on duty at Saqula
on the 2nd March, No. 852 Sapper Norman, 2/1 Cheshire Field Company, R.E., died during the journey from
Saqula to Beni Mazar. The body was taken to Minia
to-day for burial. O.C. troops and other officers in camp
followed the body to the ferry, and Lieut. R. C. Dickins,
2/4 Battalion, accompanied it by rail with an escort from
the Battalion.

O.C. 2/1 Cheshire Field Company, R.E., wrote a letter
expressing his appreciation of the action of O.C. Troops,
Beni Mazar, in sending an officer and escort to the funeral
of Sapper Norman at Minia.

The force at Beni Mazar was experimentally mobilized
and proceeded to Tambu to cover and protect the railway crossing there.

One day's rations and 120 rounds of ball ammunition
were carried by each man of the force.

One of the native transport drivers, who was attached
to the Battalion for the trip to Tambu, was arrested by the
native police ; he was released, however, at the request
of the Commanding Officer.

March 4th, 1916.

The Machine Gun Section of Lovat's Scouts was withdrawn from Beni Mazar by order of G.O.C., Minia.

A Court of Enquiry was assembled at Saqula at 10
a.m. to investigate the circumstances attending the death
of No. 852 Sapper Norman, 2/1 Cheshire Field Company
R.E., at Saqula on 2nd March. The following officers
composed the Court :

Colonel Vickers Dunfee, V.D.
Capt. W. N. Towse.
Lieut. W. H. S. Stevens.

March 5th, 1916.

MAHOMED ZABI ABD EL RAZECH invited the officers of

the Battalion to lunch ; the Regimental Band played in the Courtyard during the repast, and afterwards to the ladies of the harem. Both the officers and the members of the band were most hospitably entertained.

During the stay of the Battalion at Beni Mazar, the Beys and notables there sent all manner of gifts to the troops, amongst which were :—

2,000 eggs.
100 chickens.
2 sheep.
900 oranges.
14 turkeys.
8,000 cigarettes.
8 boxes of biscuits.
8 boxes of pineapples.
6 boxes of peaches.
6 boxes of apples.

March 6th, 1916.

The troops at Beni Mazar ceased to form part of the Minia Force, and came under the orders of Major-General DALLAS, Commanding Northern Area of Southern Force.

Sun helmets now had to be worn on all parades, and drill clothing was compulsory after 9 a.m.

The following is an extract from Force Orders :—

" As the hot weather is now commencing, special efforts must be made by all ranks to combat the fly nuisance. The strictest attention is enjoined to the destruction in incinerators of all cookhouse refuse and scraps of food and rubbish."

March 8th, 1916.

The Force at Beni Mazar was experimentally mobilised.

The alarm was sounded at 5.50 a.m., and officers were given their instructions ; a messenger was despatched for the 18 carts always kept ready by the Mamour. These carts arrived at 6.30 a.m., and in the meanwhile Companies, who were at early morning drill, were called in and breakfast was served to the whole Force.

Tents were emptied, valises and kitbags were packed,

and at 7.45 a.m. the Force paraded ; strength of Force was :

2/2 Battalion 8 officers 236 other ranks .. Total 244
2/4 Battalion 16 officers 450 other ranks .. Total 466

Twenty-three men for various reasons were left in camp, in addition to a guard of 25 N.C.O's. and men.

The Force was equipped according to instructions and carried two days' rations.

The column, with baggage carts, etc., moved off at 7.45 and proceeded to Tambu, where a defensive position was taken up ; advanced and rear guards covered the column on the march.

At 10.20 a.m. orders were received for the Force to retire and troops fell back, preceded by the transport column, to Beni Mazar, which was reached at 10.50 a.m.

No man fell out during the march.

The experiment proved very useful for instruction of all ranks ; only three carts supplied by the Mamour were late in arriving at the Camp.

Lieut. J. LOUDON, R.A.M.C., the Battalion M.O., proceeded on sick leave.

March 9th, 1916.

Capt. MARTIN, R.A.M.C., reported for duty as Battalion Medical Officer from the 1/2 S.W. Mounted Field Ambulance.

Monsieur and Madame A. C. Eysens, of Sheikh Fadl, invited some of the officers of the Battalion to lunch and to inspect the large sugar factory on the banks of the Nile. The party proceeded on horses and donkeys to the river, from whence a steam launch conveyed them to the factory.

The Commanding Officer was able to obtain half a ton of best moist sugar for the Battalion at the rate of £22 per ton.

March 11th, 1916.

Lieut. J. R. WEBSTER, the Adjutant, proceeded on three days' leave, and Lieut. W. H. S. STEVENS was appointed Acting Adjutant.

The Battalion paraded in mass on the football field for inspection by the Commanding Officer. The band and drums were in attendance.

2nd Lieut. S. DAVIS and the detachment of the 2/4 Battalion at Saqula were relieved by a detachment from the 2/2 Battalion.

March 13th, 1916.

One officer and 25 other ranks of " A " Company proceeded to Ben Hassan for field firing, under Capt. R. N. ARTHUR.

Similar parties were sent daily from the Battalion to undergo this instruction.

2nd Lieut. H. W. DENNIS and a detachment from the 2/4 Battalion relieved the detachment of the 2/2 Battalion at Saqula.

March 14th, 1916.

The detachment of the 2/2 Battalion London Regiment, under Capt. HUNTER, left Beni Mazar for Esneh.

The Commanding Officer expressed his appreciation of their fine work and good behaviour whilst under his command.

March 15th, 1916.

Capt. the Rev. C. HOLMES commenced a series of voluntary services every Wednesday evening.

A Club House was fitted up in the village, and contained officers', sergeants', and men's rooms ; there was also a dark room for photography and a canteen was fixed up in the garden.

Mirza Bey kindly lent a piano and a large quantity of furniture for the Club House.

March 17th, 1916.

Lieut. LOUDON, R.A.M.C., returned to the Battalion from leave, and Capt. MARTIN, R.A.M.C., rejoined the Field Ambulance.

A bayonet fighting and assault course was constructed for use of the Battalion.

The Club House in Beni Mazar was opened, and the Regimental Band played there from 4.45 p.m. to 6.15 p.m.

March 19th, 1916.

A medical inspection of natives was held by the Battalion Medical Officer.

:SKETCH: PLAN: OF: :DEFENCES: — :AT: — : SAQULA: BRIDGE: MARCH 1916.

BACK WATER

BRIDGE

RAISED ROADWAY

BREAK MOSQUE & CEMETERY CORNFIELD

BREAK

M.G. PIT WITH GUN

CORNFIELD

1500 YDS.

RAISED ROADWAY

COMMUNICATION TRENCH

VILLAGE

BACKWATER

SANDBAG BARRICADE WITH LOOPHOLES FOR 2 M.GS. M.G. PIT WITH GUN

CORNFIELD

BANK 20' HIGH

BANK 20 HIGH

M.G PIT

M.G.P.

BANK 20' HIGH

BEDOUIN VILLAGE

ROADWAY

TIMBER BARRICADE

ROADWAY

BOAT

SAQULA BRIDGE

BAHR YOSSF CANAL

CORNFIELD ROADWAY

ROADWAY

POLICE STATION

M.G.PITS

M.G. PIT

CORNFIELD

BANK 20' HIGH

M.G. PITS

BANK 20' HIGH

BANK 20' HIGH

M.G. PIT

HORSE LINES

YEOMANRY CAMP

INFANTRY CAMP

BACKWATER

SANDBAG BARRICADE

CORNFIELD

CORNFIELD

RAISED ROADWAY

NOTES. FIRE TRENCHES : MACHINE GUN PITS : TELEPHONES :

. M.G.

YARDS. 100 50 0 100 200 300 400 500 YARDS.

— APPROXIMATE SCALE IN YARDS. —

Saqula Bridge and Village, fortified in expectation of an attack from the Bahara Oasis

Notables and Chiefs who visited the Battalion, Upper Egypt

Garrison Duties. Parading at Sporting Club Camp, Alexandria

The Commanding Officer presented Mirza Bey with a silver cigarette case, and asked him to accept it from the officers of the Battalion as a small token of friendship and of their appreciation of his great kindness.

He also presented the Mamour of Beni Mazar, who was an old officer in the Egyptian Army and had served under the late Lord Kitchener, with a watch from the officers, together with an address as follows :—

" My dear Mamour,—Thanks to your kindness and thoughtfulness our stay at Beni Mazar has been a very happy one.

" We realise in you the character of a real soldier and a good comrade.

" We trust that this friendship so happily begun between the City of London Regiment and the inhabitants of your town will long continue.

" When the war is over and we are perhaps far away we hope you will from time to time think of your comrades from over the sea and the happy days we had together.

" I ask you on behalf of the troops here to accept this small gift, and that as the hands of this watch move round so the friendship between Egypt and our own country will daily grow stronger and stronger.

" *March*, 1916.   VICKERS DUNFEE, Colonel."

March 20th, 1916.

Thirty-five thousand cigarettes, in tins of 50, arrived for the Battalion from England ; these cigarettes were sent by friends of the Battalion at home.

Six hundred briar pipes, inscribed with the name of the Regiment, were also received ; these pipes were bought out of Battalion funds, and distributed free to the troops.

March 21st, 1916.

The following letter was received by the Commanding Officer :—

" Sir—I have the honour to offer you and the troops the small present sent by bearer.

" Hoping that it will be accepted,

" I am, Yours respectfully,

" AHMED H. EL KEESZ."

The following constituted the " small " present :—

    2 tins butter.
    40 hens.
    1,000 eggs.
    2 tins of honey.
    1,000 cigarettes.
    2 camel loads of sugar cane.

March 22nd, 1916.

A present of two footballs, two pairs of boxing gloves, some stationery and games were received from the Y.M.C.A., and were greatly appreciated by the troops.

Two large parcels of books and periodicals were also received from the Hon. Mrs. Anstruther, the Hon. Sec. to the Camps Library.

March 23rd, 1916.

An Army Post Office was established in the camp, and dealt with the following mails :—

    2/4 London.
    1/1 Lincolnshire Yeomanry.
    2/1 Cheshire Field Company R.E.

March 24th, 1916.

The Regimental Band played at Beni Mazar School.

The following letter was received by the Commanding Officer from the President of Beni Mazar School :—

" It is with the greatest pleasure that the Society has heard of your visit to its School at Beni Mazar and of recording this visit in the School Register.

" The Society has to tender you herewith the very best thanks for same.

               " H. ABD EL REZIK
                 (for the President)."

March 25th, 1916.

A route march was carried out by the Battalion

Lieut. COBUNOY and 11 other ranks of the 2/1 Welsh Field Company R.E. relieved the detachment of the 2/1 Cheshire Field Company R.E., under Lieut. MOON, at Saqula

March 26th, 1916.

The Battalion attended Divine Service at 8.30 a.m.

After the service the Commanding Officer inspected the Camp and the Club House at Beni Mazar.

March 29th, 1916.

Major V. H. SEYD was granted leave of absence, and left for Cairo in the afternoon. The Commanding Officer and all the officers of the Battalion saw him off from the station on his well-earned rest.

During the eighteen months Major Seyd had served with the Battalion he had earned the affection and regard of all ranks. He was in command of the Battalion during the evacuation from Gallipoli, and brought the Battalion safely to Mudros and Egypt.

To the Commanding Officer he proved a loyal and devoted friend ; for the comfort of the men no trouble was too great, no detail too small for his individual attention. Major Seyd indeed had the love and respect of every member of the Battalion.

March 30th, 1916.

Tents were struck and the ground exposed to the sun for a few hours.

A route march was carried out by the Battalion.

During the absence on leave of Major V. H. Seyd, Capt. R. N. Arthur acted as Second in Command of the Battalion, with the acting rank of Major.

No man in the Battalion was permitted outside his tent without a sun helmet on between 9 a.m. and 5 p.m.

April 1st, 1916.

A route march was carried out by the Battalion.

Capt. W. N. TOWSE and 2nd Lieut. F. R. C. BRADFORD were detailed as members of a Field General Court-Martial at Bahnasa.

April 2nd, 1916.

The officers of the Battalion were invited to tea by a French resident at Saft Abu Gorg.

The Regimental Band was conveyed in three carts, and six carriages were provided for the officers.

Tea was served at small tables, with most delicious

87

cakes. In the gardens banana and orange trees were in blossom, and lemons and strawberries were also growing.

April 3rd, 1916.

Mirza Bey and his brother dined in the Officers' Mess, and the following day Mirza Bey entertained the officers at dinner in his house.

A class of instruction for N.C.O.'s. was commenced, under the Regimental Sergeant-Major.

April 5th, 1916.

The following invitation was received by the Commanding Officer :

" The Judge, Magistrate, Lawyers and Headmaster of the School request the pleasure of the Colonel and all officers of the Regiment for tea at 3.45 p.m. at Beni Mazar Club."

Most of the officers of the Battalion accepted the invitation, and all were most hospitably entertained.

April 6th, 1916.

The Machine Gun Section, of the Battalion under 2nd Lieut. H. G. HICKLENTON, returned from Saqula.

The detachment of the Battalion, under Capt. W. H. S. STEVENS, was also withdrawn from Saqula, and the post was taken over by a detachment of the 1/1 Lincolnshire Yeomanry.

April 10th, 1916.

The following letter was received by the Commanding Officer from SAID MELIKA, of Beni Mazar :

" Your dear favour is now at hand. I feel very deeply sorry for your departure, and it seems to me that my sorrow will last for ever.

" Your noble feelings towards me that were clearly expressed in your letter and your kind words left a pleasant effect in my heart, which will never be forgotten.

" You thanked me for welcome and hospitality, but what welcome did I extended to you ? I have done nothing that can be mentioned beside the debt we owe the English. If we are happy or at comfort, if we enjoy peace and prosperity, if we are rich and can do any hospitality to our guests, it is to your kindness, true efforts and to the improvement you have done in Egypt since your occupation that we owe all this.

" As for you personally and your Regiment, it is very difficult for me to see you off, but I trust that you will leave Egypt only, but not our hearts. We shall always remember your kind treatment.

" Kind regards to you and best wishes to Great Britain and her Allies."

April 11*th*, 1916.

The Battalion paraded in full marching order at 8.15 a.m.

Five officers and 182 other ranks of the 2/5 Devons, under Capt. W. W. KITSON, arrived at Beni Mazar to take over the Camp, stores, etc.

The Commanding Officer sent the following letter to the NOTABLES of the District :

" On the eve of the departure of the Regiment from Beni Mazar, I should like to express to you, on behalf of my Regiment, how much we appreciate the cordial welcome and kind hospitality you have extended to us.

" We shall retain in our hearts many pleasant memories, and we trust that this happy friendship may be the means of drawing our country and yours nearer to one another."

April 12*th*, 1916.

The Battalion left Beni Mazar at 5.30 p.m. by train for Alexandria ; over 100 chiefs and notables were at the station to say " Good-bye."

April 13*th*, 1916.

The Battalion travelled all night 12-13th April, via Cairo to Alexandria, and detrained at Sidi Bisch ; from here the Battalion marched to a Camp vacated by the South African Brigade at Sidi Gaber.

Colonel VICKERS DUNFEE, V.D., took over temporary command of the 2/1 London Infantry Brigade at Sidi Gaber. The Brigade was composed as follows :

2/1 Battalion London Regiment i/c Lt.-Col. Kennard.
2/2 Battalion London Regiment i/c Lt.-Col. Holder.
2/3 Battalion London Regiment i/c Major Clarke.
2/4 Battalion London Regiment i/c Major Arthur.

April 16th, 1916.

The Battalion attended Divine Service, which was held in front of Brigade Headquarters. The Rev. W. E. DRURY, C.F., the Brigade Chaplain, officiated, and the Regimental Band played the hymns.

Colonel VICKERS DUNFEE, V.D., entertained the Commanding Officers of the Battalions of the London Brigade to dinner at Alexandria.

Capt. R. N. KEEN reported back for duty to the Battalion, and was attached to " A " Company.

April 17th, 1916.

The 2/1 London Infantry Brigade was conveyed by a series of electric trams from the Camp to the Docks at Alexandria, and embarked on H.M.T. " Transylvania " for Marseilles.

In addition to the 2/1 London Infantry Brigade, Colonial and other Imperial troops also embarked on the transport, making a total of 130 officers and nearly 3,000 other ranks.

Col. Vickers Dunfee, V.D., was O.C. Troops.
Lieut. J. R. Webster ....Ship's Adjutant.
Lieut. Bradley 2/2 Battalion ..Ship's Q.-M.
R.S.M. Haigh ....Ship's S.-M.
R.Q.M.S. Sternberg ....Ship's Q.-M. Sergt.
Lieut. Bayley, R.A.M.C. ......Senior M.O.

April 18th, 1916.

H.M.T. " Transylvania " left Alexandria Docks at 11.30 a.m. Life belts were worn constantly by all ranks.

A submarine guard of three officers and 53 other ranks was posted fore and a similar guard was also posted aft ; a third of each guard was on duty at a time on double look-out posts. A ship's guard of three N.C.O.'s and 42 men was found daily.

A deck patrol of two officers was detailed daily to parade the decks from 7 p.m. to 11 p.m. ; the officers were responsible that no lights showed seaward, that no matches were struck and that no smoking took place on deck after dusk, and that there was no singing or other noise.

Parade posts were allotted to each unit, and these posts were to be used by their respective units in case of alarm. Units were detailed to find crews for the ship's boats, but beyond these crews there was no allocation of boats for units ; in case of alarm and the boats had to be used, after the crews had taken their places and the boats had been lowered, they would be filled without distinction of unit from the troops nearest at hand.

April 20th, 1916.

A submarine alarm practice was given, and all troops proceeded to their allotted alarm posts.

The Captain of the ship expressed his approval of the way in which the troops on board turned out on the alarm being sounded. The time taken constituted a record for the ship.

April 24th, 1916.

H.M.T. " Transylvania " arrived in the Harbour Marseilles at 6.30 a.m., and the disembarkation Staff reported on board at 8 a.m.

The Battalion disembarked from the transport, entrained and left Marseilles in the afternoon.

The troop train stopped at the following Haltes Repas en route :

> ORANGE.
> MACON.
> LES LAUMES.
> MONTEREAU.

At these haltes arrangements were made so that the troops could cook their meals ; water was provided, etc.

April 26th, 1916.

The Battalion arrived at Rouen and detrained at about noon. Marching to Bruyeres Camp, and was temporarily attached to the 55th Divisional Base Depôt, under Colonel F. G. H. WIEHE.

The following is an extract from Command Orders :

" The Battalions of the 2/1 London Infantry Brigade having again become separate units, Colonel Vickers Dunfee resumed command of the 2/4 London Regiment Royal Fusiliers."

April 27th, 1916.

The Battalion was inspected by Colonel GIDEON, O.C.

Reinforcements, Rouen ; Battalion paraded in full marching order with folded ground sheets.

April 30th, 1916.
The Battalion attended Divine Service in the Cinema Hut.

2nd Lieut. E. G. LOVELL was appointed Assistant Adjutant.

May 5th, 1916.
A draft consisting of
2nd Lieut. F. R. C. BRADFORD,
2nd Lieut. C. S. G. BLOWS,
2nd Lieut. S. DAVIS,
2nd Lieut. J. W. PRICE,
and 214 other ranks left the Battalion to reinforce the 1/4 Battalion London Regiment.

The Commanding Officer bid farewell to these old comrades who had served so well and so faithfully with the Battalion during the last 20 months.

May 6th, 1916.
Capt. R. N. ARTHUR and Lieut. J. E. W. LAMBLEY, with 40 other ranks, left Rouen and proceeded to England on a week's leave.

May 10th, 1916.
Capt. W. H. S. STEVENS and Lieut. H. W. DENNIS, with 14 other ranks, left Rouen to proceed to England on a week's leave.

2nd Lieut. D. N. GIANNACOPULO was admitted to hospital.

May 13th, 1916.
Lieut. J. R. WEBSTER and 2nd Lieut. G. F. BISHOP, with 14 other ranks, left Rouen and proceeded to England on a week's leave.

2nd Lieut. E. G. LOVELL took over the duties of Adjutant while Lieut. WEBSTER was on leave.

May 14th, 1916.
A party of three N.C.O's. and 22 other ranks of the

Native Village, Beni Mazar, Upper Egypt

The Mascot of the 2/2 London Regiment which travelled to France with the Unit

VICTORY MARCH. LONDON TROOPS, 5th JULY, 1919
The 4th Battalion passing the Mansion House

Battalion proceeded to Rive Gauche Station to take over the guard duties there for one week.

Capt. R. N. KEEN was admitted to hospital.

May 16th, 1916.

Capt. H. G. STANHAM and Lieut. V. S. BOWATER left Rouen and proceeded to England on a week's leave.

May 23rd, 1916.

A draft of 133 other ranks, with Capt. W. H. S. STEVENS, and Lieut. H. W. DENNIS as conducting officers, left the Battalion and proceeded to reinforce the 1/4 Battalion London Regiment.

Another draft of 100 other ranks, under 2nd Lieut. H. G. HICKLENTON, as Conducting Officer, left the Battalion to reinforce the 1/13 Battalion London Regiment.

The Commanding Officer bid a final farewell to these troops, who had served so loyally under him for many months.

May 26th, 1916.

Capt. W. N. TOWSE and Lieut. R. C. DICKINS left Rouen and proceeded to England on a week's leave.

May 31st, 1916.

The Commanding Officer received the following letter from Lieut.-Col. STAFFORD, O.C. 1/13th Battalion London Regiment :

" May I say that the reinforcement from your unit are an excellent lot of men. They have settled down with their new comrades, and are, I think, contented and happy, and you can rest assured that everything possible will be done for their welfare and comfort."

The Regimental Band played as follows during May :

May 22nd. Y.M.C.A. Hut.
May 24th. Battalion Parade Ground.
May 25th. No. 11 Stationary Hospital.
May 29th. Y.M.C.A. No. 2 I.B.D.
May 30th. No. 11 Stationary Hospital.
May 31st. Y.M.C.A. No. 2 I.B.D.

June 1st, 1916.

Regimental Sergt.-Major HAIGH was admitted to

hospital ; his duties were taken over by Company-Sergt.-Major FISHER.

The following were the Band engagements for the month of June :

June 3rd. No. 3 I.B.D. Church Army Hut.
June 5th. No. 1 I.B.D. Y.M.C.A.
June 7th. No. 11 Stationary Hospital.
June 8th. No. 2 I.B.D. Church Army Hut.
June 10th. No. 1 Stationary Hospital.

June 3rd, 1916.

The following officers, with their respective batmen, left Rouen to proceed to the 1/4 Battalion London Regt. :

Capt. R. N. ARTHUR.
Capt. H. G. STANHAM.
Lieut. V. S. BOWATER.
Lieut. W. R. BOTTERILL.
2nd Lieut. H. W. VERNON.
2nd Lieut. B. F. L. YEOMAN.
2nd Lieut. H. G. HICKLENTON.
2nd Lieut. N. W. WILLIAMS.
Lieut. W. A. STARK.

The following officers also left Rouen and proceeded to join the 1/21 Battalion London Regiment :

Capt. W. H. S. STEVENS.
2nd Lieut. G. F. BISHOP.
2nd Lieut. H. W. DENNIS.

Lieut. and Quarter-Master J. E. W. LAMBLEY and batman proceeded to the 15th Corps A.C.C.

June 7th, 1916.

The Commanding Officer received the following letter from O.C. Central Training School, Rouen :

" So many thanks for your kind letter—it was, and always will be, a pleasure to do anything for your Battalion. I shall remember it always as one of the smartest and most keen that I have seen ; the turn out of the men was astonishingly fine.

" It is for me to thank you for all the help you have given us with your officers and N.C.O.'s., who have been so useful.

94

" Good luck to the 2/4 London, and may you yet have the pleasure of re-forming them.

"E. HARVEY JARVIS, Major."

June 22nd, 1916.

Colonel VICKERS DUNFEE reported at Rouen on returning from leave and was posted to the 1/22 Battalion London Regiment.

Capt. W. N. TOWSE and Lieut. R. C. DICKINS were both posted to the 1/21 Battalion London Regiment, and Lieut. J. R. WEBSTER, the Adjutant, after clearing up all details connected with the Battalion, was instructed to join the 1/4 Battalion London Regiment.

All remaining N.C.O's. and men of the 2/4 Battalion were transferred to the 1/4 Battalion London Regiment as reinforcements.

LAST BUT NOT LEAST :
THE LADIES' ASSOCIATION

AN old member of the 4th Battalion—one of a number left behind in Malta, when that unit left for France on January 2nd, 1915, and whose pen has often contributed to the production of the annual *Regimental Gazette* —writes :

The history of the war service of the 2/4th Battalion would not be complete without brief references to the invaluable work rendered to the four Battalions by the Ladies' Association and Prisoners of War Care Committee, also to the welcome home accorded to the cadre of the Battalion by the City of London and the Borough of Shoreditch, and to the magnificent reception given by the people of London to the troops of the Capital.

Only a member of the Ladies' Association and of the Prisoners of War Committee could do justice to the labour of patriotism and love that they performed for the best part of five anxious years. Unfortunately for the completeness of this diary, the ladies prefer to let their work speak for itself, as indeed it has done daily in the families of the prisoners of war and of those gallant men who gave their lives for freedom, or sustained wounds that incapacitated them temporarily and in some cases permanently. None but the mothers and widows of these heroes can fittingly testify to the loving care shown to them by these ladies in their time of anguish, and in their anxieties before the pension arrangements were working smoothly. To Mrs. CARTE DE LAFONTAINE (the Chairman); Mrs. VICKERS DUNFEE, Mrs. H. W. MEREDITH, Miss LORDEN (the Hon. Secretaries); the other members of the Committee, and to the visitors a deep debt of gratitude is due. Every member of the Battalion will treasure with pride the memory of the self-sacrificing work of these ladies.

Not the least praiseworthy service was the reception and tea which they gave in the Stationers' Hall on February 25th, 1919, to 250 returned prisoners of war. Many of these men acknowledged that but for the parcels of comforts which they received their captivity would have been unbearable.

It was in the highest degree appropriate that the ladies were also responsible for arranging with the Rector of St. Sepulchre's Church, Holborn Viaduct, for the holding of the Memorial Service for the officers and men of the three Battalions who had made the great sacrifice. On that occasion—Saturday, March 1st, 1919—the Rev. Canon EDGAR SHEPPARD, K.C.V.O., D.D., of the Chapels Royal, and chaplain to the Regiment, paid an eloquent and touching tribute to departed comrades (many of whom he had addressed at church parades), and also offered words of sacred comfort to the bereaved.

WELCOME HOME OF THE CADRE

As to the welcome home to some fifty officers and men of the cadre on May 27th, 1919, a word of praise is due to Lieutenant and Quartermaster E. S. TOMSETT for the excellent arrangements which he made for that historic occasion. Lieut. Tomsett, after two years or more of service with the 1/4th Battalion in Malta and France, was appointed Officer-in-Charge of the Depôt at Shaftesbury Street. There, in addition to discharging routine duty, he has taken a leading part in forming the Old Comrades' Association, and has conducted a heavy correspondence with relatives of missing men. Lieut. Tomsett for many years showed a genius in organising social events for the 1/4th Battalion when it was commanded by Colonel Dunfee, but he outshone his record in planning the details of this welcome home. One noticeable feature was the massing of the school children of Shoreditch in the streets leading to the Depôt, the youngsters making the welkin ring with their shrill cheers. The cadre arrived in London Bridge Station from Newhaven shortly after one o'clock, the Lord Mayor and Colonel VICKERS DUNFEE being amongst the company who greeted the little detachment, under the command of Lt.-Colonel A. F. MARCHMENT.

A large contingent of discharged members of the Battalions fell in behind, and, headed by the band, under Drum-Major MUNDAY, the column marched through the City, the Lord Mayor (Colonel the Rt.Hon. SIR HORACE B. MARSHALL, P.C., LL.D.), who is Hon. Colonel of the Battalion, being at the Mansion House to take the salute. On the parade ground at the Depôt, the Mayor of Shoreditch (H. BUSBY BIRD, Esq.,) gave officers and men a hearty reception, and thanked them and their demobilised comrades for the service they had rendered in preserving the civilisation of the world, and in keeping their homes free from violation. Lieut. Tomsett read a list of the many honours gained in war, and appealed to all for any information that they could furnish with regard to missing men. The stirring ceremony concluded, at the call of Lieut. Tomsett, with the singing of the " Doxology " as an expression of thankfulness for freedom from invasion, followed by the " National Anthem."

THE MARCH PAST H.M. THE KING

A day that will never fade from the memory of the 650 members of the 4th Battalion who were privileged to take part therein was Saturday, July 5th, 1919, when detachments of all the Battalions of the Royal Fusiliers (City of London Regt.) and the units of City and County of London marched past His Majesty King George at Buckingham Palace. The pride which the 4th Battalion took in the triumphal progress, through the decorated streets packed with cheering people, was enhanced by the knowledge that Colonel VICKERS DUNFEE, as one of the hon. secretaries of the Lord Mayor's Reception Committee, had taken the leading part in planning the arrangements for the welcome so magnificently accorded by the populace. From Chelsea Barracks to the Tower of London the cheers rang out without ceasing from spectators massed behind the ranks of Volunteers, the Regular and Special Police, Cadets, Boy Scouts, and other organisations. The climax was reached on ¦Constitution Hill, where 13,000 school childen gave the troops, uniformed and demobilised, a musical and cheering reception. This was repeated in St. Paul's Cathedral Churchyard, where over 3,000 children chosen from the elementary schools of the City and central districts, were entertained by Colonel and Alderman SIR CHARLES WAKEFIELD.

The procession of troops took one and a quarter hours to pass any given spot, and for that period the Lord Mayor (SIR HORACE MARSHALL) stood before the Mansion House taking the salute amid a storm of enthusiasm that at times drowned the music of the bands. By the side of his Lordship stood the Sheriffs (Sir BANISTER F. FLETCHER and Col. Sir WILLIAM R. SMITH, M.D.) and Colonel EVELYN WOOD, D.S.O. Others present were the Lady Mayoress, Miss Marshall,

98

Alderman Sir E. Cooper and Lady Cooper, Alderman Sir V. Bowater, Alderman Sir L. Newton, and Mrs. Vickers Dunfee.

Inspired by the fact that all eyes were upon them, the " Lord Mayor's Own " went past the world-famed home of the Capital's Chief Magistrate with sprightly step and steady ranks. Their marching was not one whit less admirable than was the case when they passed the dais at Buckingham Palace. At that point the men were almost entranced by the beauty of the scene presented by the Sovereign, the Queen and the Royal Family. The charm of the spectacle was fully visible only to one in the ranks, and so much were the men engrossed by it that numbers failed to notice the applause that greeted their marching from wounded soldiers and other privileged onlookers opposite the dais.

With a rapidity that testified to healthy appetites, the various City units no sooner reached the Tower than they set their faces in the direction of the buildings in which they were to be entertained at luncheon. An exception was the various Royal Fusilier battalions, who were regaled in the Tower Moat, where GENERAL SIR IAN HAMILTON, G.C.B., D.S.O., received the Lord Mayor. The Fourth were entertained in the scarcely less famed Guildhall by the Lord Mayor, who spent a quarter of an hour with them before visiting—with Colonel Dunfee, the Lady Mayoress and Mrs. Dunfee, etc.—the other units that come within the cognisance of the City T.F. Association. The band of the Volunteer Battalion, which has trained at Shaftesbury Street since their Territorial predecessors embarked for the stern test of the greatest war in history, added to the *éclat* of the occasion, the arrangements for which added further laurels to Lieut. Tomsett, who acted as toast master.

In the regrettable absence through illness of MAJOR BURNETT (The C.O., who bore the burden of the command during the greater part of the 1/4 Battalion's service in France), MAJOR DUNCAN TEAPE asked the guests to honour the health of the Lord Mayor, their hon. Colonel. This was done, with musical honours. Speaking at first with emotion, SIR HORACE MARSHALL expressed the pride that he felt in being their hon. Colonel. Having watched their career during the past four and a half years with the deepest interest, he could say that the City was proud of them, and would never forget their valour and pluck. He admired the splendid way in which they had marched that day.

Again cheers broke out for the hon. Colonel, and the climax was reached when SERGT.-MAJOR R. HARRIS proposed a vote of thanks to the Lord Mayor for his hospitality, and said they were proud to hear his Lordship say such kind things to them. Musical honours were once more rendered, followed by a similar distinction for Colonel Dunfee and for Mrs. Dunfee. In response, the Lord Mayor took the vote as intended for the Lady Mayoress, and proceeded : " Here is our dear old friend, Colonel Vickers Dunfee. Let us give one more cheer for him. No one has had more to do or taken more trouble and pains to organise the march to-day than he." When the further cheers had subsided, COLONEL DUNFEE replied that he deeply appreciated so magnificent a welcome. He had spent thirty or forty years in the 4th London, and those present to-day had helped him to make it good in discipline, strong in numbers, and ready to do anything and go anywhere. Whatever he and his wife could do for them was done with the utmost pleasure.

With a further cheer for the Lord Mayor's party on their departure, the never-to-be-forgotten day shortly afterwards came to an end. Outside the Guildhall there were many re-unions of Old Comrades.

OUR DIVISIONAL GENERAL IN GALLIPOLI

PARIS, Major-General Sir Archibald, K.C.B. ; Croix de Commandeur Legion d'honneur, 1916 ; Croix de Commandeur Ordre du Leopold, 1917 ; Croix de Guerre. Entered Royal Marine Artillery, 1879 ; Captain, 1890 ; Major, 1898 ; Lieut.-Colonel, 1908 ; Brevet-Colonel, 1905 ; Colonel 2nd Commandant, 1915 ; Major-General, 1915 ; Adjutant Militia, 1894-99 ; Chief Instructor R.M. Academy, 1903-5 ; Naval Intelligence Department, 1899-1900 ; Special Service, Rhodesian Field Force, 1900-02 ; served in South Africa, 1900-02 (mentioned in despatches twice, Brevet Lieut-Colonel, Queen's medal four clasps, King's medal two clasps) ; General Officer Commanding R.N. Division at defence of Antwerp, 1914 (mentioned in despatches thrice) and during Dardanelles Campaign, and later in France ; severely wounded, 1916.

OUR BRIGADIER - GENERAL IN GALLIPOLI

MERCER, Major-General Sir David, K.C.B., Adjutant-General Royal Marine Forces, 1916. Entered R.M.L.I. 1883 ; Adjutant Portsmouth Division, 1891-5 ; Staff-Officer, Depôt R.M., Deal, 1899-1903 ; D.A.A.G., R.M., 1903-8 ; A.A.G., R.M., 1911-14 ; Brigadier-General commanding 1st R.N. Brigade, R.N. Division, 1914-16 ; served throughout the operations in Gallipoli (mentioned in despatches twice, C.B.) and elsewhere, 1915-18 (K.C.B.) ; Officer Legion of Honour.

RECORD OF OFFICERS

ARTHUR, R. N., MAJOR : Malta, Alex., Gal., S. Egypt, France. Served with 1/4 Batt. London Regt. in France. Attached, as 2nd in Command, to 2/6 Lancashire Fusiliers, 6th Lancashire Fusiliers, 2/7 Lancashire Fusiliers, 2/8 Lancashire Fusiliers, London Scottish.

BLOWS, C. S. G., 2ND LIEUT. : Gal., S. Egypt, France. Served with 1/4 Batt. London Regt. in France, and killed in action, Sept. 9th, 1916.

BOTTERILL, W. R., A/CAPT. : Malta, Alex., Gal.. S. Egypt, France. France, Oct. 7th, 1917, to Nov. 16th, 1918. 86th Battery, 32nd Brigade R.F.A. Wounded May 7th, 1918. Awarded Military Cross, May 7th, 1918.

BOWATER, V. S., CAPT. : Malta, Alex., Gal., S. Egypt, France. France, Apr., 1916, until June, 1917, when invalided to U.K. ; then attached to Staff H.Q., London District.

BRADFORD, F. R. C., 2/LIEUT. : Malta, Alex., Gal., S. Egypt, France. Served with 1/4 Batt. London Regt. in France, and fell in action on Somme, July 1st, 1916.

COATES, L. C., CAPT. (TEMP. MAJOR R.A.F.) : Malta, Alex., Gal., France. Transferred to R.F.C., Sept., 1916. In France with No. 5 Squadron, March, 1917. Wounded in aerial combat with the late Baron von Richthofen, leading a squadron of seven Albatross scouts.

DARRINGTON, C. P., LIEUT. : Malta, Alex., Gal., France. Joined unit at Malta, Aug. 20th, 1915. Evacuated Gallipoli Nov. 29th, 1915, to U.K., H.T. " Morea." Died of wounds received at Angreau, Nov. 6th, 1918.

DAVIES, S. N., LIEUT. : Malta, Alex., Gal. In hospital at Mudros (jaundice). Invalided to U.K. with strained heart, Apr., 1916. After three months leave in U.K., detailed for light duty as accountant in War Office, Contracts Branch, attached as Costings Accountant to R.A.C.D., Feb., 1918.

DAVIS, S., Capt. : Alex., Gal., S. Egypt, France. Transferred to 1/4 Batt. London Regt. from Rouen until July 1st, 1916, when wounded at Hebuterne. Invalided U.K. Drafted to France, June 15th, 1917, and joined new 2/4 Batt. Wounded Sept. 22nd, 1917, at St. Julien, near Ypres. Awarded Military Cross, Oct., 1917.

DENNIS, H. W., Capt. : Malta, Alex., S. Egypt, France. Served in France with 142 Trench Mortar Battery—2nd in command. 4th Army Troops T.M.B. (O.C.) " Y " 56 T.M.B. and 102 T.M.B. (O.C.). After 2/4 Batt. was broken up, continued on active service in France and Belgium, through Somme, 1916, 1917 and 1918, including Battles of Arras and Vimy Ridge, March, 1918 ; Soissons, July, 1918 ; Kimmel, and continuous open fighting until Nov. 10th, 1918, finishing up on banks of Scheldt. Wounded, May, 1918. Awarded Military Cross. Mentioned in despatches.

DICKINS, R. C., Capt. : Malta, Alex., Gal., S. Egypt, France. In France with 21st Batt. London Regt. until wounded at High Wood, Oct. 15th, 1916. Joined new 2/4 Batt. in June, 1917. Wounded at Paschendale, Oct. 21st, 1917.

DICKINS, L., Capt. : Malta, Alex., Gal. 3rd Res. London Regt., Feb. 8th, 1917. Attached Aldershot Command, Labour Corps, Sept., 1917. Wounded in head, Dec. 21st, 1915. Relinquished commission on account of wounds, Feb. 2nd, 1918.

DUNFEE, V., Col. : Malta, Alex., Gal., S. Egypt, France. Attached 1/22 London Regt., Vimy. June to Aug., 1916, given command of 4th Res. Batt. at Fovant, and on this unit being broken up was posted to 1st Res. Batt. London Regt. until demobilized, Dec., 1918. Mentioned in despatches, Gallipoli, and for the training of recruits in U.K.

DYNE, C. F., Lieut. : Malta, Alex., Gal., S. Egypt, France, India. Transferred to 1/4 London Regt. Sent to 3rd G.B. Bedford Regt., Burma, May, 1918. Served in Burma Military Police in N.W. Frontier. Punitive measures against Kuki Tribes (Oct. 1918 to May 1919). On garrison duty in India.

GIANNACOPULO, D. N., Lieut. : Malta, Alex., Gal., S. Egypt, France. Appointed Interpreter Officer with

XII Corps. Control Post Interpreter Officer with XII Corps. A/D.A.P.M. Interpreter Officer with XII Corps. Salonica Expedy. Force.

HAIGH, G. D., LIEUT. : Malta, Alex., Gal., S. Egypt, France. Gazetted 2/Lieut. to 3rd London Regt., March 28th, 1917. Served with that unit in Belgium and France, at Ypres, La Fere, etc. Adjutant of 58th Divisional Wing, Apr., 1918, to July. Captured on Somme near Chipilly on Aug. 8th, 1918, whilst commanding " B " Coy. 3rd London Regt. Prisoner of war in German hands chiefly at Kamstigall, East Prussia (Baltic Coast), until repatriated. Landed from Danzig at Leith on Dec. 13th, 1918. Disembodied on May 4th, 1919.

HAMILTON, W. H., MAJOR : India, Mesopotamia, and Persia. Proceeded to India, July, 1916. Served with 1/4 Hants. Regt. in Mesopotamia and Persia from Sept. 23rd, 1917, to present date. Now in command No. 2 B.B. Makina, Mesopotamia.

HAYWOOD, W. G., MAJOR : Malta. Invalided to U.K. from Malta through illness.

HICKLENTON, H. G., LIEUT. : Malta, Alex., Gal., S. Egypt, France. Served in France to July 1st, 1916, when wounded. Invalided U.K. With 3rd Res. Batt., Sept. 1st, 1917, to Nov. 22nd, 1918 ; then to 344 Prisoners of War Coy., B.E.F.

KEEN, R., CAPT. : Malta, Alex., Gal., France. Posted to 1/4 Batt. London Regt., and served with unit on Somme. Wounded, Oct. 8th, 1916 : shell wound, left groin ; bullet, right thigh.

LAMBLEY, J. E. W., CAPT. AND Q.-M. : Malta, Alex., Gal., S. Egypt, France. Transferred to 15th Corps Cyclists Batt. at Heilly, Somme, on June 4th, 1916, and served with that unit until June 3rd, 1918, when admitted to hospital with neurasthenia, brought on by shell shock. On discharge from hospital in Sept., 1918, gazetted to Yorkshire Dragoons at Bantry, Ireland, then to Command Depôt, Scarborough ; disembodied Jan. 6th, 1919.

LIMPENNY, CAPT. :

LOVELL, E. G., CAPT. : Malta, Alex., Gal., S. Egypt,

France. Transferred to M.T., A.S.C., Nov. 1916. Proceeded to France in Feb., 1917, with 276th Siege Battery Ammunition Column, R.G.A. Attached to 44th Brigade R.G.A. from May, 1917, to July, 1918. Invalided U.K., July, 1918.

MOORE, G. H., CAPT. : Malta, Alex., Egypt (Upper and Lower). Oct., 1915, to Apr., 1916, G.H.Q., 3rd Echelon E.E.F. O.I.C. Records. Apr., 1916, to Sept., 1916, G.H.Q. I (d) Censoring 1st Echelon, E.E.F. March, 1917, to Aug., 1917, P. of W. Camp, Heliopolis. Conducting troops to India. Jan. to March, 1917. Attached 1st Batt. R. Irish Regt., Oct., 1917, to Jan., 1919.

MORRIS, H., CAPT. : Malta, Alex., Gal. O.C. Convalescent Camp, Alnwick, 1916-1917. Adjutant to 4th Batt. Devon Vol. Regt., Apr., 1917, to July, 1918. Wounded, Gallipoli, 1915. South African Medal (4 clasps).

PARKHOUSE, H., CAPT. : Malta, Alex., Egypt, Palestine. Detained at G.H.Q., 3rd Echelon M.E.F., in charge of Records. March, 1916, G.H.Q., E.E.F., 1st Echelon Canal. Attached G.H.Q. Intelligence, March, 1916, to Oct., 1916. O.C. Western Frontier Force, Base D., Oct., 1916, to June, 1917. Attached to R.A.O.C. Officer in charge of Anti-Gas Factory, June, 1917, to date.

PARR, MAJOR R.A.M.C. : Malta. Transferred from 1/4 to 2/4 Batt. in Malta. Invalided to U.K. on account of sickness.

PRICE, J. W. P., CAPT. : Alex., Gal., S. Egypt, France. Served with 1/4 Batt. London Regt. in France. Somme, Gommecourt, Arras, Cambrai, St. Quentin, and Mauberge. Wounded June 28th, 1916, and Sept. 9th, 1916.

READ, F. C. J., CAPT. : Malta, Alex., Gal., France. Served with 1/4 Batt. London Regt. in France. 13th Batt .L.N. Lancs. Regt. in U.K. Wounded, Somme, Sept. 8th, 1916.

SEYD, V. H., MAJOR : Malta, Alex., Gal., S. Egypt, France, Salonica, and Palestine. Joined 2/23 London Regt. on June 1st, 1916, as 2nd in Command. France from 26th June, 1916, to Dec. 14th, 1916. Salonica from Dec. 14th, 1916, to June 14th, 1917. Egypt and Palestine from June

18th, 1917, to June 23rd, 1918. France from July 5th, 1918, to Aug. 12th, 1918. Mentioned in General Allenby's Despatch, Jan. 16th, 1918.

SHARP, A. G., 2/Lieut. : Malta, France. After serving in Malta for a short time was sent to 3/4 Batt. London Regt., and eventually joined 1/4 in France.

STANHAM, H. G., Capt. : Malta, Alex., Gal., S. Egypt, France, Palestine. Joined 1/4 Batt. London Regt. from Rouen. Gommecourt, Leuze Wood. Wounded Sept. 9th, 1916, and invalided U.K. Drafted 3rd Res. to Egypt, Nov. 23rd, 1917, 2/6 London Regt. Took part in operations Valley of Jordan, June, 1918. Joined 1/4 Norfolk Regt. in Syria. Returned to Egypt, 2nd in Command 1st Norfolk Regt. Demobilized March 6th, 1919.

STARK, W. A., Capt. : Malta, Alex., Gal., S. Egypt, France. Served with 1/4 Batt. London Regt. in France, with new 2/4 Batt. in France and Belgium, 1916 and 1917; 2/10 London Regt., Belgium, 1918 ; 1/4 Batt., Belgium, 1919 ; Army of the Rhine, 1919. Wounded by shell burst June 28th, 1916, and gunshot wound left knee, Sept. 20th, 1917.

STEVENS, W. H. S., Capt. : Malta, Alex., Gal., S. Egypt, France. Served with 1/22 Batt. London Regt., Vimy Ridge, Bully, Souchey, Somme. Wounded shoulder, neck and jaw (machine gun).

STILLWELL, E. H., Major : India. Remained in London as O.C. Depôt. Drafted to India, 1916, 2nd in Command 23rd (North Western) Batt. London Regt.

THOMAS, N. L., Capt. : Malta, Gal., S. Egypt, France. With 29th Div. Details, Mustafa Barracks. Collected and conducted to France 1,150 troops. Served with 1/15 Batt. London Regt. in France. Wounded Sept. 15th, 1916.

TOWSE, W. N., Capt. : Malta, Alex., Gal., S. Egypt, France. Enlisted Artists Rifles. Received commission Dec., 1914. Attached 1/21 Batt. London Regt. (1st Surrey Rifles) on return from Egypt. Killed, High Wood, Sept. 15th, 1916. Shot through the head whilst leading his Company in the attack.

VERNON, H. W., Lieut. : Malta, Alex., Gal., S. Egypt, France. With 1/4 Batt. London Regt. Hebuterne, Fonquevillers and Somme, Joined R.A.F., June 1st, 1918. Graduated as 2nd Class Operations Pilot. Transferred to Home Defence Squadron, Essex, Nov. 2nd, 1918. Wounded Leuze Wood, Sept. 9th, 1916, left elbow (bullet).

WEBSTER, J. R., Capt. and Adjt. : Malta, Alex., Gal., S. Egypt, France. Served with 1/4 Batt. London Regt. in France, and killed in action Sept. 9th, 1916, on the Somme near Ginchy.

WELLBY, E. V., Major : Remained in U.K. as Adjutant with 3/4 Batt. London Regt. Instructed in April, 1915, to raise 4/1 London Regt. Left for administration work in Egypt, Apr., 1917.

WILLIAMS, N. W., A/Capt. : Malta, Alex., Gal., S. Egypt, France. Joined 2/4 Batt. in Malta. Transferred to 1/4 Batt. London Regt. Wounded at Fonquevillers, July, 1916 (back). Seconded to M.G.C., Dec., 1916. Appointed Assistant Area Gas Officer M.G.T.C., Jan., 1918. Area Gas Officer, 1918.

WOOD, A. E., Major : Unfit for General Service. Retained in U.K., and served on East Coast with Defence Troops. Invalided from the Service, May 17th, 1919.

YEOMAN, B. F. L., Lieut. : Malta, Alex., Gal., S. Egypt, France. Served in France, and wounded on Somme July, 1st, 1916 ; again at Monchy, July, 1917. Transferred to R.F.C., Dec., 1917. Killed at Witney (Oxon), May 11th, 1918.

RECORD OF PERSONNEL

ABRAHAMS, S., Pte. : Mudros, S. Egypt, France. Draft from Devonport, Nov. 15th, 1915. Killed in action.

ACUM, W. H. A., Cpl. : Malta, Alex., Gal., S. Egypt, France. Joined Depot Band 6 I.B.D., thence to Staff Band Cyclist Base Depot.

ADAMS, F. G., Pte. : Malta, Alex., Gal., S. Egypt, France. Served 2 years 13th Batt. R.F. in France and Belgium, and finally to 6th Batt. R.F. in Ireland. Wounded Apl. 20th, 1917, Oct. 4th, 1917, Aug. 23rd, 1918.

ADAMSON, H. J., L/Cpl. : Malta, Alex., Gal., S. Egypt, France. Joined 1/4 London Regt., Gommecourt, July 1st, 1916. Battle of Somme, Leuze Wood, invalided U.K., Sept. 14th, 1916. Blackdown 29th London and Labour Corps. Discharged June 25th, 1918. Wounded Sept. 9th, 1916, left foot, right hand.

ADIE, W. J. :

AINSLEY, L. C. : Malta, Alex., Gal., S. Egypt, France. Attached 1/13 London Regt. Transferred to 4th London. Somme, July 1st, 1916. Reported missing Sept. 9th, 1916, after an attack east of Albert.

AKAM, G., Pte. : Malta, Alex., Gal., S. Egypt, France. Attached 1/13 London Regt. until July, 1916, when transferred to 1/4 London Regt. Mentioned in despatches Oct., 1918.

AKERS, W. J., L/Cpl. : Malta, Alex., Gal., S. Egypt, France. Attached 1/13 London Regt. until June 22nd, 1916. Admitted to Hospital, L.C.D., Seaford, 29th London, Guildford, R.D.C., Hunstanton.

ALDER, — : Malta, Alex., Gal. Evacuated sick to Malta, to U.K., March 28th, 1916.

ALDERSLADE, H. J. : Malta, Alex., Gal., S. Egypt, France. Joined 1/4 London Regiment.

ALEXANDER, L. J., Pte. : Mudros. Embarked Devonport Nov. 15th, 1915 ; May 13th, 1916, D.A.G., Alexandria. Transferred 1/4 London Regt. in France, 13th

Batt. R.F. Returned to U.K. to 2/5 Essex. Drafted 11th Essex, France, until Sept. 15th, 1918. Wounded leg and arm.

ALLEN, A. E., PTE. : Malta, Alex., Gal. Invalided from Gallipoli Nov. 20th, 1915 ; to U.K. April 24th, 1916. Joined 1/4 London Reg. Hurdcott, June, 1916.

ALLEN, C., PTE. : Malta, Alex. Invalided to U.K. Sept. 15th, 1915. H.T. " Egypt." Joined 4/4 London Regt., Salisbury. Transferred to 2/1 Herts. Regt., Darlington. 23rd Cheshire Regt., and proceeded with it to France. G.S.W. right arm and chest

ALLEN, F. H. J. : Malta, Alex., Gal., S. Egypt, France. Transferred to 1/4 London Regt. Joined Chinese Labour Batt. Wounded hip and face, July 1st, 1916

ALLEN, J. A., CPL. : Malta, Alex., Gal., France. Invalided from Gallipoli Oct. 8th, 1915. Served with 1/4 London Regt. in France, Sept., 1916, to Feb., 1917. Reserve Batt., Torquay. Labour Batt. March, 1917, to Apl., 1918. 146 Labour Coy., and 685 Home Service Coy. G.S.W. left lung and thigh and left forearm.

ALLPORT, W. E., PTE. : Malta, Alex., Gal., S. Egypt, France. Killed in action Battle of Somme, July 1st, 1916. Recommended for D.C.M.

ALLUM, R., SERGT. : Malta, Alex., Mudros, S. Egypt, France. Embarked April 14th, 1916, with horses for Marseilles. Discharged Sept. 27th, 1917. Wounded on Somme Sept. 12th, 1916. Arm and shoulder.

AMOS, F. W., C.S.M. : Malta, Alex., Gal., S. Egypt, France. Transferred to 1/4 Batt. London Regt., from July, 1916 ; served in every engagement until Nov., 1916. Arras, Cambrai, Ypres, Oppy Wood. Wounded leg and finger. Awarded Belgian Croix de Guerre. Mentioned in Despatches, Cambrai, Arras, Returned to England, Sept., 1918, 6 months' rest, war-worn. Attached to Graduate Batt. at Newmarket till demobilized, Feb. 20th, 1919.

ANDREWS, W., PTE. : Malta, Alex., Gal., S. Egypt, France. Drafted to 1/4 Batt. London Regt. Invalided U.K. July 1st, 1916. Drafted to new 2/4 Batt. London Regt. France, Nov. 5th, 1917. L.C.D., Seaford, until demobilized. Taken prisoner March 21st, 1918, but escaped. Shell shock, July 1st, 1916. Gassed, Albert, Aug. 8th, 1918. Slight thigh wound.

ANDREWS, W. H. : Malta, Alex., Gal., S. Egypt, France. Invalided to U.K., May 7th, 1916.

ANNEREAU, G. H., L/Cpl. : Malta, Alex., Gal., S. Egypt, France. Gunshot wound right thigh, Sept. 20th, 1916. Killed in action, April 16th, 1917.

ARCHER, F. C., Pte. : Malta, Alex., Gal., S. Egypt, France. Transferred 1/4 Batt. London Regt., and served continuously in France and Belgium. Gassed Oppy Wood, 1918.

ARMSTRONG, A., Pte. : Malta, Alex., Gal., S. Egypt, France. Transferred to 1/13 Batt. London Regt. Killed in action, Leuze Wood, Sept. 9th, 1916.

ASHWORTH, J. H., Sergt. : Malta, Alex., Gal., S. Egypt, France. Transferred 1/4 London Regt. until Oct., 1916 In Hospital, dysentery, Oct., 1916, to Aug., 1918, at Blackdown. 1st Res. London Regt. Demobilized April 7th, 1919.

ATKINS, J. W., Pte. : Malta, Alex., Gal., S. Egypt, France. Transferred to 1/4 Batt. London Regt. 3rd (R.), Farnborough. Marked B2 and drafted to Waterways and Docks, R.E. Wounded Aug. 16th, 1917. Awarded M.S.M. Aug., 1917, for throwing live grenade out of trench.

ASKEW, R., Bandsman : Malta, Alex., Gal., S. Egypt, France. Drafted to Base Band, Rouen.

AYLMER, W. C., Pte. : Malta, Alex., Gal., S. Egypt, France. Transferred to 1/4 Batt. London Regt. at Hebuterne. Finally drafted to a Labour Coy. Wounded on Somme, G.S.W. left shoulder.

BAGG, A. E., L/Cpl. : Malta, Alex., Gal., S. Egypt, France. Transferred to 1/4 Batt. London Regt. Killed in action Leuze Wood, Aug. 9th, 1916.

BAILEY, P. J., 2nd Lieut. : Malta, Alex., Gal., S. Egypt, France. Transferred to 1/4 Batt. London Regt. as Cpl. Promoted Sergt., Sept., 1917. Served with 21st O.C.B. Nov., 1917, to March, 1918. Commission in R.N.A.S. ; acted as pilot in R.A.F. Wounded July 1st, 1916, Gommecourt.

BAKER, H. W., Pte. : Malta, Alex., Gal., S. Egypt, France.

Transferred to 1/4 Batt. London Regt. Slight shell wound, July 6th, 1916.

BAKER, C. R., L/CPL. : Malta, Alex., Gal. Invalided U.K. H.T. " Nevassa," Dec. 10th, 1915. Served in France from April, 1918.

BAKER, H. M., CPL. : Malta, Alex., Gal., S. Egypt, France. Killed in action in France, May 6th, 1917.

BAKER, A. C., CPL. : Malta, Alex., Gal., S. Egypt, France. Transferred 1/4 London Regt. Attached 151 Labour Coy. Wounded.

BALDOCK, A. J., L/CPL. : Gal., S. Egypt, France. Draft from England Nov. 15th, 1915. Transferred Tank Corps, 1917, and served in France with same. Wounded 3 times.

BALL, G. F. : Malta, Alex., Gal. Left Malta for Dardanelles Aug. 11th, 1915. Served with Line of Communication, Signal Coy., R.E., in Salonica and Dedeagatch (Bulgaria). Died Nov. 30th, 1918, from pneumonia.

BALL, C., PTE. : Malta, Alex., Gal. Left Malta Aug. 11th, 1915, for Dardanelles. Served with Signal Coy., R.E Lines of Communication.

BALON, H. E. :

BARBER, B. R. : Gal., S. Egypt, France. Draft from England, Nov. 15th, 1915.

BARNES, E. F., CPL. : Malta, Alex., Gal., S. Egypt, France. Extracts from his comrades' letters :—" He, being in command of the Platoon, was just going to get out of our second line when he was shot through the head. He died instantaneously without a groan. He was the bravest boy I have ever met." " Ernie advanced in the best of spirits, and leading his men like a man." Killed in action, Oct. 7th, 1916.

BARNES, F., L/CPL. : Malta, Alex., Gal., S. Egypt, France. Joined 1/4 Batt. London Regt. from Rouen, and served with this unit continuously.

BARNES, T. S., PTE. : Malta, Alex., Gal., S. Egypt, France. Transferred to 1/4 Batt. London Regt., and served with that unit to Nov., 1916. Invalided U.K. and transferred to 261 R.D.C., Birmingham.

BARNEY, C. H. : Malta, Alex., Gal. Transferred to Regular A.S.C., April 17th, 1916.

BARR, W. A., C.Q.M.S. : Malta, Alex., Gal., S. Egypt, France. Served in France continuously after Batt. was broken up. Wounded Gallipoli, 1915. France, July 1st, 1916.

BARR, H., PTE. : Malta, Alex., Gal., S. Egypt, France. Transferred to 1/4 Batt. London Regt. Wounded and taken prisoner at Gommecourt, July 1st, 1916. Repatriated Dec. 17th, 1918. G.S.W. left side and back.

BARR, N. :

BARRETT, C. B., 2ND A.M. : Malta, Alex., Gal., S. Egypt, France. Transferred to 1/4 Batt. London Regt. L.C.D., Seaford. Joined R.F.C., served in Italy with 66th Squadron as Wireless Mechanic ; transferred Jan. 1st, 1918, to 42nd Squadron. Returned to France, March, 1918, and served with advance troops until Armistice. Wounded at Hebuterne July 1st, 1916.

BARRON, T., PTE. : Malta, Alex., Gal. Detached to 8th Army H.-Qrs. Served in Palestine ; transferred to 1/20 London Regt. Invalided from Egypt Jan. 22nd, 1919.

BARRY, D. : Malta, Alex., Sick at Mudros. Invalided U.K. H.T. " Aquitania," Nov. 25th, 1915.

BARTLETT, F. E., CPL. : Malta, Alex., Gal., S. Egypt, France. Attached to 1/13 London Regt. Wounded Hebuterne, June 19th, 1916. G.S.W. severe compound fracture lower jaw. In hospital ever since.

BASERGA, J., PTE. : Malta, Alex., Gal., S. Egypt, France. Attached 1/21 London Regt., on Vimy Ridge. Took part in Somme battles ; wounded at High Wood, Sept. 15th, 1916. Right leg amputated.

BATCHELOR, A. E., SERGT. : Malta, Alex., Gal., S. Egypt, France. Transferred to 1/4 London Regt. Attached 1/3 London Regt. until 1918, when posted to an O.C.B., Gidea Park. Wounded May 17th, 1917 ; shrapnel right leg.

BATT, J. S., PTE. : Malta, Alex., Gal., France. Wounded G.S.W., Nov. 3rd, 1915.

BEARE, E. E., LIEUT. : Malta, Alex., Gal., S. Egypt, France. Transferred 1/4 London Regt. until Jan., 1917, when he joined O.C.B. Gazetted to 2nd Devonshire Regt., and served again in France. Wounded Mar. 2nd, 1918.

BEARE, H. C., Cpl. : Malta, Alex. Invalided to U.K., H.T. " Asturias," Nov. 4th, 1915. Attached 29th Batt. until discharged on account of ill-health, Jan., 1918.

BEARMAN, W., L/Cpl. : Malta, Alex., Gal., S. Egypt, France. Transferred to 1/4 Batt. London Regt. In Battle of Somme. Noted for a commission. Killed in action, July 1st, 1916.

BECKETT, A. R., C.Q.M.S. : Malta, Alex., Gal., S. Egypt, France. Attached to N. Hants. Labour Coy. Attached 10th K.O.S.B.

BEESLEY, F. W. G. : Gal., S. Egypt, France. Draft from England, Nov. 15th, 1915 ; Mar. 4th, 1916, sent to Cyprus for convalescent treatment ; May 31st, 1916, rejoined unit at Rouen. Bullet wound right eye, Dec. 23rd, 1915. Wounded in France, July 4th, 1916. Died at Military Hospital, Monmouth.

BELL, T. : Malta, Alex., Gal. Batman to Capt. Moore. Struck off strength, Mar. 17th, 1916.

BENJAMIN, N., Pte. : Malta, Alex., Gal., S. Egypt, France. Attached to 1/13 London Regt. Engaged at Hebuterne, July 1st, 1916. Demobilized Oct. 22nd, 1917. Wounded severely July 18th, 1916.

BERRYMAN, G., Pte. : Malta, Alex., Gal., S. Egypt, France. Invalided U.K. after being wounded. Transferred to Tank Corps ; drafted to France again June, 1917. Took part in advance with 7th Batt. Tank Corps. Wounded left wrist, Sept. 7th, 1916. Drafted home, Jan. 1st, 1919.

BIRD, A. F., Pte. : Malta, Alex., Gal., S. Egypt, France. Transferred 1/4 London Regt. until Oct., 1916. Wounded on Somme and spent 12 months in Hospital before discharged from service in consequence of wounds. Shell shock and wound in foot.

BENSTEAD, G. A., Pte. : Malta, Alex., Gal., S. Egypt, France. Transferred 1/4 London Regt., Hebuterne, Somme, Laventie, Arras, Ypres ; acted as Batt. Scout. Wounded. Mentioned in despatches. Divisional Card of Honour, Sept. 23rd, 1918.

BIRD, E., Pte. : Malta, Alex., Gal., S. Egypt, France. Attached to 1/13 London Regt. to July 1st, 1916. Slightly wounded. Rejoined 1/4 London Regt. until Sept., 1916. Transferred to 2/4 Norfolk Regt., U.K. Thence to Royal Warwicks in France. Wounded at Ypres, Aug., 1917. Returned to France, March, 1918, and joined Royal Berks until end of campaign. Wounded twice.

BLAKE, G., DRUMMER : Malta, Alex., Gal., S. Egypt, France. Killed in action, Gallipoli, Dec. 21st, 1918.

BLAKE, W. A., BANDSMAN : Malta, Alex., Gal., France. Joined Staff Band, Rouen.

BOLTON, J. : Gal., S. Egypt, France. Draft from England Nov. 15th, 1915.

BONE, H. : Malta, Alex., Gal., S. Egypt, France.

BOSWELL, C. W., PTE. : Gal., S. Egypt. Draft from England, Nov. 15th, 1915. Transferred to Reserve Unit U.K., April 28th, 1916.

BOWLEY, O., PTE. : Gal., S. Egypt, France. Draft from Devonport, Nov. 15th, 1915. Killed in action Gommecourt, July 1st, 1916.

BOVEY, A., CPL. : Malta, Alex., Gal., S. Egypt, France. Transferred to 1/4 London Regt. until March 27th, 1918. Wounded right leg, left thigh and buttock.

BOXALL, H., BANDSMAN : Malta, Alex, Gal., S. Egypt, France. Joined Base Depot Band, Rouen.

BRAIN, F. E. : Malta, Alex., Gal., S. Egypt, France.

BRIGHT, A. H., ARMR.-SERGT. : Malta, Alex., Gal., S. Egypt, France. A.O.C., A.O.D. Workshops, Le Havre. Invalided U.K. Dec. 23rd, 1916. Attached as Armr.-Sergt. to 3rd Bedfordshire Regt., Felixstowe, till discharged, Mar. 5th, 1919. Jaundice, dysentery, and heart trouble.

BOYDEN, N., CLR.-SERGT. : Malta, Alex., Gal., S. Egypt, France. Posted to M.G.S., and served with it to end of War.

BRIGNELL, S. V., CPL. : Malta, Alex, Gal., S. Egypt, France. Enlisted at age of 15, and served with 2/4 Batt. until broken up at Rouen. Transferred to 1/4 London Regt. Discharged Dec., 1918. Wounded three times : 1st Gallipoli, 2nd on Somme in 1916, 3rd in Aug., 1918.

BROWN, W. Y., PTE. : Malta, Alex., Gal., S. Egypt,

France. Attached 1/21 London Regt. Awarded Military Medal.

BRISLAND, H. L. : Malta, Alex., Gal., S. Egypt, France. Transferred to 1/4 London Regt. Invalided U.K. In hospital at Cosham. Joined 4th Res. Batt. at Hurdcott ; drafted to a Labour Batt. and discharged Feb. 1st, 1918. Wounded slightly Aug. 16th, 1916, and again Sept. 25th, 1916.

BRITTON, R. W. A. : Malta, Alex., Gal., S. Egypt, Mesopotamia.

BROAD, E. W. B., PTE. : Malta, Alex., Gal., S. Egypt, France. Hebuterne and Les Boeufs Wood. Discharged Feb. 12th, 1917. Three shrapnel wounds in back, Oct. 7th, 1916.

BROAD, J. : Malta, Alex., Gal., S. Egypt.

BROOKER, W. J. : Malta, Alex., Gal., S. Egypt, France. Transferred to 1/4 Batt. London Regt. Killed in action, Leuze Wood, Sept. 20th, 1916.

BROOKS, P. : Malta, Alex., Gal. Invalided to U.K. from Alex., April 17th, 1916.

BROWN, H. R., PTE. : Malta, Alex., Gal., S. Egypt, France. Drafted 1/13 London Regt. Killed in action on Somme, July 1st, 1916.

BROWN, A. : Malta, Alex., Gal., S. Egypt, France.

BROWN, W. Y. : Malta, Alex., Gal., S. Egypt, France.

BROWN, J. S. : Malta, Alex., Gal. Invalided to Malta, thence to U.K., Dec. 31st, 1915.

BROWN, T. H.: Malta, Alex., Gal. Wounded at Gallipoli, Dec. 23rd, 1915. Invalided to U.K., H.T. " Galika," May 24th, 1916.

BROWN, W. G. : Malta, Alex., Gal., S. Egypt, France.

BRUCE, C. P., SERGT. : Malta, Alex., Gal., S. Egypt, France. Transferred to 1/4 London Regt. Drafted Oct. 1st, 1918, to 8th London Regt. Wounded Sept. 9th, 1916.

BRUNTON, A. : Malta, Alex., Gal., S. Egypt, France. Enlisted in Malta (Cook). Invalided to U.K. May 7th, 1916.

BRUTON, V. C. W., SERGT. : Malta, Alex., Gal., S. Egypt, France.

BUDGEON, C. W., Pte. : Malta, Alex., Gal., S. Egypt, France. Drafted to 1/13 London Regt. After July 1st, 1916, transferred to 1/4 London Regt., and served with it throughout the War. Two Divisional Cards of Honour.

BULLINGER, W. D., Sergt. : Malta, Alex., Gal., S. Egypt, France. Transferred 1/4 London Regt. Invalided U.K., L.C.D., Seaford, to June 30th, 1917. Joined 3rd (R.) London Regt. Attached to 9th London Regt. in France, Sept. 30th, 1918, until end of War. Wounded Leuze Wood, Sept. 9th, 1916. G.S.W. right side ; shrapnel in back.

BUNKER, H. C. G., L/Cpl. : Malta, Alex., Gal., S. Egypt, France. Attached to 1/13 London Regt. In Oct., 1916, transferred to 1/4 London Regt. Discharged through wounds received in action. Wounded five times. Awarded M.S.M. Twice mentioned in despatches.

BUNNELL, W. J. : Gal., S. Egypt, France. Draft from England, Nov. 15th, 1915.

BURFORD, D. : Malta, Alex., Gal., S. Egypt, France. Attached 1/13 London Regt. until mortally wounded, July 1st, 1916 ; died July 11th, 1916.

BURNS, V. M., Pte : Malta, Alex., Gal. Invalided to Malta, thence to U.K., H.T. " Mauritania." Discharged medically unfit, Aug. 3rd, 1916.

BUSH, H. : Malta, Alex., Gal. Invalided to U.K., H.T. " Dwanka " (March 14th, 1916). Rejoined at Hurdcott, June, 1916. Transferred 2/1 Herts Regt., Oct., 1916, and in Jan., 1917, to 114 Labour Coy. France, Feb., 1917, to Nov., 1917, when joined 62 Coy. R.D.C., Dover. Demobilized Feb. 5th, 1919.

BUTLER, H. A., Pte. : Malta, Alex. Invalided to U.K., H.S. Egypt, Oct. 22nd, 1915. Served at home with Res. Batt. Joined 1/3 London Regt. in France, Oct. 8th, 1916. Wounded April 10th, 1917. G.S.W. right thigh and right hand. Thigh amputated April 30th, 1917.

BUTLER, H. A., Pte. : Malta, Alex., Gal., S. Egypt, France. Transferred to 1/4 London Regt. Invalided U.K. July 5th, 1916. Rejoined in France, April 21st, 1917, and served there until Dec. 8th, 1918. Demobilized Dec. 30th, 1918.

BUTTERWORTH, A. R., Pte. : Malta, Alex., Gal., S. Egypt, France. Wounded in head.

BYWOOD, J. C., Pte. : Malta, Alex., Gal., S. Egypt, France. Served for three years with the 1/4 London Regt. Wounded in left arm.

CABLE, C. : Gal., S. Egypt, France. Draft from Devonport, Nov. 15th, 1915.

CAIN, G. W., Sergt. : Malta, Alex., Gal., S. Egypt, France. Transferred to 1/4 London Regt. until discharged with trench fever, March 11th, 1918. Mentioned in despatches, July 1st, 1916, for carrying wounded to place of safety under shell fire.

CAMP, W. F., Pte. : Malta, Alex., Gal., S. Egypt, France. Transferred to A.S.C., Nov. 1st, 1917 ; invalided U.K., June 1st, 1917. Wounded July 1st, 1916.

CAPEL, G. J. S., Cpl. : Malta, Alex., Gal. France. Transferred to 1/4 London Regt., and, after seeing considerable service, was taken prisoner, March 28th, 1918. Wounded Gallipoli in wrist. France, face and ankle.

CARN, J. : Malta, Alex., Gal., S. Egypt, France.

CAPEL, E. A. : Malta, Alex., Gal., S. Egypt, France. Transferred 21st London Regt. Wounded Sept., 1916, High Wood. Killed in action at Ypres, June 7th, 1917.

CAPERN, H. J. : Malta, Alex. Invalided to U.K., Oct. 26th, 1915.

CAPON, R. : Gal., S. Egypt, France. Draft from Devonport, Nov. 15th, 1915.

CARPENTER, C., Pte. : Malta, Alex., Gal., S. Egypt, France. Gommecourt, Somme, 1916, Laventie, Arras, Cambrai, 1917, Vimy Ridge, Mons, 1918.

CARTER, C. E. : Malta, Alex., Gal., S. Egypt, France. Transferred to 1/4 London Regt. Commission in 2/1 London Regt., April, 1917. Wounded on Somme, July 1st, 1916. Killed in action, Aug. 20th, 1917, near Ypres. Mentioned in dispatches Dec. 24th, 1917, for distinguished service in the field. Officially recommended for the V C.

CARTER, A. J. H., Sergt. : Malta, Alex., Gal., S. Egypt, France. Wounded July 1st, 1916, at Gommecourt Wood.

Gave 1½ pints of blood to save a wounded comrade. Killed in action, Sept. 18th, 1918.

CATFORD, J. : Malta, Alex., Gal., S. Egypt, France.

CATHERINES, J. E., Pte. : Malta, Alex., Gal., S. Egypt, France. Drafted to 1/13 London Regt. Wounded Sept. 7th, 1916. Drafted to Labour Corps. Discharged July 9th, 1918. G.S.W. right wrist.

CAVALIER, J., Pte. : Malta, Alex., Gal., S. Egypt, France. Wounded twice.

CEARNS, F. E., Pte. : Malta, Alex., Gal., S. Egypt, France. Transferred to 1/4 London Regt. in Jan., 1916. Joined Trench Mortar Battery, 168 Brigade. Wounded March 7th, 1917. Rejoined 1/4 London Regt. in France, June 11th, 1917. Killed in action Aug. 13th, 1917.

CHALLIS, F. : Malta, Alex., Gal., S. Egypt, France. Transferred 1/4 London Regt. till Feb., 1917. Transferred R.A.O.C.

CHANDLER, H., L/Cpl.: Malta, Alex., Gal., S. Egypt, France. Invalided to U.K., Feb. 6th, 1916. Transferred to King's Liverpool Regt. and served in France till Feb. 2nd, 1919. Wounded right hand.

CHANDLER, S. R., Lieut. K.R.R.C. : Malta, Alex., France. Embarkation Staff, Alexandria, Aug. 27th, 1915. Served with 18th Batt. K.R.R.C. in France. Wounded left arm, left hand disabled.

CHAPMAN, F. W. Pte. : Malta, Alex., Gal., S. Egypt, France. Transferred to 1/4 London Regt. Killed in action Sept. 24th, 1916.

CHAPMAN, C. : Gal., S. Egypt, France. Draft from Devonport, Nov. 15th, 1915.

CHEEK, F. S., Pte. : Malta, Alex., Gal., S. Egypt, France. Transferred to 1/4 London Regt. In hospital May 25th, 1916. L.C.D., Seaford, to Nov., 1916. Transferred to 676 Labour Coy.

CHICK, A. G., Pte. : Malta, Alex., Gal. Killed in action, Nov. 22nd, 1915.

CHIPPS, S. E. : Malta, Alex., Gal., S. Egypt, France. Wounded on Somme, July 1st, 1916 ; Gal., Dec. 18th, 1915. Died at Sandgate Hospital, July 20th, 1916. Buried at Kingston-on-Thames.

CHIRNSIDE, E. A., Sergt. : Malta, Alex., Gal., S. Egypt, France. Drafted to 1/13 London Regt. in Aug., 1916 ; transferred to 1/4 London Regt. Invalided to U.K., Nov. 9th, 1916. Transferred to 10th Res. London Regt. as Musketry and Lewis Gun Instructor. Wounded at Laventie left leg (slight).

CHOPPING, S., Bandsman : Malta, Alex., Gal., S. Egypt, France. Transferred to Base Band, Rouen.

CHUBB, L. J., Cpl. : Malta, Alex., Gal. Invalided to U.K., March 23rd, 1916. Oct. 2nd, 1916, rejoined (Res.) Battn. Jan., 1917, transferred H.A.C. Composite Battn. Nov. 1917, transferred to M.H.S. Accountants and served with this unit in France.

CHURCH, S., Pte. : Malta, Alex., Gal., S. Egypt, France. Joined Res. Batt. Drafted to 2/1 Herts Regt. Nov. 11th, 1916, thence to 406 Agriculture Coy. Wounded G.S.W. right shoulder (bullet in chest).

CHURCHWARD, R. H. : Malta, Alex., Gal., S. Egypt, France.

CLAMMER, R. C., Sergt. : Malta, Alex., Gal., S. Egypt, France. Transferred 1/4 London Regt., and served to the end of the War with the Batt. Wounded Sept. 26th, 1916, June 13th, 1917, Aug. 16th, 1917. Awarded D.C.M. and M.M. Mentioned in despatches April 9th, 1918, Oct. 15th, 1918.

CLARIDGE, L. B., Pte. : Malta, Alex., Gal., S. Egypt, France. Transferred to 1/4 London Regt. Mortally wounded May 30th, 1915 ; died May 31st, 1916.

CLARK, C. D. : Malta, Alex., Gal., S. Egypt, France.

CLARK, E. A. - Malta, Alex. Embarkation Staff, Alexandria, Aug. 27th, 1915.

CLARK, F. B., Pte. : Malta, Alex., Gal., S. Egypt, France. Transferred to 1/4 London Regt. Gommecourt Wood, Ypres, 1917. Oppy Wood until retreat, March 28th, 1918. Wounded shrapnel right elbow, and shrapnel head and left eye destroyed.

CLARKE, A. A. : Malta, Alex., Gal., S. Egypt, France.

CLARKE, A. W. : Malta, Alex., Gal., S. Egypt, France.

CLEMMENS, R., 2/Lieut. : Malta, Alex., Gal., S. Egypt, France. Transferred 1/4 London Regt. until Oct. 7th,

1916. 3rd Res. Batt. London Regt., Nov. 27th, 1916, to July 5th, 1917. No. 4 O.C.B., July 5th, 1917, to Oct. 30th, 1917. Commissioned in 10th London Regt. Embarked for Egypt, Jan. 22nd, 1918. Joined 1/10th London Regt. in Palestine. Joined 2/10 Batt. in France, June 13th, 1918. Invalided U.K., Nov. 19th, 1918. Wounded Somme, Oct. 7th, 1916, and Somme, Aug. 29th, 1918.

CLEMENTS, A. G. W., L/Cpl. : Malta. Clerk on H.Q. Staff, Malta Command.

COGGER, G. : Malta, Alex., Gal., S. Egypt, France. France until Jan. 26th, 1919.

CLIFTON, A. G. : Malta, Alex. Invalided to U.K., H.S. " Mauretania," Nov. 4th, 1915.

COATES, S. G., Cpl. : Malta, Alex., Gal., S. Egypt, France. Transferred to 1/4 Batt. London Regt., and served with the Unit throughout the War. Demobilized Feb. 13th, 1919. Gassed Aug. 28th, 1918, right of Arras. Awarded M.M.

COGGINS, R. F., 2nd Air Mechanic : Malta, Alex., Gal., S. Egypt, France. Transferred to 1/4 London Regt. from Rouen until May 2nd, 1917. Joined Res. Batt., Blackdown. Transferred R.A.F., Dec. 8th, 1917. Served as Wireless Operator and Observer. Wounded, shell shock, G.S.W., left arm.

COLE, G. : Malta, Alex., Gal., S. Egypt, France.

COLE, H., Pte. : Malta, Alex., Gal. : Invalided to U.K,, Jan. 25th, 1916, H.S. " Grantully Castle," transhipped to H.S. " Britannic " at Naples. Pte. Cole had 22 years' continuous service to the 1st Tower Hamlets and 4th V.B. R.F.

COLE, J. G. F., Pte. : Malta, Alex., Gal., S. Egypt, France. Somme, July 1st, 1916, 168th M.G.C. Arras, April 9th, 1917, Cambrai, Nov. 20th, 1917 ; Oppy Wood. Invalided to P. of W. Camp. Demobilized Jan., 1919. Wounded slightly.

COLES, A. G. : Malta, Alex., Gal., S. Egypt, France.

COLLYER, A. W., Pte. : Malta, Alex., Gal., S. Egypt, France. Attached 1/13 London Regt., and transferred to 1/4 London Regt., July 1st, 1916, and served with it throughout the remainder of War.

COMPTON, E. F.: Gal., S. Egypt, France. Draft from Devonport, Nov. 15th, 1915.

CONWAY, A. S., CPL.: Malta, Alex., Gal., S. Egypt, France. Transferred 1/4 London Regt. from Rouen. Wounded left foot Aug. 9th, 1916. Reported missing, Aug. 16th, 1917; presumed killed.

COLLINGE, S.W., PTE.: Gal., S. Egypt, France. Draft from Devonport, Nov. 15th, 1915. Killed in action.

CONACHY, P., CPL.: Malta, Alex., Gal., S. Egypt, France. Transferred 1/4 London Regt. from Rouen; in U.K., March 22nd, 1918, to Sept. 30th, 1918. Wounded Somme, 1916, Arras, 1917; gassed 1918.

CONNELLY: Malta, Alex.

COOK, G. H., PTE.: Malta, Alex., Gal., S. Egypt, France. Transferred from Rouen to 1/4 London Regt. Wounded on Somme, Sept. 9th, 1916. Rejoined 1/3 London Regt. in France, June 6th, 1917. Wounded right arm.

COOK, W. J., PTE.: Malta, Alex., Gal., S. Egypt, France Transferred from Rouen to 1/4 London Regt. Invalided U.K., Oct., 1916. Joined 3rd Res. Batt. March, 1918. Transferred to R.A.S.C. Wounded Sept. 22nd, 1916 and Oct. 8th, 1916.

COOPER, A. J.: Malta, Alex., Gal., S. Egypt, France. Killed in action.

COOPER, L. A.: Malta, Alex., Gal., S. Egypt, France.

COPE, W. C.: Malta, Alex., Gal. Killed in action, Oct. 8th, 1915.

CORBET, S. J., SERGT.: Malta, Alex., Gal., S. Egypt, France. Attached to 1/13 London Regt. from Rouen. Transferred to 1/4 London Regt., July 1st, 1916, and served throughout the War. Wounded left arm; partial disablement.

CORDELL, G.: Malta, Alex., Gal., S. Egypt, France.

CORNISH, E. J., CPL.: Malta, Alex., Gal., S. Egypt, France, N. Russia. After being wounded was transferred to 29th London Regt., and drafted to Murman Coast. Wounded shrapnel through shoulder.

CORRIGAN, G. A.: Malta, Alex., Gal., S. Egypt, France.

COTTRELL, A.: Malta, Alex., Gal., S. Egypt, France.

COUSINS, F. W. : Malta, Alex., Gal., S. Egypt, France. Killed in action Gommecourt, July 1st, 1916.

COUZENS, L. W., Driver : Malta, Alex., Gal., S. Egypt, France. Transferred to 1/4 London Regt.

COURTHOLD, J., Pte. : Malta, Alex., Gal., S. Egypt, France. Invalided to U.K. from the Somme, Sept., 1916. After 6 months in hospital sent to L.C.D., Seaford, and then to Reserve Batt. at Blackdown. Transferred to 29th London Regt. R.F. at St. Osyth, Essex, July, 1917. Discharged medically unfit, Oct. 20th, 1917. Wounded Sept. 10th, 1916, right thigh, shrapnel.

COX, E. C., Sergt. : Malta, Alex., Gal., S. Egypt, France. Drafted on June 14th, 1918, to North Russian Expd. Force.

COX, O. H., L/Cpl. : Malta, Alex., Gal., S. Egypt, France. Transferred from Rouen to 1/4 London Regt. from Nov., 1916, to June, 1917, in England with 3rd Res. Batt. Afterwards attached to 1/4 Cambs. Regt. 2/6 (Cyc.) Suffolk Regt., 5th (Res.) South Staffs. Regt.

COX, E. C., Sergt. : Malta, Alex., Gal., S. Egypt, France. Invalided U.K., Aug., 1916. Drafted to 29th London Regt. and sailed for N. Russia June 16th, 1918. Mentioned in despatches in Russia.

CRABB, R. F., Pte. : Malta, Alex., Gal., S. Egypt, France. Died of wounds Sept. 8th, 1916.

CRACKNELL, G. : Malta, Alex., Gal. Killed in action, Dec. 3rd, 1915.

CRAWFORD, F., Cpl. : Malta, Alex., Gal., S. Egypt, France. Transferred 1/4 London Regiment. Somme, July 1st, 1916 ; Arras, 1917 ; Ypres, Aug., 16th, 1917 ; Oppy Wood, March 28th, 1918. School of Signalling, Dunstable. Discharged Oct. 24th, 1918. Wounded right wrist, Sept. 9th, 1916.

CRONIN, E. : Malta, Alex., Gal., S. Egypt, France.

CROOK, S. : Malta, Alex., Gal., S. Egypt, France. Killed in action Sept. 9th, 1916.

CROUCH, A. E., Capt. : Malta, Alex., Gal., S. Egypt, France. Transferred 1/4 London Regt. Received commission at St. Omer, Dec. 31st, 1916. Joined 13th London Dec. 31st, 1916. In England, Feb. 21st, 1918, to Oct. 30th, 1918.

CROUCH, A. J., Pte. : Malta, Alex., Gal., S. Egypt, France. Transferred to 1/4 Batt. London Regt. Mortally wounded, Combles, Sept. 20th, 1916.

CROWDER, J. : Malta, Alex., Gal., S. Egypt, France. Invalided to U.K. May 7th, 1916.

CROWE, L. E. : Malta, Alex., Gal. Invalided to U.K., H.S. " Oxfordshire," Feb. 11th, 1916.

CUNDRICK, G. R., Pte. : Malta, Alex., Gal., S. Egypt, France. G.S.W. left arm, July 1st, 1916.

CUNNINGHAM, W. H. : Malta, Alex., Gal., S. Egypt, France.

CUNNINGTON, G., Pte. : Malta, Alex., France. Mortally wounded Sept. 8th, 1916.

CURD, W. : Malta, Alex., Gal. Invalided to U.K., " Glengorm Castle," March 24th, 1916.

CURTIS, C. J. : Malta, Alex., Gal., S. Egypt, France. Killed in action, Sept. 7th, 1916.

CUSSEN, J., L/Cpl. : Malta, Alex., Gal., S. Egypt, France. Transferred 1/4 London Regt. Attached 1/3 London Regt. Attached 8th East Surrey Regt. Taken prisoner, Aug. 6th, 1918. Wounded at Leuze Wood, Sept. 9th, 1916 ; at Ypres, Aug. 13th, 1917.

CUTRESS, H., Pte. : Malta, Alex., Gal., S. Egypt, France. L.C.D., Seaford, marked B2, and transferred to R.D.C. Marked Grade 3 and posted to P. of W. Camp. Demobilized March, 1919.

CURTIS, C. J. : Malta, Alex., Gal., S. Egypt, France. Killed in action, May 16th, 1917.

CURTIS, J., Pte. : Malta, Alex., Gal., S. Egypt, France. Wounded in France.

DAIN, H. G., Pte. : Malta, Alex., Gal., S. Egypt, France. Attached 1/13 London Regt. Invalided U.K. and discharged from Army Aug. 17th, 1917. Wounded July 1st, 1916. Five wounds by high explosive.

DAINTON, S. C., Cpl. : Malta, Alex., Gal., S. Egypt, France. Transferred 1/4 London Regt. Wounded Somme, 1916. Rejoined Batt. and served until end of War. Wounded right hand and thigh.

DAINTRY, S., L/CPL. : Malta, Alex., Gal., S. Egypt, France. Killed in action, July 1st, 1916.

DAINTRY, E., SERGT. : Malta, Alex., Gal., S. Egypt, France. Transferred 1/4 London Regt. Discharged April 16th, 1918. Wounded Leuze Wood, Sept. 9th, 1916. G.S.W. left hand and left shoulder.

DALEY, W., PTE. : Malta, Alex., Gal., S. Egypt, France. Wounded once.

DALMAN, S., PTE. : Malta, Alex., Gal., S. Egypt, France. Transferred 1/4 London Regt. and served with Batt. ever since.

DALSTON, W. : Malta, Alex., Gal., S. Egypt, France.

DANN, J. H., PTE. : Malta, Alex., Gal. Invalided U.K., H.S. " Nevassa," Jan. 28th, 1916, and transferred to R.D.C.

DAVIDSON, J. S. : Malta, Alex., Gal., S. Egypt. France. Attached 1/13 London Regt., Hebuterne, July 1st, 1916. Transferred to 1/4 London Regt., Jan., 1917. Wounded, Sept. 9th, 1917 ; was Capt. Webster's runner at the time he was killed. Returned to France, July 23rd, 1917. Returned to U.K. Jan. 29th, 1918. Joined 15th O.C.B., Romford. Wounded right and left leg.

DAVIES, W. L., PTE. : Malta, Alex., Mudros, France Transferred 1/4 London Regt. Discharged Feb. 2nd, 1917. Wounded Aug. 26th, 1916, shrapnel in knee joint

DAVIS, T. : Malta, Alex., Gal., S. Egypt, France. Transferred to Essex Regt. Discharged July 13th, 1917. Paralysis of left arm, result of injuries received in action.

DAVIS, D. E., SERGT. : Malta, Alex., Gal., S. Egypt, France. Transferred 1/4 London Regt., and served with it until Aug., 1918. Awarded M.M.

DAVIS, H. J. : Malta, Cairo, France. Dec. 1st, 1915, to H.T. " Abdul Monayor " for Western Frontier for duty with H.Q. Staff.

DAVIS, J. E., CPL. FARRIER : Malta, Alex. Invalided to U.K., Oct. 26th, 1915. Drafted to 4/1 Cambs. Regt.

DAVIS, W. R. : Malta, Alex., Mudros, France.

DAY, C. E., L/CPL. : Malta, Alex., Gal., Palestine. Drafted to 1/10 London Regt. Transferred to R.A.S.C., and served under General Staff 75th Division.

DEAN, E. R., Pte. : Malta, Alex., Gal., S. Egypt, France. Transferred 1/4 London Regt. Wounded G.S.W. in back, Aug., 1916. G.S.W. left leg (amputated) Sept., 1916.

DEAN, T. : Gal. Draft from Devonport, Nov. 15th, 1915. Invalided to U.K., H.S. " Oxfordshire," Feb. 11th, 1916.

DENT, F. : Malta, Alex., Gal., S. Egypt, France. Transferred to 1/4 Batt. London Regt. Somme, Leuze Wood, Guillemont, Laventie, Arras, March, 1917. Rejoined Unit March 1st, 1918, until July, 1918 ; returned to U.K. to O.C.B., Fermoy, Ireland. Wounded Aug. 16th, 1917.

DEVO, W., Pte. : Malta, Alex., Gal., France. Invalided to U.K., Dec. 25th, 1915. H.S. " Aquitania." Served on re-calling up in France. Discharged, disabled, Dec., 1918. Wounded left hand (disabled).

DEWELL, A. E., C.S.M. : Malta, Alex., Gal., France. Transferred 1/4 London Regt. Invalided U.K., April, 1917. Joined 3rd Res. Batt. Draft to new 2/4, Nov., 1917, to March, 1918. Posted 1/6 London Regt. Still serving Army of Occupation (Rhine).

DOE, A., Driver : Malta, Alex., Gal., S. Egypt, France. Transferred 1/4 London Regt. Served throughout the War.

DIXON, J. R. : Malta, Alex., Gal., S. Egypt, France. Invalided U.K., May 7th, 1916.

DOLLIMORE, H. N., Sergt. : Malta, Alex., Gal., S. Egypt, France. Transferred 1/4 London Regt., Gommecourt Wood, Somme, Arras, Ypres, Aug., 16th 1917. Wounded at Gommecourt Wood, July 1st, 1916 ; Ypres, Aug. 16th, 1917.

DOSSETT, F. J., Pte. : Malta, Alex., Gal., S. Egypt, France. Attached 1/13 London Regt. Discharged Aug. 16th, 1916. Wounded G.S.W. left hand, with loss of three fingers.

DOUGHTY, A. J., Pte. : Malta, Alex., Gal., S. Egypt, France. Attached 1/13 London Regt. Transferred 1/4 London Regt., 3rd Res. Batt 13th Labour Coy, 6th Labour Coy., 250 Divisional Employment Coy. Wounded Sept. 9th, 1916, on Somme.

DOWDING, H. S. : Malta, Alex., Gal. Invalided to U.K., H.S. " Panama," Feb. 20th, 1916.

DOWLING, H. W., Pte. : Malta, Alex., Gal., S. Egypt. Invalided to U.K., H.S. " Oxfordshire," Feb. 11th, 1916.

DOWSETT, G. J., L/Cpl. : Gal., S. Egypt, France. Draft Devonport, Nov. 15th, 1915. Transferred 1/4 London Regt. from Rouen until taken prisoner at Oppy Wood, Arras. Wounded at Guillemont and at Cambrai.

DRISCOLL, L. R., Pte. : Malta, Alex., Gal., S. Egypt, France. Transferred 1/4 London Regt. Demobilized Feb. 24th, 1919. Wounded 1st Somme, 2nd Ypres.

DROSTLE, E. G., Pte. : Malta, Alex., Gal., S. Egypt, France. Leuze Wood, Combles, Laventie, Gommecourt. Blown up July 1st, 1916.

DUDLEY, L. : Malta, Alex., Gal., S. Egypt, France. Transferred to 1/4 London Regt., Hebuterne, Somme. Wounded Oct. 7th, 1916, at Les Boeufs. Discharged on account of wounds, Aug., 1917. Wounded twice.

DUNNING, G. A., 2A/M. : Malta, Alex., Gal., S. Egypt, France. Transferred 1/4 London Regt. Posted 29th London Regt., thence to 101 Agricultural Coy., Maidstone ; 363 Coy., Sutton. Transferred to R.F.C. as Mechanic. Wounded July 1st, 1916, at Hebuterne, G.S.W. lower right ribs.

DUCK, C., Pte. : Malta, France. Served for 2½ years in France with 1/4 and 1/3 London Regt. Wounded severely May 4th, 1917.

DURKIN, J., Pte. : Malta, France. Drafted to U.K., 3rd Res. Batt. at Torquay ; thence to 151st Labour Coy. in France, and served 23 months with that Unit.

EATON, R. G., Sergt. : Malta, Alex., Gal., S. Egypt, France. Transferred 1/4 Batt. London Regt. Posted to 1/1 London Regt., Jan., 1918. Wounded Sept. 8th, 1916 (Gas), and April 1st, 1918.

EDNEY, S. T., Pte. : Malta, Alex., Gal., S. Egypt, France. Killed in action July 1st, 1916.

EDWARDS, V. M., Cpl. : Malta, Alex., Gal., S. Egypt, France. Transferred 1/4 London Regt. Transferred, May 5th, 1917, to 512 Field Coy. R.E., and served in the 56th Division to end of War.

EDWARDS, S. A., A/R.S.M. : Malta, Alex., Mudros,

France. Attached Intelligence Corps, June 23rd, 1916, 4th Army, thence to 5th Army ; July 15th, 1918, to 10th Royal Fusiliers. Was Service W.O. Army Intelligence until demobilized, April 18th, 1919. Awarded M.S.M., June, 1918.

EDWARDS, A.R. : Malta, Alex., Gal. May 24th, 1916, invalided to U.K., H.S. " Galika."

EKE, G., Pte. : Malta, Alex., Gal., S. Egypt, France. Transferred 1/4 Batt. London Regt. at Hebuterne. Wounded Oct. 7th, 1916, right knee.

ELKINGTON, E. H., Sergt. : Malta, Alex., Gal., S. Egypt, France. Killed in action, Oct. 7th, 1916.

ELLIOTT, John, Lieut. : Malta, France. Gazetted to 1/4 Batt. London Regt. France Dec., 1915, to June, 1916, with 1/4 London Regt. Loaned to Admiralty for administrative work, 1918. Discharged on account of injury, Feb. 19th. Injury to knee, June, 1916.

ELSBURY, M. E., Sergt. : Malta, Alex., Gal., S. Egypt, France. Transferred 1/4 London Regt. Served continuously in France until Aug., 1918, when sent home on exchange (war worn).

ELVIDGE, E. P. E., L/Cpl. : Malta, Alex., France. Missing since Sept. 9th, 1916.

EMES, W. G., C.S.M. : Malta, Alex., Gal. Jan. 17th, 1916, invalided to U.K., H.S. " Mauretania." Drafted to 4th Res. Batt., Jan., 1917. Transferred to 13th L.N. Lancs. Discharged by Medical Board.

ENEVER, F. A. : Malta, Alex., Gal., France.

ENGLISH, W. C., Cpl. : Malta, Alex., Gal. Nov. 6th, 1915, invalided to U.K., H.S. " Hunslit." Transferred R.A.M.C. (M.T.) at Blackdown. Demobilized, March 19th, 1919.

ENGLISH, T. H., Pte. : Malta, Alex., Gal., S. Egypt, France. June 3rd, 1916, attached to 15th " A " Cyclist Corps until April 17th ; invalided to U.K. and drafted to 166th Labour Coy. ; disembodied March 6th, 1919.

ENTICNAP, E., L/Cpl. : Malta, Alex., Gal., S. Egypt, France. Invalided to U.K., Sept. 1st, 1916, to May 1st, 1917. Drafted to France until March 22nd, 1918, when reported missing.

ESCHMANN, D. : Malta, Alex., Gal., France. Dec. 30th, 1915, to Malta with jaundice. Rejoined unit Alex., April 13th, 1916.

ESCHMANN, S. C., LIEUT. : Malta, Alex., Gal., France. Returned U.K., Aug., 1916, to Cadet School at Oxford. Commissioned in 4th Suffolk Regt., Dec. 19th, 1916 ; attached later to R.F.C. as Observer, and saw much service in France.

ETHERIDGE, G., L/CPL. : Malta, Alex., Gal., S. Egypt, France. Transferred to 1/4 London Regt. Invalided U.K. Rejoined 1/4 London Regt. March, 1917, and served with unit to March 23rd, 1919. Wounded on Somme.

EVANS, T. H., BANDSMAN : Malta, Alex., Gal., S. Egypt, France. Jan. 1st, 1916, invalided to Malta, jaundice. Rejoined unit March 25th, 1916. Joined Base Band, Rouen.

EVANS, A. J., CPL. : Malta, Alex., Gal., S. Egypt, France. Drafted to 1/13 London Regt. Transferred to 5th Essex Regt. Killed in action, Aug. 23rd, 1918.

EVANS, J. B. : Malta, Alex., Gal. Nov. 11th, 1918, returned to U.K. to take up commission, H.T. " Mashobra."

EVANS, W. T., L/CPL. : Malta, Alex., Gal., S. Egypt, France. Transferred 1/4. Discharged by Medical Board, March 31st, 1917. Wounded Sept. 7th, 1916.

EXCELL, S. H., L/CPL. : Malta, Alex., Egypt. Attached Indian Exped. Force, Suez Canal, Sept., 1915, to Dec. 23rd, 1916, Ismailia. Discharged M.B., June 9th, 1917.

EYLES, G., PTE. : Malta, Alex., Gal., S. Egypt, France. Posted 2/3 London Regt. Invalided U.K. Returned to France Sept., 1917, until Aug. 8th. 1918. Wounded (1st) June, 1916, (2nd) Aug., 1918.

FEAKES, C. W., PTE. : Malta, S. Egypt.

FELLOWS, A. E. : Malta, Alex., Gal., S. Egypt, France.

FENNER, G., SERGT. : Malta, Alex., Gal. March 28th, 1916, invalided to U.K., H.S. " Formosa." Served two years with 151 Labour Coy.

FENNELL, W. : Malta, Alex., Gal., S. Egypt, France. Killed in action.

FERGUSSON, V. A., SERGT. : Malta, Alex., Gal., S. Egypt, France. Transferred to 1/4 London Regt., Hebuterne, Gommecourt Wood, Leuze Wood, Le Transloy, Ypres, Cambrai, 1917. Taken prisoner, March 28th, 1918, Oppy, and worked behind German lines five months. Repatriated Dec. 28th, 1918. Wounded Oct. 7th, 1917.

FERRY, R. S., PTE. : Malta, Alex., Gal., S. Egypt, France. Served in France 2 years 7 months. Discharged Jan. 7th, 1919. Wounded May 8th, 1917.

FIELD, H. F., L/CPL. : Malta, Alex., Gal. May 12th, 1916, invalided U.K., H.S. " St. Patrick." Served with 3rd (R) Batt. ; transferred March, 1917, to 151 Labour Coy. in France.

FISHER, E., C.S.M. : Malta, Alex., Gal., S. Egypt, France. Transferred 1/4 London Regt. from Rouen. Transferred to 151 Labour Coy., March 1st, 1917, and served for remainder of War in France. Wounded G.S.W. head, shell wound in back.

FITKIN, H., CPL. : Malta, Alex., Gal., France. Nov. 27th, 1915, invalided U.K., H.S. " Dunvegan Castle." Transferred to Dorset Regt. Drafted to France with Manchester Regt. Taken prisoner March 21st, 1918, at St. Quentin, and after 12 months exchanged and sent to U.K. and discharged.

FITT, A., 2/LIEUT. : Malta, Alex., Palestine and Syria. Remained in Egypt (unfit). Transferred to 20th Garrison Batt., thence to Labour Corps. Granted Temp. Commission, and served with 71 Coy. E.L.C., Tripoli, Syria.

FITZGERALD, A. C., GUNNER R.F.A. : Malta, Alex., Gal., S. Egypt, France. Transferred 1/4 London Regt., Hebuterne, July 1st, 1916, Gommecourt, Somme. Invalided U.K., Oct., 1916, to 3rd R. Batt. Transferred to R.F.A., Nov., 1917, and served in Ireland.

FITZWALTER, A., BANDSMAN : Malta, Alex., Gal., S. Egypt, France. Joined Base Band, Rouen.

FLANAGAN, C. W. : Gal., France. Draft Devonport, Nov. 15th, 1915. Returned to U.K., Feb. 11th, 1916, H.T. " Magnificent." Drafted to 7th Leicesters in France. On May 27th, 1918, he was acting as S.B. His party was surrounded by Germans, and he was shot through the head (although unarmed) by a German officer and killed.

FLEET, E., L/CPL. : Malta, Alex., Mudros, S Egypt,. France.

FLETCHER, H. J. : Malta, Alex., Gal., S. Egypt, France.

FLOWERS, H. R., BANDSMAN : Malta, Alex., Gal., S. Egypt, France. Joined Base Band, Rouen.

FLEXEN, E. J., PTE. : Malta, Alex., Gal., S. Egypt, France. Transferred 1/4 London Regt. from Rouen. Invalided U.K., Sept., 1916. Returned to France and served with unit until demobilized, Feb. 26th, 1919. Wounded Sept. 9th, 1916, on Somme.

FLYNN, O. : Malta, Alex., Gal., S. Egypt, France.

FORSTER, H. J., BANDSMAN : Malta, Alex., Gal., S. Egypt, France. Joined Base Band, Rouen.

FOSH, A. H., PTE. : Malta, Alex., Gal., S. Egypt, France. Transferred 1/4 London Regt. from Rouen. Invalided U.K., Aug. 8th, 1916. Discharged unfit, March 27th, 1917.

FOSTER, H., CPL. : Malta, Alex., Gal., S. Egypt, France. Drafted to 1/13 London Regt. from Rouen. Transferred to 1/4 London Regt., July 30th, 1916. Discharged M.B., April 12th, 1917. Wounded left arm, Leuze Wood, Sept. 9th, 1916.

FOWKE, A. C., PTE. : Malta, Alex., Gal. Dec. 14th, 1915, invalided to U.K., H.S. " Mauretania." Discharged medically unfit, Sept., 1916.

FOXEN, J. E., CPL. : Malta. On Postal Censor's Staff for 4½ years. Attached 1st W. Yorks. from June 30th, 1916, to Jan. 18th, 1919.

FREED, J. : Malta, Alex., Gal., S. Egypt, France.

FREEMAN, H., L/CPL. : Malta, Alex., Gal., S. Egypt, France. Drafted to 1/13 London Regt. from Rouen, and transferred to 1/4 Batt. London Regt. Wounded twice and gassed once.

FROST, F. A. : Malta, Alex., Gal., S. Egypt, France.

FULLER, C., CPL. : Malta, Gal., S. Egypt. 25th Res. Rifle Brigade, Cornwall. Demobilized Jan., 1919.

FURLONG, H., PTE. : Malta, Alex., Gal., S. Egypt, France. Italy May 6th, 1916. Transferred to 1/4 London Regt. Drafted to 3rd Dorsets and 5th Dorsets. Twelve months in Italy. Wounded three times. Back, right arm and side,

GAGAN, J., Sergt. : Malta, Alex., Gal., S. Egypt, France. Transferred to 146 Labour Coy., March 24th, 1917. Chinese Labour Coy., Feb. 14th, 1918. Wounded twice.

GAGE, E. W., Drummer : Malta, Alex., Gal., France. May 22nd, 1916, invalided to U.K., H.S." Braemar Castle." Joined 1/4 Batt., Jan, 1917, until Feb., 1919.

GALLOWAY, T., Riflmn. : Malta, Alex., Gal., S. Egypt, France. Transferred on account of wound to 151 Labour Coy., March 28th, 1917, and to 12th London Regt., June 5th, 1918. Wounded once.

GAME, C. G., Sergt. : Malta, Alex., Gal., S. Egypt. Wounded G.S.W. left forearm.

GAME, C. J., Cpl. : Gal., S. Egypt, France. Draft from Devonport, Nov. 15th, 1915. Served 2 years 2 months after leaving Rouen. Wounded once.

GANCY, W. : Malta, Alex., Gal., S. Egypt, France.

GARVEY, J. S., Pte. : Malta, Alex., Gal., S. Egypt, France. Transferred to 1/4 London Regt. from Rouen. Invalided U.K., L.C.D., Seaford. Drafted to Labour Corps. Draft to Boulogne, Nov., 1917. Attached to R.E. to end of War. Wounded shell shock July, 1916, and Aug., 1916.

GARVEY, J., Pte. : Malta, Alex., Gal., France. Drafted to R.D.C., May, 1917. 18th Glos., June, 1918. Discharged Aug. 21st, 1918. Wounded twice, left leg and shoulder.

GATE, R. E. : Malta, Alex., Gal. Killed in action in Gal., Nov. 21st, 1915.

GARDINER, A. E. : Malta, Alex., Gal., S. Egypt, France. Wounded, leg. Killed in action,May 29th, 1917. Awarded M.M.

GARDINER, S., L/Cpl. : Malta, Alex., Gal. Accidentally killed in Bombing School. Buried at Pink Farm, Gallipoli.

GARNETT, J., Pte. : Malta, Alex., Gal., S. Egypt, France. Transferred to 1/4 Batt. London Regt. until wounded, Sept. 25th, 1916. Rejoined Oct., 1916, and transferred to Tank Corps, Jan., 1917, to Nov., 1917, when wounded and invalided to U.K. Marked B2 and remained as instructor to Dec. 17th, 1918, when discharged. Wounded, Sept. 25th, 1916, right shoulder ; Nov. 20th, 1917, right eye (lost sight of).

GARRETT, H. A., L/CPL. : Malta., Alex. Nov. 6th, 1915, invalided to U.K., H.S. " Goorka."

GARRETT, A. W., CPL. : Malta, Alex., Gal. Invalided from Gallipoli three days before evacuation, classified P.B.2. Transferred to 20th R. Bde., thence to A.P. Dept., continuing to serve in Egypt.

GATFORD, H., CAPT. : Malta, Alex., France. Jan. 17th, 1916, embarked on H.T. " Maniton " to take up commission in England. Gazetted July 2nd, 1916, in R.E. Drafted to France, Feb., 1917, until Oct., 1918, when transferred to G.H.Q. Wireless School, 2nd Army, to end of War.

GAZELEY, G. C. : Malta, Gal., S. Egypt, France. Drafted to Bedfordshire Regt. and thence to Lancashire Regt. Buried St. Sever Cemetery, Rouen.

GEORGE, W. : Malta, Alex., Gal., S. Egypt, France.

GEORGE, R. : Malta, Alex., Gal., S. Egypt. Invalided U.K., result of accident at Beni Mazar. Discharged M.B., Jan. 25th, 1918.

GERRISH, J. H., PTE. : Malta, Alex., Gal., S. Egypt, France. Transferred 1/4 Batt. London Regt., Gommecourt, Somme, Laventie, Arras, Cambrai, Ypres, Vimy, Bullecourt, Mons.

GIBBINS, H. C., L/CPL. : Malta, Alex., Gal., S. Egypt. France. Wounded at Gommecourt, July 1st, 1916. Transferred to 6th Dorsets. Wounded twice. Awarded M.M.

GIBSON, ERIC McLEOD, LIEUT. : Malta, Egypt, France. Gazetted 2nd Lieut. July 20th, 1915, in 1st Batt. London Regt. Left Malta for U.K., Aug., 1915. Joined 2/1 Batt. in Egypt. Joined 1/1 Batt., May, 1916. Joined 2/7 Batt. Middlesex Regt., Canterbury. Rejoined 2/1 Batt. in France, Aug. 13th, 1918. Ministry of Munitions Tool Dept. Wounded G.S.W., neck, May 27th, 1916 ; G.S.W. face, June 26th, 1916.

GILBERT, W. J., PTE. : Malta, Alex., Gal. Killed in action Gallipoli, Dec. 8th, 1915.

GILRUTH, W., SERGT. : Malta, Alex., France. Oct. 22nd, 1915, invalided U.K., H.S. " Egypt." Drafted to France, Dec., 1916. Vimy, Ypres, Cambrai. Killed in action, March 14th, 1918. Honourably mentioned in Div. Orders.

GINN, W. F., BANDSMAN : Malta, Alex., Gal., S. Egypt, France. Joined Base Band, Rouen.

GINN, S. S. S., BANDSMAN : Malta, Alex., Gal., S. Egypt, France.

GLOVER, C. R., LIEUT. : Malta, Alex., Gal., France. Invalided to U.K., H.S. "Aquitania," Dec. 25th, 1915 Commissioned in 2/1 London Regt. Served in France. Invalided out of Army, Jan. 15th, 1919.

GOLLOP, U. R. R., PTE. : Malta, Alex., Gal., S. Egypt, France. Joined Base Band, Rouen.

GOOCH, D. F., SERGT. : Malta, Alex., Gal., S. Egypt, France. Transferred to Base Depot, Harfleur, thence to 1/4 Batt. London Regt., and all engagements to Oct. 8th, 1916. Invalided to U.K. and returned to France. Died of wounds, Nov. 26th, 1917.

GOODWIN, E. H. : Malta, Alex., Gal., S. Egypt, France.

GORROD, W. R., CPL. : Malta, Alex., Gal., S. Egypt, France. Transferred 1/4 Batt. London Regt. Invalided U.K., Nov. 2nd, 1916. Instructor 3rd Res. Batt. until June 1st, 1918, when discharged on medical grounds.

GORROD, S. M., SERGT. : Malta, Alex., Gal., S. Egypt, France. Transferred to 1/4 Batt. London Regt. from Rouen Killed in action on Somme, Sept. 7th, 1916.

GOUDGE, E. S., PTE. : Malta, Alex., Gal., S. Egypt, France. Transferred 1/4 Batt. London Regt. from Rouen, and served continually with the unit until Jan. 26th, 1919, when demobilized.

GOULD, E. C., PTE. : Malta, Alex., France. Oct. 26th, 1915, invalided to U.K., H.S. "Galika." Served in France with M.G.C. Obtained honourable mention in Div. Card.

GOULD, H., CPL. : Malta, Alex., Gal., S. Egypt, France. Transferred 1/4 Batt. London Regt. from Rouen. Somme, 1916 ; Ypres, 1917 ; Cambrai, Arras, 1918. Wounded arm and back, 1916 ; left thigh, 1916, right thigh, 1917, neck, 1918.

GOSTLIN, F. W., PTE. : Malta, Alex., Gal., S. Egypt, France. Wounded left arm, May 28th, 1916.

GRAHAM, R. B., L/CPL. : Malta, Alex., Gal., S. Egypt. Invalided U.K., Oct., 1916, for clerical employment as result of Medical Board.

GRAHAM ROE, A. C., 2ND LIEUT. : Malta, Alex., Gal.,

S. Egypt, France. Attached 20th (P.S. Batt.) in France ; sent to O.C.B., U.K., Aug. 25th, 1916. Gazetted 2nd Lieut. Jan. 25th, 1917. Left for France, March 16th, 1917. Killed in action, April 28th, 1917.

GRAVES, R. G., Sergt. : Malta, Alex., Gal., S. Egypt, France. Transferred 1/4 Batt. London Regt. from Rouen. Invalided U.K. Served in England for 2 years. Drafted to France to 2/8 Batt. London Regt. Wounded on Somme.

GREEN, H. B., 2nd Lieut. : Malta, Alex., Gal., S. Egypt, France. Left France, June, 1916, to O.T.B., Lichfield. Gazetted Nov., 1916, to 7th Batt. Worcesters. Left for France, Dec., 1916. Distinguished himself in field. Killed in action, April 13th, 1918, at Neuve Eglise.

GREEN, W. J., Pte. : Malta, Alex., Gal., S. Egypt, France. Transferred to 1/4 Batt. London Regt. from Rouen. Gommecourt, Somme, Laventie, Richbeourg. Wounded G.S.W. left side of head and forearm.

GREEN, G. : Malta, Alex., Gal., S. Egypt, France. Transferred 1/4 Batt. London Regt. from Rouen. In U.K., Aug. 12th, 1916, to June 11th, 1917. Drafted 1/3 Batt. London Regt. until Aug. 16th, 1917. Invalided out of Army, April, 1918. Wounded (1) right arm, (2) shoulder, (3) back.

GREEN, G. A., Cpl. : Malta, Alex., Gal., S. Egypt, France. Transferred to 1/4 Batt. London Regt. from Rouen. Sept. 1916, invalided to U.K., and employed as clerk at War Office. Wounded Sept. 18th, 1916, at Leuze Wood.

GREGORY, A. R. : Gal., S. Egypt, France. Draft from Devonport, Nov. 15th, 1915.

GRIFFIN, S. R. : Malta, Alex., Gal. : Dec. 23rd, 1915, killed in action by shell.

GRIFFITH, A. C., Pte. : Malta, Alex., Gal., S. Egypt, France. Killed in action Oct. 8th, 1918.

GURR, A., Pte. : Malta, Alex., Gal., S. Egypt, France. Transferred 1/4 Batt. London Regt. from Rouen. Reported missing July 1st, 1916 ; presumed dead.

HADFIELD, S., Pte. : Malta, Alex., Gal., S. Egypt, France. Transferred 1/4 Batt. London Regt. from Rouen.

Served in France to Cambrai. Taken prisoner Nov. 24th, 1917. Repatriated Dec. 7th, 1918. Wounded (1) Gallipoli (2) and (3) France.

HAGGIS, H. W., L/Cpl.: Malta, Alex. Jan. 1st, 1915, invalided to U.K., H.T. " Glengorm Castle." Became I. of M. 4th Res. Batt. Discharged July 31st, 1917.

HALDANE, D., Pte. : Malta, Alex., Gal. Dec. 30th, 1915, G.S.W. in head. Died at Malta, Jan. 4th, 1916.

HALE, W. T. : Malta, Alex., Gal., S. Egypt, France.

HALL, A. W., L/Cpl. : Malta, Alex., Gal., S. Egypt, France. Drafted to 1/13th Batt. London Regt. from Rouen. Invalided U.K. Drafted March, 1917, to Labour Coy. in France. R.D.C., Dec., 1917. Demobilized, Jan. 22nd, 1919. Wounded right cheek and gassed.

HALL, S. J., Pte. : Malta, Alex., Gal., S. Egypt, France. May 12th, 1916, invalided U.K. Drafted to 100 Prov. Batt. July 1st, 1916. R.D.C., April 17th, 1917, to end of War.

HALLETT, G., Pte. : Malta, Alex., Gal., S. Egypt, France. Transferred 1/4 Batt. London Regt. from Rouen. Invalided U.K., July, 1916. Returned to France. Wounded, Ypres, Aug. 16th, 1917. Continued service to March 28th, 1918, when taken prisoner.

HANNAY, H. T., 2/Lieut. : Malta, Alex., Gal., S. Egypt, France. Transferred 1/4 Batt. London Regt. from Rouen. Wounded July 17th, 1916. Killed in action March 28th, 1918.

HARE, W. H., L/Cpl. : Malta, Alex., Gal., S. Egypt, France. Transferred to 1/4 Batt. London Regt. from Rouen. Wounded (1) July 3rd, 1916, (2) Aug. 17th, 1917. Killed in action, March 28th, 1918.

HARDINGHAM, A. E., Pte. : Malta, Alex., Gal., S. Egypt, France. Transferred 1/4 Batt. from Rouen. Invalided U.K., July, 1916, and joined Res. Batt. L.C.D., Seaford. Discharged unfit, Aug. 8th, 1917. Wounded G.S.W. right leg and shoulder, Gommecourt Wood, July 1st, 1916.

HARPER, R. A., 2/Lieut. : Malta, Alex., France. May 23rd, 1916, drafted from Rouen to 1/13 London Regt, No. 2 O.T.B. Pembroke College, Cambridge, Dec. 1st,

1916. Gazetted, April 27th, 1917, 2/1 London Regt. Drafted France, June 7th, 1917. Mortally wounded, Sept. 14th, 1917.

HARPER, T., Sergt. : Malta, Alex., France. Oct. 22nd, 1915, embarked sick for U.K., H.S. " Egypt." Drafted to France in 1916. Killed in action, May 28th, 1918, in night raid.

HARRIE, W. G., Pte. : Malta, Alex., Gal., S. Egypt, France. May 6th, 1916, drafted from Rouen 1/4 Batt. London Regt. and served with Batt. until mortally wounded Oct. 7th, 1916. Wounded thigh, Oct. 7th, 1916. Died Oct. 13th, 1916.

HARRIS, J., Pte. : Malta, France. Wounded once.

HARRIS, N., Pte. : Malta, Alex., Gal., S. Egypt, France. May 23rd, 1916, drafted from Rouen to 1/13 London Regt. Wounded three times.

HARRIS, H., Pte. : Malta, Alex., Gal. Dec. 10th, 1915, invalided to U.K., H.S. " Nevassa."

HAWKINS, G. A., Cpl. : Malta, Alex., Gal., S. Egypt, France. Transferred to 1/4 Batt. London Regt. from Rouen. Returned to France, Feb., 1917.

HAWKINS, F. H., Pte. : Malta, Alex., Gal., S. Egypt, France. May 23rd, 1916, transferred 1/4 Batt. London Regt. from Rouen. Gommecourt, Somme, Arras, Cambrai, Ypres, Vimy. Served to end of War. Twice gassed.

HAWKINS, A., Pte. : Malta, Alex., Gal., S. Egypt, France. May 6th, 1916, transferred to 1/4 Batt. London Regt. from Rouen. Served throughout and demobilized March 28th, 1919.

HAYES, G. F., Pte. : Malta, Alex. March 22nd, 1916, embarked at Alexandria, H.T. " Tunisian," for U.K. Discharged on account of age.

HAYLETT, S., Pte. : Malta, Alex. Gal. March 28th, 1916, invalided to U.K., H.S. " Formosa." Discharged M.B., July, 1916.

HAYNES, H. S., Cpl. : Malta, Alex., Gal., S. Egypt, France. Transferred 1/4 Batt. London Regt. from Rouen until 7th Oct., 1916. Transferred R.A.F., April 1st, 1918. Wounded Dec. 23rd, 1915, G.S.W. left leg in Gallipoli ; G.S.W. left shoulder on Somme.

HAZEL, E. J., O.R. Sergt. : Malta. Transferred on medical grounds from 1/4 Battn. in Malta. Volunteer Long Service Medal.

HAZEL, L. J. : Malta, Alex., Gal. March 26th, 1916, invalided U.K., H.S. " Egypt."

HEAD, S. W. : Malta, Alex., Gal., S. Egypt, France. May 6th, 1916, transferred 1/4 Batt. London Regt. from Rouen.

HEATHCOTE, J. C. (Sewell), Pte. : Malta, Alex., Gal., S. Egypt, France. May 23rd, 1916, transferred 1/4 Batt. London Regt. from Rouen.

HEATH, E. J., Capt. : Malta, Alex., Gal., S. Egypt, France. May 23rd, 1916, transferred to 1/13 London Regt. until invalided to U.K. Commission Labour Corps, 1917. Wounded at Zillebeck. Mentioned in despatches, Nov., 1917.

HEDDESHEIMER, E. G., Sergt. : Malta, Alex., Gal., S. Egypt, France. Transferred to 1/4 Batt. London Regt. from Rouen. Killed in action on Somme, Oct. 7th, 1916.

HEDDESHEIMER, H. J., C.S.M. : Malta, Alex., Gal., S. Egypt, France. Transferred 1/4 Batt. London Regt., Guillemont, buried by shell. Invalided to U.K., L.C.D., Seaford. Discharged M.U., Nov. 17th, 1917.

HEDGER, F. : Malta, Alex., Gal., S. Egypt, France. May 6th, 1916, transferred 1/4 Batt. London Regt. from Rouen.

HEED, A. R. : Malta, Alex., Gal. Dec. 9th, 1915, wounded. Jan. 28th, 1916, invalided to U.K., H.S. " Essequibo."

HEMBROW, W. J. : Malta, Alex., Gal., S. Egypt, France. May 23rd, 1916, transferred to 1/4 Batt. London Regt. from Rouen. Wounded July 1st, 1916, and May 3rd, 1917.

HENSMAN, W. C. : Malta, Alex., Gal., S. Egypt, France. May 23rd, 1916, transferred to 1/4 Batt. London Regt. from Rouen. Missing, presumed killed, July 1st, 1916.

HERBERT, J., Pte. : Alex., Gal., S. Egypt, France. May 7th, 1916, invalided U.K., from Rouen. Discharged from 2/4 Batt. as being under age, and joined up again in the 3rd Northamptons.

HERRIDGE, A. J., C.S.M. : Malta, Alex., Gal., S. Egypt, France. Transferred to 1/4 Batt. London Regt. at Rouen. Wounded (1st) face in Gallipoli, (2nd) back and leg, Aug. 17th, 1916. Killed in action, Sept. 9th, 1916.

HEWITT, E. C., PTE.: Malta, Alex., Gal., S. Egypt, France. June 3rd, 1916, transferred to 1/4 London Regt. at Rouen, and took part in all engagements to Sept. 30th, 1916. Invalided U.K. (fever). Substituted April 4th, 1917. Wounded slightly July 1st, 1916.

HEY, D. H., PTE.: Malta, Alex., Gal., France. Died of wounds received on Somme, Sept. 11th, 1916. Buried in La Neuville Cemetery, Corbie.

HEYES, G., SERGT.: Malta, Alex., Gal., S. Egypt, France. May 6th, 1916, transferred to 1/4 London Regt. from Rouen, and served with Batt. in every engagement. Awarded M.M. and three Distinguished Service Cards, March, August and Nov., 1918.

HICK, W. S.: Malta, Alex., Gal., S. Egypt, France. May 6th, 1916, transferred to 1/4 London Regt. from Rouen.

HIGGINS, E., PTE.: Malta, Alex., Gal., S. Egypt, France. May 6th, 1916, transferred to 1/4 London Regt. from Rouen. Wounded once. Killed in action, Oct. 8th, 1916.

HILLMAN, W.: Malta, Alex., Gal., S. Egypt, France. May 23rd, 1916, drafted to 1/13 London Regt. from Rouen. Died of wounds, April 9th, 1917, at Telegraph Hill, Arras.

HILTON, F. A., PTE.: France. Unfit to sail with Batt. on Dec. 23rd, 1914. Served in France, March 31st, 1918, to Jan. 19th, 1919. Transferred to 1/20 London Regt.

HILLIER, H. D., PTE.: Gal., S. Egypt, France. Draft from Devonport, Nov. 15th, 1915. May 6th, 1916, drafted from Rouen to 1/4 Batt. London Regt. Wounded at Gommecourt, Aug. 1st, 1916 (lost leg).

HINDE, W. J., PTE.: Malta, Alex., Gal., S. Egypt, France. Transferred to 1/4 Batt. London Regt. from Rouen Hebuterne, Somme, Leuze Wood, Givenchy. Killed in action, Sept. 9th, 1916.

HINKINS, W., PTE.: Malta, Alex., Gal., S. Egypt, France. Transferred to 1/4 Batt. London Regt. from Rouen. Bazancourt, June, 1916; Les Boeufs, Oct. 7th, 1916. Drafted to new 2/4 Isle le Hamel, June 17th. Ypres, Sept. 20th, 1917. Drafted to U.K. as B3 from wounds. Wounded left arm and hand, Oct. 7th, 1916; and right ankle, Sept. 20th, 1917.

HIRTH, R. E., L/Cpl.: Malta, Alex., Gal., S. Egypt, France. Drafted to 1/13 Batt. London Regt., and later transferred to 1/4 Batt. London Regt., after discharge from hospital, transferred to 1st Middlesex Labour Coy., and served in France with the unit.

HODGES, W. T., Sapper: Malta, Alex., Gal., S. Egypt, France. May 23rd, 1916, drafted to 1/13 Batt. London Regt. from Rouen. Invalided to U.K., June, 1916. Joined 3rd Res. Transferred to R.E. I.W. & D., Nov. 15th, 1917. Wounded, June 6th, 1916.

HOLDGATE, L. A., Sergt.: Malta, Alex., Palestine. Aug. 30th, 1915, detailed for duty with G.H.Q. Staff, followed by post of O.R.S., 40th R.F.

HOLDSWORTH, A., Sergt.: Malta, Alex., Gal., France. March 25th, 1916, invalided to U.K. from Malta, H.S. " Egypt." Joined 3rd Res. Batt. Drafted 149 Labour Coy. in France, April 4th, 1917, to Jan. 30th, 1919. Wounded in Gallipoli, Dec. 31st, 1915.

HOLINSKI, A. R.: Malta, Alex., Gal., S. Egypt, France. May 23rd, 1916, drafted to 1/13 London Regt. from Rouen.

HOLLAND, W., Pte.: Malta, Alex., Gal., S. Egypt, France. May 6th, 1916, transferred to 1/4 London Regt from Rouen. Wounded 4 times.

HOLMES, E. (known as A. Chapman), Pte.: Malta, Alex., Gal., S. Egypt, France. Killed in action, Sept. 9th, 1916.

HOLTHAM, B., Pte.: Malta, Alex., Gal., S. Egypt, France. May 23rd, 1916, transferred 1/4 London Regt., and served in all engagements with this unit to March 28th, 1918, when taken prisoner.

HONIG, W., C.S.M.: Malta, Alex., Gal., S. Egypt, France. Transferred to 1/4 London Regt., and served with unit until end of War. Awarded M.M.

HOOKE, R. S., Cpl.: Malta, Alex., Gal., S. Egypt, France. May 23rd, 1916, transferred to 1/4 London Regt. from Rouen. Wounded (1) head, July 2nd, 1916, (2) mortally wounded, Nov. 25th, 1917.

HOUNSLOW, C., Bandsman: Malta, Alex., Gal., S. Egypt, France. Joined Base Band, Rouen.

HOUSDEN, S. G., Cpl. : Malta, Alex., Gal., S. Egypt, France. May 6th, 1916, transferred to 1/4 London Regt. from Rouen. Wounded Oct. 20th, 1915. Killed in action, March 28th, 1918.

HOWELL, W. : Malta, Alex., Gal., S. Egypt, France. May 6th, 1916, transferred to 1/4 London Regt. from Rouen.

HOWARD, H. W. : Malta, Alex., Gal., France. May 5th, 1916, transferred to 1/4 London Regt. from Rouen.

HUDDY, S. C., Signaller : Malta, Alex., Gal., S. Egypt, France. May 6th, 1916, transferred to 1/4 London Regt. from Rouen. Shell shock, Bazancourt, June 25th, 1916. Drafted to L.C.D., Seaford. Discharged by T.M.B., March 16th, 1917.

HUGGENS, C. F., C.S.M. : Malta, Alex., Gal., S. Egypt, France. Transferred to 1/4 London Regt. from Rouen. Invalided U.K. Joined 3rd Res. Batt. at Torquay. Returned to France, March 28th, 1917, with 147 Labour Coy. until Jan. 15th, 1919. Wounded Somme, Sept. 9th, 1916. Mentioned in despatches, Nov. 7th, 1917 : Coolness under fire.

HUGHES, H., Sergt. : Malta, Alex., Gal., S. Egypt, France. Transferred 1/4 London Regt. from Rouen. Died of wounds in head, Apr. 15th, 1917, No. 20 Casualty Clearing Station, France.

HUMPHRIES, F., Pte. : Malta, Alex., Gal., S. Egypt, France. May 23rd, 1916, transferred 1/4 Batt. London Regt. from Rouen. Stayed 6 months in France, and drafted to 686 H.S. Employment Coy. Wounded once.

HUNT, F., Pte. : Malta, Alex. : Oct. 21st, 1915, invalided to U.K., H.S. " Aquitania." Joined 4th Res. at Salisbury. Drafted to France with 1/3rd London Regt. Wounded, G.S.W. chest. Discharged M.B. May 17th, 1917.

HUNT, C. J., Sergt. : Malta, Alex., Gal., S. Egypt, France. May 6th, 1916, transferred to 1/4 London Regt. from Rouen. Evacuated and in hospital to Feb., 1917. Posted for duty S.D.5, War Office. Wounded June 14th, 1916. Awarded Serbian Medal for valour.

HUNTINGFORD, B., Pte. : Malta, Alex., Gal., S. Egypt, France. May 6th, 1916, transferred to 1/4 London Regt from Rouen. Apr. 16th, 1916, invalided to U.K., shell shock. Discharged M.B., Dec. 28th, 1917.

HURDLE, A. R., SAPPER (SIGNALS) : Malta, Alex., Gal., S. Egypt, France. May 6th, 1916, transferred to 1/4 Batt. London Regt. from Rouen. Invalided U.K. Drafted to 4th Res. at Salisbury. Transferred to 2/1 Herts., thence to R.E. Returned to France, Nov. 25th, 1917, to 8th Signal Coy. Joined 61st Div. Sig. Coy., Oct. 4th, 1918. Wounded at Hebuterne, May 30th, 1916.

HUSSEY, S. E., CPL. : Malta, Alex., Gal., S. Egypt, France. Transferred to 1/4 London Regt. from Rouen. Invalided to U.K. Transferred R.D.C., Blandford, Jan. 18th. Joined 3rd Res. Batt. Drafted to 1/4 Batt., April, 1918. Returned to U.K., Nov. 8th, 1918, for O.T.B. Wounded, July 1st, 1916 (foot), Aug. 1st, 1916 (right arm).

HYDE, L. R., SERGT. : Malta, Alex., Gal., S. Egypt, France. Sergt. of M.G. Section, and then transferred to 1/4 Batt. London Regt. from Rouen, until Les Boeufs, where wounded, Oct. 7th, 1916, Beaulieu Wood, while leading the Coy. In hospital 6 months and convalescent 6 months. G.S.W. left ankle. Awarded M.M.

HYDE, H. E. : Malta, Alex., Gal., S. Egypt, France. May 23rd, 1916, transferred to 1/4 London Regt. from Rouen.

IDDENDEN, C., SERGT. : Malta, Alex., Gal., S. Egypt, France. Transferred to 1/4 London Regt. from Rouen, until March 28th, 1918, when invalided U.K. Joined 1st Res. Batt., Aug. 14th, 1918. Present at Arras, Ypres, Cambrai, Oppy Wood. Finally S. Instructor Brigade School, Blackdown. Wounded (1) Hebuterne, (2) Leuze Wood, (3) Oppy.

IRELAND, W. BANDSMAN : Malta, Alex., Gal., S. Egypt, France. Joined in Malta from 1/4 Batt. Drafted back to 1/4, and joined Batt. Band at Rouen.

IRVING, W. W. : Malta, Alex.

IRWIN, A. W. : Malta, Alex. Dec. 14th, 1915, invalided to U.K., H.S. " Tagus."

ISZATT, C. : Malta, Alex., Gal., S. Egypt, France. May 23rd, 1916, transferred 1/4 Batt. London Regt. from Rouen, and served in all actions to Sept. 18th, 1916, Leuze Wood. In hospital to May, 1918, and then discharged by M.B. Wounded once.

JACOBS, F., PTE. : Malta, Alex., Gal., S. Egypt, France. May 6th, 1916, transferred 1/4 Batt. London Regt. from Rouen. Wounded on Somme, knee. Killed in action, May 7th, 1917.

JACKSON, G. : Malta, Alex., Gal., S. Egypt, France. Jan. 25th, 1916, invalided to U.K., H.S. "Formosa."

JACKSON, R. W. : Malta, Alex. Oct. 21st, 1915, invalided to U.K., H.S. "Aquitania."

JAKINS, A. W., L/CPL. : Malta, Alex., Gal., S. Egypt, France. May 23rd, 1916, drafted to 1/13 London Regt. from Rouen, and served in all engagements to Oct. 7th, 1916. Killed in action, Oct. 7th, 1916.

JAMES, F., L/CPL. : Malta, Alex., Gal., S. Egypt, France. May 23rd, 1916, transferred to 1/4 London Regt. from Rouen, and served in all engagements to Arras, May 12th, 1917, when wounded. Nine months in hospital. Posted to 367 H. S. Labour Coy. Discharged Jan. 8th, 1919.

JAMES, A. E., L/CPL. : Malta, Alex., Gal., S. Egypt, France. May 23rd, 1916, transferred to 1/4 London Regt. from Rouen until Sept. 8th, 1916. Invalided to U.K. with shell shock. In hospital to Jan. 4th, 1917. Rejoined 3rd Res. Batt., Torquay. Attached Recruiting Headquarters War Office, as Clerk, Feb. 8th, 1917. National Service Oct. 19th, 1917. Discharged Dec. 14th, 1918.

JAQUES, S. D., L/CPL. : Malta, Alex., Gal., S. Egypt, France. May 23rd, 1916, transferred to 1/4 London Regt. from Rouen, and served with unit throughout the War. First as Signaller and afterwards as O.R. clerk.

JEFFERIES, W. J., PTE. : Malta, Alex., Gal., S. Egypt, France. Dec. 7th, 1915, died of wounds received in action, Gallipoli.

JENKINS, R., PTE. : Malta, Alex., Gal., S. Egypt, France. Transferred to 1/4 Batt. London Regt. from Rouen and served with unit until Mar., 1918, when returned to U.K. for rest, gassed.

JERVIS, C., L/CPL. : Malta, Alex., Gal., S. Egypt, France. May 23rd, 1916, transferred to 1/4 London Regt. from Rouen, and served continuously with unit until taken prisoner, March 28th, 1918.

JOHNSTON, G., L/CPL. : Malta, Alex., Gal., S. Egypt,

France. May 23rd, 1916, transferred to 1/4 London Regt. Invalided to U.K., marked C1. Transferred 151 Labour Coy. until demobilized, Feb. 7th, 1919. G.S.W. right shoulder, Dec. 9th, 1915 ; knee, July 1st, 1916.

JOHNSON, J. : Malta, Alex., Gal. March 29th, 1916, invalided to U.K., H.S. " Carisbrooke Castle."

JOHNSTON, W. C. : Malta, Alex., Gal., S. Egypt, France. Transferred to 1/4 Batt. London Regt. from Rouen.

JOLLY, W. J., SERGT. : Malta, Alex., Gal., S. Egypt, France. May 20th, 1916, invalided to U.K. from Rouen, result of accident. Transferred to hospital, and thence to L.C.D., Seaford, 100th Prov. Batt., Guildford, became Coy. O.R. clerk.

JONES, H. C., PTE. : Malta, Alex., Gal., S. Egypt, France. Transferred to 1/4 Batt. London Regt. from Rouen. Somme, July 1st, 1916 ; Leuze Wood, Sept. 15th, 1916 ; severely wounded, Sept. 16th, 1916, and died at Rouen, Oct. 16th, 1916.

JOSEPH, W. (GANEY), PTE. : Malta, Alex., Gal., S. Egypt, France. Transferred 1/4 London Regt. from Rouen, May 6th, 1916. Drafted to R.D.C. in June, 1918, sent to 18th Gloucester Regt., found unfit, and discharged Aug. 31st, 1918. Wounded left leg and shoulder.

JOSEPHS, B., PTE. : Malta, Alex., Gal., S. Egypt, France. Transferred to 1/4 Batt. London Regt. from Rouen. Injured Aug. 16th, 1917.

JOSLIN, H. J., CPL. : Malta, Alex., Gal., S. Egypt, France. Transferred 1/4 London Regt. from Rouen. Transferred to M.G.C., April 1918. Took part in advance into Germany. Demobilized May, 1919. Wounded at Arras, 1916.

JUDSON, W. A., A/R.S.M. : Malta, Alex., Gal., S. Egypt, France. Transferred to 1/4 Batt. London Regt. from Rouen, and served until Sept. 9th, 1916, when wounded. Discharged from hospital Jan. 6th, 1917. Joined 3rd Res. Battn., marked B3, and transferred to War Office as Clerk. Wounded, G.S.W. back and right forearm.

KATZ, C. : Malta, Alex., Gal., S. Egypt, France. May 23rd, 1916, drafted to 1/13 London Regt. from Rouen. Killed in action, July, 1916.

KECK, C., PTE. : Malta, Alex., Gal., S. Egypt, France.

May 23rd, 1916, drafted to 1/13 London Regt. from Rouen. Transferred to 1/4 London Regt. on Somme, La Bassée, Arras, 1917, Cambrai, Arras, 1918. Wounded slightly.

KEEP, A.P., DRUMMER : Malta, Alex., Gal., S. Egypt, France. May 23rd, 1916, drafted to 1/13 London Regt. from Rouen. Killed in action, July 1st, 1916.

KELSEY, F., PTE. : Malta, Alex., Gal., S. Egypt, France. Transferred 1/4 London Regt. from Rouen, May 6th, 1916. Killed in action, Apr. 10th, 1917. Buried Monchy Military Cemetery, near Arras.

KENNEDY, W., PTE. : Gal., S. Egypt, France. Draft from Devonport, Nov. 15th, 1915. May 6th, 1916, transferred to 1/4 London Regt. from Rouen. Wounded three times.

KENNEDY, F. H. : Malta, Alex. Gal. Dec. 26th, 1915, invalided to U.K., H.S. " Aquitania."

KENT, E. G. : Malta, Alex., Gal., France.

KILLBY, C. : Malta, Alex., Gal., S. Egypt, France. May 23rd, 1916, transferred to 1/4 London Regt. from Rouen, and served with unit until seriously wounded, Sept. 7th, 1916. Discharged, July 25th, 1917. Wounded shrapnel, abdomen, Sept., 7th 1916.

KILLICK, H. N., L/CPL. : Malta, Alex., Gal., S. Egypt, France. May 6th, 1916, transferred to 1/4 London Regt. from Rouen. Wounded Somme, 1916. Six months in hospital, and then transferred to R.D.C. Rejoined 1/4 Batt., March, 1918, and served to end of War. Wounded muscle of right arm (destroyed), Sept., 1916.

KING, W. A., SERGT. : Malta, Alex., Gal., S. Egypt, France. Transferred to 1/4 London Regt. from Rouen. Awarded M.M. Killed in action, Aug. 16th, 1917.

KNIGHT, L. A., SERGT. : Malta, Alex., Gal., N. Egypt, Salonika. H.Q. Staff (Chief Clerk) R.Q.M.S., Mudros. Invalided to U.K. from Salonika, Apr., 1918. Discharged unfit, Sept., 1918.

KNIGHT, C. W. : Malta, Alex., Gal., S. Egypt, France. May 6th, 1916, transferred to 1/4 Batt. London Regt. from Rouen.

KNIGHT, W. : Malta, Alex., Gal. Nov. 18th, 1915, died of dysentery.

KNIGHTLY, G. E., Pte. : Malta, Alex., Gal., S. Egypt, France. May 6th, 1916, transferred to 1/4 Batt. London Regt. Killed in action, Somme, Sept. 8th, 1916.

KNIGHTLY, A. V., Cpl. : Malta, Alex., Gal., France. March 23rd, 1916, invalided to U.K., H.S. " Dunluce Castle." Joined 3rd Res. for 6 months. Drafted new 2/4 Batt. in France, Sept., 1917 joined 3rd Res. Batt., and with the unit until demobilized. Wounded, Ypres, Sept. 20th, 1917.

KNOWLES, R., Sergt. : Malta, Alex., Gal., S. Egypt, France. Transferred 1/4 Batt. London Regt. from Rouen. Invalided U.K. Discharged from hospital, Nov., 1916. Joined 3rd Res. Batt. and attached for duty to R.E. until Aug., 1917. Transferred 314 Works Coy. for duty with W. D. Land Agent. Demobilized 25th March, 1919. Wounded. G.S.W. left leg, Leuze Wood, Sept. 10th, 1916.

LAKE, W., Pte. : Malta, Alex., Gal., France. Nov. 16th, 1915, invalided U.K., H.S. " Dunvegan Castle." Spent 12 months in hospital, and then to 3rd Res. Batt. Drafted to Employment Coy., France, July 29th, 1917.

LANNING, C. F. : Malta, Alex. Jan. 18th, 1916, died of peritonitis.

LAMBERT, F. A., C.S.M. : France. Rejected for Foreign Service by Medical Board at Maidstone. Served both at home and in France from Jan. 24th, 1917, with new 2/4 until taken prisoner, March 23rd, 1918. Wounded (neck).

LARDNER, S., Cpl. : Malta, France. Transferred to Devon Batt., 1916, and Labour Corps, 1917.

LARKIN, F. S., Sapper : Malta, Alex., Gal., S. Egypt, France. May 23rd, 1916, transferred to 1/13 London Regt. from Rouen, then to 2/1 Cambs. R.E. Signals. Wounded shrapnel.

LAST, A. S., Pte. : Malta, Alex., Gal., S. Egypt, France. May 6th, 1916, transferred to 1/4 Batt. London Regt. from Rouen. Mortally wounded and died in France, May 6th, 1916.

LAWRENCE, W., Drummer : Malta, Alex., Gal., S. Egypt,'' France. Oct. 26th, 1915, invalided to U.K., H.S. " Galekap.

LAW, H., Pte. : Malta, Alex., Gal., S. Egypt, France. May 6th, 1916, transferred to 1/4 Batt. London Regt. from Rouen. Served until killed in action.

LAWTON, A., C.Q.M.S.: Malta, Alex., Gal., S. Egypt, France. Transferred 1/4 Batt. London Regt. from Rouen. Demobilized, Jan. 21st, 1919. Wounded, Beauraines, Apr. 4th, 1917 (head).

LEE, F. C., PTE.: Malta, Alex. Oct. 21st, 1915, invalided to U.K., H.S. "Aquitania."

LEE, C.: Malta, Alex., Gal., S. Egypt, France. May 6th, 1916, transferred to 1/4 Batt. London Regt. from Rouen. Invalided U.K. Joined 3rd Res. until March 19th, 1917, when drafted to Tank Corps. Wounded, Fontqueviller, July 5th, 1916.

LEFTLEY, A. W.: Malta, Alex., Gal., S. Egypt, France. May 23rd, 1916, transferred to 1/4 Batt. London Regt. from Rouen.

LEHEC, A., PTE.: Malta, Alex., Gal., S. Egypt, France. Dec. 10th, 1915, invalided from Gallipoli, injury to foot. May 23rd, 1916, drafted 1/13 London Regt. from Rouen. Transferred 1/4 Batt. London Regt., and served with that unit until wounded, Ypres, Aug. 16th, 1917. Three months in hospital. Joined 3rd Res. Batt. and drafted to a Labour Batt. Wounded twice.

LEMON, J. H.: Malta, Alex., Gal., S. Egypt, France. May 6th, 1916, transferred 1/4 Batt. London Regt. from Rouen.

LENNARD, A. J.: Malta, Alex., Gal. March 29th, 1916, invalided U.K., H.S. "Carisbrooke Castle." Discharged by M.B., Sept. 4th, 1916.

LESTER, A. E., 2ND LIEUT.: Malta, Alex., Gal., S. Egypt, France. Transferred to 1/4 Batt. London Regt. from Rouen. Recommended for and granted commission in 1/13 London Regt., Dec. 27th, 1916. Gommecourt, Somme, 1916, Arras, 1917, Ypres, 1917, Bourlon Wood, Cambrai, 1917, Vimy, 1918. Awarded M.C. for conspicuous gallantry while in command of raiding party. Wounded (1st) Gallipoli, (2nd) Oppy Wood. Reported wounded and missing, May 8th, 1918.

LESTER, G. E., LIEUT.: Malta, Alex., Gal., S. Egypt, France. Transferred 1/4 London Regt. from Rouen. Granted commission and joined new 2/4 Batt. Wounded three times, Gommecourt, Passchendale, Sept. 26th, 1917, and La Fae. Taken prisoner, March. 21st, 1918, when wounded.

LEVY, A. F., PTE.: Malta, Alex., Gal., S. Egypt, France.

May 23rd, 1916, transferred 1/4 London Regt. from Rouen. Transferred to Tank Corps, Jan., 1917. Wounded (1st) slightly in Gallipoli, (2nd) neck in France. Killed while fighting his tank, "Jacob," March 25th, 1918.

LEWIN, A., Sapper : Malta, Alex., Gal., Palestine. Transferred to 19th Rifle Brigade, and then to 360 Coy. R.E. Wounded, Jan. 4th, 1916 (slight).

LEWIS, R. W. J., Sergt. : Malta, Alex., Gal., France. Drafted from Rouen to 1/22 Batt. as groom to Col. Dunfee, afterwards joined Reg. Transport, and became Transport Sergt. ; was in France to end of campaign. Wounded in Gallipoli (head).

LEWIS, E. W., L/Cpl. : Malta, France. Returned from Malta, Sept., 1916. Transferred to 25th Rifle Brigade, thence to 4th (R.) Wilts. to 5th Suffolk, proceeded to France, Aug., 1917. Returned March, 1918. Back to France, July, 1918. Demobilized, Jan. 28th, 1919. Wounded, Ypres, Aug. 27th, 1917.

LIGHTFOOT, E. H., Cpl. : Malta, Alex., Gal., S. Egypt, France. May 6th, 1916, transferred to 1/4 Batt. London Regt. from Rouen. Wounded, Sept. 9th, 1916. Invalided to U.K., June 18th, 1918. Joined 33rd Batt. Rifle Brigade; returned to France, July 3rd, 1918.

LINDSEY, S. G., Bandsman : Malta, Alex., Gal., S. Egypt, France. Joined Base Band, Rouen.

LINGWOOD, R. T., Sergt. : Malta, Alex., Gal., S. Egypt, France. May 23rd, 1916, drafted from Rouen to 1/13 London Regt., until July 1st, 1916. Invalided to U.K., July 30th, 1916. Transferred to 29th London Regt., thence to R.D.C. Wounded, concussion whilst in advance sap.

LINTOTT, A. W., Sergt. : Malta, Alex., Gal., S. Egypt, France. May 23rd, 1916, transferred 1/4 London Regt. from Rouen until Nov. 24th, 1917, when wounded and taken prisoner. Repatriated Jan., 1919. Awarded M.M.

LIVINGSTONE, A. H., Pte. : Malta, Alex., Gal., S. Egypt, France. May 23rd, 1916, transferred to 1/4 Batt. London Regt. from Rouen, and served with this unit until March 26th, 1918. Discharged by M.B. Sept. 25th, 1918, neurasthenia.

LLOYD, F. W., Cpl. : Malta, Alex., Gal., S. Egypt, France. May 6th, 1916, transferred 1/4 Batt. London

Regt. from Rouen. Somme, Arras, Ypres, 1917, Cambrai through German offensive, 1918. Came to England, and on return was posted to 1/3 London Regt. Obtained two Divisional Mentions.

LOCKE, F. W., PTE. : Malta, Alex., Gal., S. Egypt, France. May 6th, 1916, transferred 1/4 Batt. London Regt. from Rouen. Killed in action, France, Apr. 16th, 1917.

LONERAGAN, A. : Malta, Alex., Gal. Killed in action, Dec. 3rd, 1915.

LOVICK, C. T., L/CPL. : Malta, Alex., Gal., S. Egypt, France. May 23rd, 1916, transferred to 1/4 London Regt. from Rouen, and took part in all operations to Nov., 1917. Gave a pint of blood to comrade ; returned to L.C.D., Shoreham, from Blackdown. Was transferred to Grenadier Guards. Joined 3rd G.G. in France, and marched to Cologne.

LOWNES, D.D., PTE. : Gal., S. Egypt, France. Draft from Devonport, Nov. 15th, 1915. May 6th, 1916, transferred to 1/4 Batt. London Regt. from Rouen, and in all engagements to Feb. 22nd, 1917, when wounded at Richeburg. Invalided home. Rejoined again, June 12th, 1917. Posted 1/3 London Regt. Wounded, Ypres, Aug. 14th, 1917. Rejoined again Feb. 14th, 1918. Taken prisoner, March 22nd, 1918.

LUPSON, G., SAPPER : Malta, Alex., Gal., S. Egypt, France. Transferred to 1/4 Batt. London Regt. from Rouen. Afterwards served with 1/3, 2/1, 2/3. Finally transferred to Field Survey Coy. R.E. Wounded twice, gassed once.

LUTON, A. E., PTE. : Malta, Alex., Gal., S. Egypt, France. May 23rd, 1916, transferred to 1/4 London Regt. from Rouen. Wounded, Somme, July 1st, 1916. Missing, presumed dead, Oct. 7th, 1916.

MACKINTOSH, A., PTE. : Malta, Alex., Gal., S. Egypt, France. May 6th, 1916, transferred 1/4 London Regt. from Rouen. Invalided U.K. Joined 3rd Res. Batt. Returned to France, Sept. 2nd, 1917. Spent 5 months in hospital with wounds, L.C.D., Shoreham, thence to R.A.M.C. Wounded twice.

MADGETT, T., PTE. : Malta, Alex., Gal., S. Egypt,

France. May 23rd, 1916, drafted to 1/13 London Regt. from Rouen. Gommecourt, July 1st, 1916, Somme, Neuve Chapelle, Arras, 1917. Wounded Passchendale.

MAIDMENT, G. H. : Malta, Alex. Oct. 22nd, 1915. Embarked for U.K., H.S. " Egypt."

MALES, A., Cpl. : Malta, Alex., Gal. Jan. 22nd, 1916, invalided to U.K., H.S. " Marama." Discharged M.B., July 7th, 1917. Wounded in Gallipoli, Dec. 9th, 1915.

MALLETT, J., Pte. : Malta, Alex., Gal., S. Egypt, France. June 3rd, 1916, transferred 1/4 London Regt. from Rouen. Mortally wounded Combles, Sept. 9th, 1916. Buried at Corbie Cemetery.

MALLINDINE, T. : Malta, Alex., Gal. Killed in action, Gallipoli, Dec. 20th, 1915.

MANDALL, G. H., Cpl. : Malta, Alex., Gal., S. Egypt, France. Transferred to 1/4 London Regt. from Rouen. Wounded Apr. 9th, 1917. In hospital to March 11th, 1918, when discharged by M.B. Wounded twice, (1st) right arm, (2nd) G.S.W. right hand.

MANNING, P. W. : Malta, Alex., Gal., S. Egypt, France. May 23rd, 1916, drafted to 1/13 Batt. London Regt.

MANNING, W. C., L/Cpl. : Malta, Alex., Gal., France. Dec. 26th, 1915, invalided to U.K., H.S. " Aquitania." Transferred to Tank Corps, Jan. 12th, 1917. Wounded once shrapnel.

MANSBRIDGE, K. : Malta, Alex., Gal., S. Egypt, France. May 3rd, 1916, invalided from hospital, Malta to U.K., H.S. " Northland."

MASKELL, T. J., Drummer : Malta, Alex., Gal., S. Egypt, France. May 23rd, 1916, drafted to 1/13 Batt. London Regt. from Rouen. Wounded head and spine. Died of wounds, July 7th, 1916.

MARTIN, J. A., Pte. : Malta, Alex., Gal., S. Egypt, France. Transferred to 1/4 Batt. London Regt. from Rouen. Invalided U.K., Oct. 24th, 1917. Drafted 1/3 Batt., Jan. 30th, 1918, to 1/2 London. Demobilized, Jan. 8th, 1919. Wounded, Somme, Sept. 9th, 1916, and Sept. 27th, 1918.

MASON, T., Pte. : Malta, Alex., Gal., S. Egypt, France. Transferred 1/4 Batt. London Regt. from Rouen. Went into hospital. Rejoined Aug. 5th, 1916. Buried twice and wounded once. Reported missing, Aug. 16th, 1916, presumed killed.

MASON, F., BANDSMAN : Malta, Alex., Gal. Invalided U.K., and drafted to 29th London. Wounded, shell shock.

MASON, S. H., CPL. : Malta, Alex., Gal., S. Egypt, France. May 6th, 1916, transferred to 1/4 Batt. London Regt. from Rouen, and served in all engagements until Sept. 26th, 1918. Gommecourt, 1916, Somme, 1916, Arras, 1917, Cambrai, 1917, Ypres, 1917, Oppy, 1918, Bullecourt, 1918, Cambrai, 1918. Wounded Sept. 26th, 1918, at Canal du Nord.

MASTERS, J. F., L/CPL. : Malta, Alex., Gal., S. Egypt, France. May 23rd, 1916, transferred to 1/4 Batt. London Regt. from Rouen. Invalided U.K., July 1916, and posted to 3rd. Res. Batt. London Regt. Draft to 151 Labour Coy., France, March, 1917, to end of War. Wounded July 1st, 1916, head and shoulders (shrapnel).

MATTHEWS, A. : Malta, Alex., Gal., S. Egypt, France. Transferred 1/4 Batt. London Regt. from Rouen, May 6th, 1916. July 1st, 1916, in attack on Gommecourt, was wounded and lay in a shell hole for 14 days before being relieved. Twelve months in hospital before being finally discharged, Jan. 21st, 1918.

MAUNDER, L. R., PTE. : Malta, Alex., Gal., S. Egypt, France. May 6th, 1916, transferred to 1/4 Batt. London Regt. from Rouen. Gommecourt, Somme, Leuze Wood, Combles. Wounded Les Bœufs. Laid for five days before being picked up. Ten months in hospital ; then discharged by M.B. Wounded Oct. 20th, 1915, at Cape Helles.

MAY, R. J., LIEUT. : Malta, Alex., Gal., S. Egypt, Salonica. Nov. 11th, 1915, embarked N.R. " Mashobia " for U.K. to take up commission. Gazetted Feb. 22nd, 1916. Sailed for Salonica Apr. 7th, 1916. Invalided U.K., March 17th, 1917. Wounded, shell concussion.

MAYNARD, C. F., L/CPL. : Malta, Alex. Oct. 26th, 1915, invalided to U.K., H.S. " Galeka." Discharged permanently unfit, Oct. 3rd, 1918.

MAYSTON, S. H. : Malta, Alex., Gal., S. Egypt, France. May 23rd, 1916, draft from Rouen to 1/13 Batt. London Regt.

McDERMOTT, C.: Malta, Alex., Gal., S. Egypt, France. Transferred to 1/4 Batt. London Regt. from Rouen.

McLACHAN, T. J., SERGT.: Malta, Alex., Gal., S. Egypt, France. Transferred to 1/4 Batt. London Regt. from Rouen, and served with unit throughout War. Buried and slightly wounded.

McDONALD, C. W., PTE.: Malta, Alex., Gal., S. Egypt, France. May 23rd, 1916, transferred to 1/4 Batt. London Regt., thence to London Scottish and Labour Coy. and 207 P.O.W. Coy., France. Wounded head.

MEAN, P. E., L/CPL.: Malta, Alex., Gal., S. Egypt, France. May 23rd, 1916, transferred to 1/4 Batt. London Regt. from Rouen. Killed in action July 1st, 1916.

MELVILL, G. H., 2/LIEUT.: Malta, Alex., Gal., S. Egypt, France. May 23rd, 1916, draft from Rouen to 1/13 Batt. London Regt. 3rd Res. Batt., Sept. 18th, 1916, to July, 1917; 22nd O.C.B. from July 17th, to Sept. 1917. Attached to 20th Middlesex from July, 1918, to date. Wounded, July 1st, 1916.

MERRETT, A. J.: Malta, Alex., Gal. Dec. 31st, 1915, invalided to U.K., H.S. "R. d'Italia." Posted to 16th Essex, 29th Middlesex, 595 Employment Coy. Wounded, shell shock.

MEYERS, S. A., 2/LIEUT.: Malta, Alex., Gal., S. Egypt, France. May 23rd, 1916, draft from Rouen to 1/13 Batt. London Regt. Invalided U.K., July, 1916. Joined 3rd Res. Batt. at Hurdcott. Joined O.T.B., Pembroke, Cambridge. Drafted to France, June, 1917. Wounded, Somme, July 1st, 1916. Killed in action, Oct. 26th, 1917.

MIALL, W. G.: Malta, Alex. Aug. 30th, 1915, to Cairo for duty H.Q. Staff. Dec. 1st, 1915, to Western Frontier.

MILLS, A., CPL.: Malta, Alex., Gal., S. Egypt, France. May 23rd, 1916, drafted from Rouen to 1/13 London Regt. Wounded in hand, June, 1916.

MILTON, A., L/CPL.: Malta, Alex., Gal., S. Egypt, France. May 23rd, 1916, transferred 1/4 London Regt. from Rouen until wounded, Oct. 7th, 1916. Joined 3rd Res. Batt., Sept., 1917. Transferred R.A.O.C., Woolwich. Wounded left thigh and shrapnel in head (steel helmet saved his life).

MILTON, E., PTE. : Malta, Alex., Gal., S. Egypt, France. May 23rd, 1916, drafted from Rouen to 1/13 Batt. London Regt., thence to 1/4 London Regt. Transferred March, 1917, Royal W. Surrey, and invalided to U.K. Wounded, G.S.W. right thigh, July 1st, 1916, and in head, 1918.

MILLWARD, C., PTE. : Malta, Alex., Gal., France. May 23rd, 1916, transferred to 1/4 Batt. London Regt. from Rouen. Killed in action, July 1st, 1916.

MOLES, J. W., PTE. : Malta, Alex., Gal., S. Egypt, France. Nov. 27th, 1915, invalided to U.K., H.S. " Guildford Castle." Discharged Dec. 19th, 1916. Wounded, Oct. 23rd, 1915, right side, Gallipoli.

MONTAGUE, H. C., PTE. : Malta, Alex., Gal., S. Egypt, France. May 6th, 1916, transferred 1/4 Batt. London Regt. from Rouen. Killed in action, Somme, July 1st, 1916.

MORETON, G. A., CPL. : Malta, Alex., Gal., S. Egypt, France. On return from France transferred to R.A.F. as Motor Driver. Wounded Les Bœufs, Oct. 7th, 1916. G.S.W., left elbow and thigh.

MORBURY, P. T. : Malta, Alex., Gal., S. Egypt, France. May 23rd, 1916, transferred to 1/4 Batt. London Regt. from Rouen.

MOORE, W., DRUMMER : Malta, Alex., Gal., S. Egypt. Feb. 2nd, 1916, invalided to U.K., H.S. " Nevassa." Discharged by M.B., Aug. 18th, 1917.

MOORE, C. H., CADET : Malta, Alex., Gal., S. Egypt, France. May 23rd, 1916, transferred to 1/4 Batt. London Regt. from Rouen. In hospital, July 1st, 1918. Transferred to 13th R.F. Posted to R.A.F. Cadet Wing, Aug., 1918. Wounded, Nov., 1916.

MORING, S. A. : Malta, Alex., Gal., S. Egypt, France. May 23rd, 1916, drafted from Rouen to 1/13 London Regt. Shot through lungs ; died Sept. 24th, 1916 ; buried, at Etaples.

MORISON, F., PTE. : Malta, Alex., Gal., S. Egypt. In convalescent home, Egypt, when Batt. left. Joined 19th Garrison R.B. to June, 1918 ; then to 810 Employment Coy.

MORISON, A., PTE. : Malta, Alex., Gal., S. Egypt, France.

May 6th, 1916, transferred to 1/4 Batt. London Regt. from Rouen. Wounded, Somme, July 1st, 1916. In hospital to Feb., 1917. Posted to 29th R.F. and to 401 Labour Coy., June, 1917. Returned to France, Apr., 1918, to 86 Labour Coy.

MORRISON, A. F. : Malta, Alex., Gal., S. Egypt, France. May 6th, 1916, transferred to 1/4 London Regt. from Rouen. Served with Batt. to March 28th, 1918, when taken prisoner. Repatriated, Dec. 20th, 1918.

MARTER, P. W., L/CPL. : Malta, Alex., Gal., S. Egypt, France. May 6th, 1916, transferred to 1/4 London Regt. from Rouen. Served with Batt. until wounded Ypres, Aug. 16th, 1917. Transferred to M.G.C., May, 1918. Returned to France to 15th Batt. M.G.C.

MORRELL, R. H., PTE. : Malta, Alex., Gal., S. Egypt, France. Transferred to 1/4 Batt. London Regt. from Rouen to Sept. 5th, 1916, and from Apr. 3rd, 1917, to March 21st, 1918. Remainder of time in England. Wounded G.S.W., right hand ; G.S.W., right thigh.

MORRIS, F., PTE. : Malta, Alex., Gal., S. Egypt, France. May 6th, 1916, transferred to 1/4 Batt. London Regt. from Rouen. Killed in action, Somme, July 1st, 1916.

MORPHEW, H. K. : Malta, Alex., Gal., S. Egypt, France. Transferred to 1/4 Batt. London Regt. from Rouen. Wounded, Dec. 31st, 1915, slightly, in Gallipoli.

MORSE, C. : Malta, Alex., Gal. Dec. 26th, 1915, invalided to U.K., H.S. " Aquitania."

MORTLOCK, H. A., L/CPL. : Malta, Alex., Gal., S. Egypt, France. Transferred to 1/4 Batt. London Regt. from Rouen. Mortally wounded Sept. 9th, 1916 ; died, Sept. 11th, 1916.

MORTON, E. R., CPL. : Malta, Alex., Gal., S. Egypt, France. Transferred to 1/4 Batt. London Regt. from Rouen. Mortally wounded on May 12th, and died next day.

MOSELY, T., SERGT. : Malta, Alex., Gal., S. Egypt, France. Transferred to 1/4 London Regt. from Rouen. Drafted to Portsmouth for 12 months. Proceeded to France, Jan., 1918. Wounded Dec. 9th, 1915, Gallipoli. Killed in action on Somme, Aug. 9th, 1918.

MOTT, L. B., Pte. : Malta, Alex., Gal., S. Egypt, France. May 23rd, 1916, transferred to 1/4 Batt. London Regt. from Rouen until Battle of Somme, when he was attached to 168 Inf. Bde. H.Qrs. Took part in every battle in which Bde. was engaged. Wounded, Dec. 18th, 1915, Gallipoli.

MOTT, E. : Gal. Nov. 15th, 1915, draft from Devonport. March 22nd, 1916, sent to U.K. for duty with Res. Unit., H.T. " Tunisian."

MUDGE, H. L. J., Sergt. : Malta, Alex., Gal., S. Egypt, France, Portuguese E. Africa. Transferred to 1/4 Batt. London Regt. from Rouen, and came from U.S.A. to enlist. Wounded France, May, 1917. Killed in action, Apr. 13th, 1918, at Medo, E. Africa.

MULLER, F. E. : Malta, Alex. Gal., S. Egypt, France. May 23rd, 1916, transferred to 1/4 Batt. London Regt. from Rouen.

MUNDY, S., Sergt. Drummer : Malta, Alex., Gal., France. Feb. 11th, 1916, invalided to U.K., H.S. " Oxfordshire." Joined 4th and 3rd Res. Batts. and then drafted to 13th North Staffords in France.

MUTTON, V. E., Signaller : Malta, Alex., Gal., S. Egypt, France. May 23rd, 1916, transferred to 1/4 Batt. London Regt. from Rouen to May, 1917. Invalided U.K. Joined new 2/4 Batt. March 29th, 1918 ; afterwards to 2/2 and 1/3 London Regt. Wounded (shell) right arm, May, 1917.

MYLREA, E. C., L/Cpl. : Malta, Alex., Gal., S. Egypt, France. May 23rd, 1916, drafted from Rouen to 1/13 London Regt. until Aug., 1916 ; then transferred to 1/4 London Regt. Invalided U.K. and joined 3rd Res. Dec. 1916, as C2, transferred to 151 Labour Coy., France, March, 1917. Demobilized, Jan. 30th, 1919. Wounded, Somme, Sept., 1916.

NEAL, J., Pte. : Malta, Alex., Gal., S. Egypt, France. Transferred to 1/4 Batt. London Regt. from Rouen to June 23rd, 1917. Invalided medically unfit. Served with 5th Army A.O.C. to Dec., 1917, and then sent to U.K. (sick), and then served with 367 H.S. Coy. Wounded left leg, July 1st, 1916. Buried in Mine Crater, Oct., 1916 (permanent injury), Feb. 5th, 1917, slight hand wounds.

NEAME, D.C. : Malta, Alex., Gal., S. Egypt, France.

NEIL, B. : Malta, Alex., France. May 23rd, 1916, drafted from Rouen to 1/13 London Regt.

NEWMAN, A. J., SIGNALLER : Malta, Alex., Gal., S. Egypt, France. May 23rd, 1916, transferred to 1/4 London Regt. from Rouen. July, 1916, invalided to U.K. Joined 3rd Res., Blackdown, June, 1917. Went to hospital for operation to foot. Drafted France, March 28th, 1918. Attached 7th Buffs to end of War. Wounded, Hebuterne, July 1st, 1916.

NICKLESS, F., PTE. : Malta, Alex., Gal., S. Egypt, France. May 6th, 1916, transferred to 1/4 Batt. London Regt. from Rouen. Served for 2 years 3 months. Discharged M.B., Aldershot, Aug. 28th, 1918. Gassed, Sept. 7th, 1916. G.S.W. left leg, Oct. 7th, 1916.

NICHOLSON, W. T. : Malta, Alex., Gal., S. Egypt, France. May 23rd, 1916, transferred to 1/4 Batt. London Regt. from Rouen. Wounded, Nov. 24th, 1915, head, Gallipoli.

NORTH, J., PTE. : Malta, Alex., Gal., S. Egypt, France. May 23rd, 1916, transferred to 1/4 Batt. London Regt. from Rouen, and served with unit until taken prisoner, Nov. 30th, 1917. Wounded twice in right leg.

NOTTAGE, E. H. : Malta, Alex., Gal., S. Egypt, France. May 6th, 1916, transferred to 1/4 Batt. London Regt. from Rouen. Wounded, head, Gallipoli. Left eye and right lung destroyed on Somme, July 1st, 1916. In hospital till 6th Jan., 1918, when he died after terrible suffering.

NORTON, T. : Malta, Alex., Gal., S. Egypt, France. Dec. 6th, 1916, invalided from Gallipoli, Jan. 3rd, 1916, to U.K., H.S. " Britannia."

NORTON, N. : S. Egypt, France. Nov. 15th, 1915, draft from Devonport. May 23rd, 1916, transferred to 1/4 Batt. London Regt. from Rouen.

NYE, G., CPL. : Malta, Alex., Gal. Nov. 14th, 1915, invalided from Gallipoli to U.K., H.S. " Nevassa." Attached to 4th Res., Hurdcott. Discharged July, 1916.

O'HANLON, S. : Malta, Alex., Gal., S. Egypt, France. May 6th, 1916, transferred to 1/4 Batt. London Regt. from Rouen. Killed in action, July 1st, 1916.

OSBORN, J., CPL. : Gal., S. Egypt, France. May 6th, 1916, transferred to 1/4 Batt. London Regt. from Rouen.

Transferred to Tank Corps, Feb. 14th, 1916. Demobilized, March 19th, 1919.

OSBORNE, D., PTE.: Malta, Alex., Gal., S. Egypt, France. May 6th, 1916, transferred to 1/4 Batt. London Regt. from Rouen. Discharged April 2nd, 1917. Wounded, Dec. 9th, 1915 (slightly) in Gallipoli, and at Hebuterne.

OSBORN, A., CPL.: Malta, France. Remained at Malta with Bde. H.Qrs. Returned to U.K. Draft to France to 1/4 Batt. London Regt., Feb., 1916. Invalided U.K., Aug., 1916. Returned to France, July, 1917, to 7th Buffs. Invalided U.K., trench fever, Sept., 1918. Discharged, Dec. 30th, 1918.

OUGH, R. J., PTE.: Malta, Alex., Gal., S. Egypt. Discharged medically unfit, Aug., 1916. As a Batman he earned the gratitude of the C.O.

O'BRIEN, J., PTE.: Gal., S. Egypt, France. May 23rd, 1916, draft from Rouen to 1/13 Batt. London Regt., thence to 1/4 London Regt. Invalided U.K., Oct., 1916; then to L.C.D., Seaford; 3rd Res., Blackdown. Returned to France, Oct. 14th, 1917, to 20th London. Invalided U.K., Dec. 10th, 1917. Discharged, Apr. 18th, 1918. Wounded Oct. 7th, 1916, on Somme and at Cambrai. Awarded D.C.M.

OVERTON, T.: Malta, Alex., Gal., S. Egypt, France. May 6th, 1916, transferred to 1/4 Batt. London Regt. He volunteered to go " over the top " to bring in a wounded man, and never returned. It was a brave action. Presumed killed.

OXLEY, H. J. W., CPL.: Malta, Alex., Gal., S. Egypt, France. Transferred to R.E., Calais.

PAGE, H. F., 2/LIEUT.: Malta, Alex., Gal., S. Egypt, France. May 23rd, 1916, transferred to 1/4 Batt. London Regt. from Rouen. O.C.B., Gailes. Gazetted 2/Lieut. 4th K.O. Royal Lancaster Regt., Sept. 26th, 1917. Drafted to India in spring of 1918 to 2/6 Sussex Regt., Lahore. Divisional Card of Honour for service in field, Oct. 7th, 1916.

PAGE, G. H., BANDMASTER: Malta, Alex., Gal., S. Egypt, France. July, 1916, joined Base Band, Rouen, as Bandmaster. Wounded once in left leg.

PARISH, F. : Malta, Alex., Gal., S. Egypt, France. Transferred to 1/4 Batt. London Regt. from Rouen.

PARKIN, F. W. : Malta, Alex., Gal., France. Oct. 30th, 1915, invalided to Malta and to U.K., Dec. 4th, 1915, H.S. " Mauretania." Served in France with 1/3 and 1/4 London. Wounded, G.S.W. in thigh and compound fracture, and discharged.

PARRIS, J. F., Pte. : Malta, Alex. Sept. 15th, 1915, invalided to U.K. Joined 3rd Res., and employed in D.O.R.E. as Clerk. Demobilized, Jan. 9th, 1919.

PAPPS, C. A., Pte. : Malta, France. Remained in Malta for two years, and served in France 1 year 9 months. Wounded right hand.

PARROTT, A. R. : Malta, Alex., Gal., S. Egypt, France. Transferred to 1/4 Batt. London Regt. from Rouen.

PARSONS, F. W., Pte. : Malta, Alex., Mudros, S. Egypt, France. May 23rd, 1916, transferred to 1/4 Batt. London Regt. from Rouen. Completed 2 years 7 months in France. Demobilized, Dec. 18th, 1918.

PARSONS, N. : Malta, Alex., Gal., S. Egypt, France. May 23rd, 1916, transferred to 1/4 Batt. London Regt. from Rouen.

PARTRIDGE, E. G., Cpl. : Malta, Alex., Gal., S. Egypt, France. Transferred to 1/4 Batt. London Regt. from Rouen. Invalided U.K., and rejoined at Arras, March, 1917. Invalided U.K., with 3rd Res. Batt. Demobilized, Jan. 21st, 1919. Wounded, Leuze Wood, Sept. 18th, 1916, right thigh, and at Ypres, left knee.

PAYNE, W. A., Pte. : Malta, Alex., Gal., S. Egypt, France. May 6th, 1916, transferred to 1/4 Batt. London Regt. from Rouen. Killed in action at Hebuterne, Aug. 13th, 1916.

PAYNE, H. S., 2/Lieut. : Malta, Alex., Gal., S. Egypt, France. May 23rd, 1916, drafted to 1/13 Batt. London Regt. from Rouen until Oct. 1916. Laventie, Neuve Chapelle. Feb., 1917, returned to U.K. for commission. Oct., 1917, with 10th Queen's. Drafted to France, thence to Italy. Back to France, Feb., 1918. Awarded D.C.M. Wounded on Somme, March 24th, 1918 (spinal). Died of wounds at Roehampton.

PAYNE, O.S., SERGT.: Malta, Alex., Gal., S. Egypt, France. May 23rd, 1916, drafted to 1/13 London Regt. from Rouen. Afterwards to 1/4 Batt. until invalided U.K., Aug. 4th, 1917. Joined 3rd Res. Batt. as Instructor. Drafted to France to 1/3 Batt. Demobilized Feb. 21st, 1919. Won Batt. Championship in Malta (Sports).

PAYTON, F. F., PTE.: Malta, Alex., Gal., S. Egypt, France. May 6th, 1916, transferred to 1/4 Batt. London Regt. from Rouen. Somme, Arras, 1918. Lens, with new 2/4 Batt. from Jan. 28th, 1918, to Sept. 12th, 1918, thence to 2/2 Batt. to end of War. Wounded, shrapnel, left knee, July 1st, 1916. Left arm, June 25th, 1917. Gassed, Oct. 14th, 1918.

PEACHEY, A. N., LIEUT.: Malta, Alex., Gal., France. Nov. 13th, 1915, invalided to Mudros, Dec. 26th, 1915, thence to U.K., H.S. "Aquitania." Received commission in M.G.C., Jan. 26th, 1917. Embarked for France, March 30th, 1917, 219th M.G.C. Invalided U.K., May 14th, 1917. Posted, Feb. 21st, 1918, to 73rd M.G.C. Evacuated U.K., Apr. 3rd, 1918. Still in hospital, May 30th, 1919. Wounded Bihecourt, March 22nd, 1918. Awarded M.C., March 22nd, 1918.

PEACOCK, F. D.: Malta, Alex. Sept. 29th, 1915, embarked for U.K. for commission.

PEACOCK, H., LIEUT. (M.G.C.): Malta, Alex., France, Salonica, Bulgaria, Batoum. Aug. 27th, 1915, detailed to Embarkation Staff, Alex., May 2nd, 1916, to U.K. for commission in M.G.C. Sept., 1916, served with 80th Coy., Salonica, Bulgaria, and Batoum.

PEARCE, F. W., PTE.: Malta, Alex., S. Egypt, France. May 6th, 1916, transferred to 1/4 Batt. London Regt. from Rouen. Twelve months in France. Discharged, May 15th, 1918. Amputation of toes.

PEARCE, H. J.: Malta, Alex., Gal. Dec. 4th, 1915, invalided from Gallipoli.

PEARSE, H. C.: Malta, Alex., Gal. Killed in action, Gallipoli, Dec. 9th, 1915.

PENDRILL, W., CPL.: Malta, Alex., Gal., S. Egypt, France. Transferred to 1/4 Batt. London Regt. from Rouen, May 23rd, 1916. Gommecourt, Laventie, Arras,

1917. Invalided U.K. Joined 3rd Res. Batt., July, 1917. Drafted to France, Nov., 17th, 1917, to 1/20 Batt. Invalided U.K., Nov. 30th, 1917. Wounded Gommecourt (slightly), wounded (severely), Apr. 9th, 1917. Gassed, Nov. 30th, 1917.

PENFOLD, W.:

PERRY, W. W. R., Pte. : Gal., S. Egypt, France. Nov 15th, 1915, draft from Devonport. May 6th, 1916, transferred to 1/4 Batt. London Regt. from Rouen. Wounded (1) right hand, (2) chest.

PERRY, J. E. : Gal. Nov. 15th, 1915, draft from Devonport. Dec. 30th, 1915, invalided from Gallipoli, and March 28th, 1916, to U.K., H.S. " Formosa."

PETERS, C. A., Cpl. : Malta, Alex., Gal., S. Egypt, France. May 6th, 1916, transferred to 1/4 Batt. London Regt. from Rouen until wounded, Sept., 1916. Returned to France, Jan., 1918. Wounded, G.S.W. wrists and legs.

PETRE, H. L., L/Cpl. : Malta, Alex., Gal., S. Egypt, France. Transferred 1/4 Batt. London Regt. from Rouen. Drafted to 100 Provisional Batt., Aldeburgh, thence to 6th Labour Batt., and to 368 Labour Coy. Smashed knee in France.

PHILDIUS, V., Lieut. : Malta, Alex., Gal., S. Egypt, France. May 6th, 1916, transferred to 1/4 Batt. London Regt. from Rouen to Jan., 1917. March to June, 1917, O.T.B., Oxford. Gazetted, June, 1917, 6th Middlesex Regt. France, Aug., 1917, to Feb., 1918. U.K., Feb., 1918, to Aug., 1918. France, Sept., 1918, to Jan., 1919. Wounded once.

PFEIFFER, F. C., Pte. : Malta, Alex., Gal. Died of wound to head, Nov. 8th, 1915, Gallipoli.

PHILLIPS, A. : Malta, Alex., Gal., S. Egypt, France. Dec. 4th, 1915, invalided from Gallipoli. Jan. 3rd, 1916, to U.K., H.S. " Britannic."

PHILLIPS, A. M. : Malta, Alex., Gal., S. Egypt, France. Dec. 26th, 1915, invalided Gallipoli to Malta.

PHILLIPS, W. : Malta, Alex., Gal., S. Egypt, France. Nov. 25th, 1915, invalided from Gallipoli, and Dec. 15th, 1915, to U.K., H.S. " Goorkha."

PICKETT, F. W., Pte. : Malta, Alex., Gal., S. Egypt, France. Transferred to 1/4 Batt. London Regt. from

Rouen. Mortally wounded G.S.W. head, Sept. 12th, 1916. Admitted No. 26 Hospital, Etaples. Died, Sept. 13th, 1916. Buried, Etaples Military Cemetery.

PICKFORD, G. : Malta, Alex., Gal. Invalided from Gallipoli, Dec. 30th, 1915, to Malta.

PINCH, V. E., PTE. : Malta, Alex., Gal., S. Egypt, France. Dec. 14th, 1915, invalided from Gallipoli and to U.K., Feb. 6th, 1916, H.S. " Neuralia." Drafted to France, 1917, 1/3 Batt. Returned to U.K. same year.

PIPPETT, H. A., 2/LIEUT. : Malta, Alex., Gal., S. Egypt, France. Transferred to 1/4 Batt. London Regt. from Rouen. Invalided U.K., Sept. 25th, 1916. L.C.D., Seaford, Jan. 5th, 1917. Commission in R.A.F. as Administrative Officer, Aug. 24th, 1918. Wounded, G.S.W., left arm, permanently disabled.

PITMAN, W. C., PTE. : Malta, Alex., Gal., S. Egypt, France. May 6th, 1916, transferred to 1/4 Batt. London Regt. from Rouen to July 8th, 1916. Severely wounded. In U.K., July 9th, 1916, to Oct. 17th, 1917.

PLASTER, H. D., SERGT. : Malta, Alex., Gal., S. Egypt, France. May 23rd, 1916, drafted to 1/13 Batt. London Regt. from Rouen, and then to 1/4 Batt. Invalided out with trench fever, June, 1917. Wounded both buttocks.

PLOWMAN, T. H. : Malta, Alex., Gal., S. Egypt. Dec. 10th, 1915, invalided from Gallipoli to U.K., May 12th, 1916, S.S. " Queen Alexandria."

POLLARD, T., SERGT. : Malta, Alex., Gal., S. Egypt, France. Transferred to 1/4 Batt. London Regt. from Rouen. Invalided U.K., Sept., 1916, thence to L.C.D., Seaford. Transferred to 29th London Regt. thence to 25th King's Liverpool Regt. Left for France, May, 1918. Transferred to 365 P. of W. Coy. Wounded Sept. 18th, 1916, and Oct. 2nd, 1918.

POOLE, C. : Malta, Alex., Gal., S. Egypt, France. Transferred to 1/4 Batt. London Regt. from Rouen.

POOLE, W., CPL. : Malta, Alex., Gal. Dec. 22nd, 1915, invalided with enteric fever from Gallipoli, and to U.K., Feb. 6th, 1916, H.S. " Neuralia." L.C.D., Seaford, until May 7th, 1918. O.R. Corporal, No. 21 O.C.B., Fleet, May 8th, 1918. Demobilized Jan. 20th, 1919.

POPE, T. C., Sergt. : Malta, Alex., Gal., S. Egypt, France. May 23rd, 1916, drafted from Rouen to 1/13 Batt. London Regt. to July 1st, 1916, and then posted to 1/4 Batt. London Regt. Killed in action, Les Bœufs, Oct. 7th, 1916.

PORTER, J. A., Pte. : Malta, Alex., Gal., S. Egypt. Apr. 28th, 1916, drafted to Reserve Unit, U.K., 100 Provisional Batt., Aldeburgh. Discharged by M.B., Aug. 31st, 1916.

POTTON, J. E., Pte. : Malta, Alex., Gal., S. Egypt, France. May 23rd, 1916, transferred to 1/4 Batt. London Regt. from Rouen. In all engagements on Somme, Laventie until wounded arm and leg. On leaving hospital was posted to 102 P. of W. Coy.

POWE, E. J., Pte. : Malta, Alex., Gal., S. Egypt, France. May 6th, 1916, transferred to 1/4 Batt. London Regt. from Rouen. Killed in action, Somme, July 1st, 1916.

POWELL, H. S., Mechanic R.A.F. : Malta, Alex., Gal., S. Egypt, France. Transferred to 1/4 Batt. London Regt. from Rouen. Invalided U.K., Sept. 11th, 1916, L.C.D., Seaford. Drafted to 3rd Res. A.P.C., March 19th, 1918, and to R.A.F., Apr. 1st, 1918. Wounded, G.S.W. right hand and shrapnel right leg and shoulder.

POWELL, R. G., Sergt.-Instr. : Malta, Alex., Gal., S. Egypt, France. May 23rd, 1916, drafted to 1/13 London Regt. from Rouen. Invalided U.K., and joined 3rd Res. Batt., Salisbury, Aug. 10th, 1916. Transferred to Tank Corps, March 12th, 1917, and remained with Training Staff until end of War. Wounded July 1st, 1916, shrapnel, arm.

POWELL, J. E., Cpl. : Malta, Alex., Gal., S. Egypt, France. June 3rd, 1916, transferred to 1/4 Batt. London Regt. from Rouen to U.K., Sept. 11th, 1916. L.C.D., Seaford, Jan. 6th, 1917. Returned to unit, Feb., 1918. A.P.D., March 21st, 1918. R.A.F., Apr. 1st, 1918. De-mobilized, Apr. 21st, 1919. Wounded, G.S.W. right hand and shrapnel on legs and body.

POWELL, T. A., Lieut. : Malta, Alex. Nov. 11th, 1915, embarked on H.T. " Mashobia " for U.K. for commis-sion. Gazetted 2nd Lieut. 4th London, Oct. 29th, 1915. Served with 2/5 Northumberland Fus. and 2/1 R. Bucks. Hussars.

PRATT, S. J., Cpl. : Malta, Alex., Gal., France. June 1st,

1916, invalided to U.K. under age. Joined 29th London Regt. In June, 1918, drafted to 33rd London R.B. in France.

PRATT, W. H., PTE. : Malta, Alex., Gal., S. Egypt, France. June 3rd, 1916, transferred to 1/4 Batt. London Regt. from Rouen. Served with unit until taken prisoner, March 28th, 1918.

PRESS, G., PTE. : Malta, Alex., Gal., France. May 6th, 1916, transferred to 1/4 Batt. London Regt. from Rouen. Discharged by M.B., Dec. 22nd, 1916. Wounded on Somme, July 1st, 1916.

PRICE, W., PTE. : Malta, Alex., Gal., S. Egypt, France. May 6th, 1916, transferred to 1/4 Batt. London Regt. from Rouen. Wounded shell shock and buried.

PRIDMORE, W. B., L/SERGT. : Malta, Alex., France, Russia. June 10th, 1916, invalided to U.K. from Rouen. Drafted to 29th London, Aldeburgh. Transferred to A.O.C. draft to Russia.

PRIDMORE, W. B. : Malta, Alex., Gal., S. Egypt, France. May 6th, 1916, transferred to 1/4 Batt. London Regt. from Rouen.

PRIOR, N., L/CPL. : Malta, Alex., Gal., S. Egypt, France. June 3rd, 1916, transferred to 1/4 London Regt. from Rouen, and served in France through the War. Returned Dec. 17th, 1918. Demobilized Jan. 7th, 1919.

PRIOR, W. N. : Malta, Alex., Gal. Wounded G.S.W., head, and arm amputated. Died on board H.S. " Gloucester Castle."

PRITCHARD, W., PTE. : Malta, Alex., Gal., S. Egypt, France. May 6th, 1916, transferred to 1/4 Batt. London Regt. from Rouen. Aug., 1916, drafted to 3rd, R. Suffolk Regt. for Home Defence. Wounded, Somme, Aug. 1st, 1916, left arm.

PRITCHETT, H., CPL. : Malta, Alex., Gal., S. Egypt, France. Transferred to 1/4 Batt. London Regt. from Rouen. Posted to a Labour Coy., Aug., 1918. Wounded, Jan. 12th, 1917, shrapnel in chest.

PRITCHETT, E. G. : Malta, Alex., France. Sept. 3rd, 1915, to Naval Officers Staff, Alexandria. May 6th, 1916, transferred to 1/4 Batt. London Regt. from Rouen.

PROBART, H., Pte. : Malta, France. Invalided out, July 3rd, 1917. Wounded in arm.

PYKE, W. A. G., L/Cpl. : Malta, Alex., Gal., S. Egypt, France. May 23rd, 1916, transferred 1/4 Batt. London Regt. from Rouen. Gassed twice. Divisional Card of Honour.

RADCLIFFE, H. J., Pte. : Malta, Alex. Oct. 12th, 1915, invalided U.K., " Gloucester Castle."

RAVEN, G. V., Pte. : Malta, Alex., Gal., S. Egypt, France. Transferred to 1/4 Batt. London Regt. from Rouen. Discharged by M.B. on account of wound. Wounded, July 1st, 1916, hand and leg, slightly ; and severely, shoulder and back, Sept. 25th, 1916.

RAYMENT, E. C., 2/Lieut. : Malta, Alex., Gal., S. Egypt, France. May 18th, 1916, invalided from Rouen to U.K. Six months at O.T.B., Gailles. Gazetted 2/Lieut. Cheshire Regt. Served in France, Oct. 2nd, 1918, to Nov. 11th, 1918.

RAYMOND, G. : Malta, Alex., Gal.

RAYMER, C. W. : Malta, Alex., Gal., S. Egypt, France. May 23rd, 1916, drafted to 1/13 Batt. London Regt.

RAYNER, S. E. : Gal., S. Egypt, France. Nov. 15th, 1915, draft from Devonport, Apr. 28th, 1916, invalided U.K., H.S. " Holland."

REEVE, W. J., Pte. : Malta, Alex., Gal., S. Egypt, France. May 6th, 1916, transferred to 1/4 Batt. London Regt. from Rouen. Wounded, July 1st, 1916, but remained on duty. Mortally wounded, Apr. 9th, 1917, and died, Apr. 11th, 1917.

REEVES, S. G., Pte. : Malta, Alex., Mudros, S. Egypt, France. May 6th, 1916, transferred to 1/4 Batt. London Regt. from Rouen, and served with unit to Sept., 1916, when evacuated with broken leg. Returned to France, June, 1917. Posted to 1/3 Batt., and in all engagements to March, 1918. Served with U.S. Army. Returned to 1/3 and served to end of War. Wounded slightly, Cambrai, 1917.

REID, W., Pte. : Malta, Alex., Gal., S. Egypt, France. May 6th, 1916, transferred to 1/4 Batt. London Regt.

from Rouen. Wounded, July 3rd, 1916, G.S.W., arm. Apr. 9th, 1917, wounded right hip. Aug. 15th, 1917, wounded left forearm and shoulder. Served in England to Sept., 1918, and returned to France to 20th Middlesex. Wounded three times.

REIDER, W. : Malta, Alex., Gal., S. Egypt, France. Dec. 17th, 1915, invalided to Malta. Jan. 17th, 1916, to U.K., H.S. " Italia."

RICHARDSON, G. W., PTE. : Malta, Alex., Gal., S. Egypt, France. Jan. 8th, 1916, invalided to Malta. Feb. 20th, 1916, to U.K., H.S. " Panama." Wounded, Dec. 31st, 1915, by shell face and leg. Lost his sight.

RICKETTS, W., PTE. : Malta, Alex., Gal., S. Egypt, France. Transferred to 1/4 Batt. London Regt. from Rouen. Killed in action Battle of Somme.

RIDSDALE, E. R., PTE. : Malta, Alex., Gal., S. Egypt, France. May 23rd, 1916, transferred to 1/4 Batt. London Regt. from Rouen. Somme, Passchendale, Ypres. Wounded compound fracture left arm.

RIPPIN, I. A., SERGT. MASTER COOK : Malta, Alex., Gal., S. Egypt, France. Transferred to 1/4 Batt. London Regt. from Rouen. Wounded on Somme ; left leg amputated.

ROBENTS, S. : Malta, Alex., Gal., S. Egypt, France. Transferred to 1/4 Batt. London Regt. from Rouen.

ROBERTS, W. G. : Malta, Alex., Gal., S. Egypt, France. May 6th, 1916, transferred to 1/4 Batt. London Regt. from Rouen. Killed in action, Aug. 7th, 1916, aged 19.

ROBINSON, H. J., AIR MECHANIC : Malta, Alex., Gal., S. Egypt, France. May 6th, 1916, transferred to 1/4 Batt. London Regt. from Rouen. Served through Somme offensive. Six months in hospital in England, and after joining 3rd Res. Batt., transferred to R.A.F.

ROBINSON, A. W., 2/LIEUT. : Malta, Alex., S. Egypt, France. Oct. 9th, 1915, to 3rd Echelon for Staff Duty at Alex. London Infantry Record Office, July to Nov., 1916. O.R. Sergt., 1st Res., Fovant, Torquay, Blackdown, Nov., 1916, to Nov., 1917. R.F.C. Cadet. Nov., 1917, to Feb., 1918. Gazetted 2/Lieut. R.F.C., Feb. 12th, 1918. In France as Flying Officer, June, 1918, until crash down, Aug. 7th, 1918, night raiding. Wireless School, Sept.,

1918, to March, 1919, as Assistant Adjutant. Wounded, head.

ROBERTSON, W. H. : Malta, Alex., Gal., S. Egypt, France. May 23rd, 1916, transferred to 1/4 Batt. London Regt. from Rouen.

RODD, T. R., Pte. : Malta, Alex., Mudros, S. Egypt, France. May 23rd, 1916, transferred to Div. Hospital. Wounded once.

ROERIG, R. G. : Malta, Alex., Gal., S. Egypt, France. May 23rd, 1916, transferred to 1/4 Batt. London Regt. from Rouen until Sept. 9th, 1916, when killed in action.

ROGERS, H. W., Cpl. : Malta, Alex., Gal. May 7th, 1916, invalided to U.K., and served with 16th Essex, 29th Middlesex, and finally in charge of motor transport, R.E., Sheerness.

ROGERS, E. S., Pte. : Gal., S. Egypt, France. Nov. 15th, 1915, draft from Devonport, May 6th, 1916. Transferred to 1/4 Batt. London Regt. from Rouen, and served with it until Dec., 1916. Wounded and transferred to 10th Essex, U.K. Returned to France, March 28th, 1918, and served until end of War. Three wounds.

ROGERS, J. S., Pte. : Malta, Alex., Gal., S. Egypt, France. May 23rd, 1916, transferred to 1/4 Batt. London Regt. from Rouen.

ROGERS, E. F., Bandsman : Malta, Alex., Gal., S. Egypt, France. Joined Base Band, Rouen.

ROGERS, W. E., 2/Lieut. : Malta, Alex., France. Sept. 21st, 1915, to Hospital Alexandria, Oct. 25th, 1915. Invalided to U.K. with enteric, H.S. " Delta." Drafted to France as 2/Lieut., Feb. 1st, 1918. Invalided to U.K., and on leaving hospital, reported 3rd Res., Blackdown. Wounded severely, Sept. 1st, 1918.

ROSE, V. S., Pte. : Malta, Alex., Gal., S. Egypt, France. May 6th, 1916, transferred to 1/4 Batt. London Regt. from Rouen. Served in all engagements until Oct. 7th at Les Boeufs, when he went over the top with his platoon. Reported missing, presumed killed.

ROSSINGTON, G. L., Sergt. : Malta, Alex., Gal., S. Egypt, France. Transferred to 1/4 Batt. London Regt. from Rouen, and served in all engagements without sickness or wounds to March 28th, 1918, when taken prisoner. Awarded M.M.

ROWE, J. : Malta, Alex. Nov. 19th, 1915, joined 1st Garrison Batt. Royal Irish Regt.

ROY, J. C., Sergt. : Malta, Alex., Gal., S. Egypt, France. Jan. 17th, 1916, invalided to U.K., H.S. " Glengorm Castle." Wounded, Nov. 22nd, 1915, shrapnel. Killed in action, Aug. 11th, 1918

RUBNER, C., L/Cpl. : Malta, Alex., Gal., S. Egypt, France. Transferred to 1/4 Batt. London Regt. from Rouen. Demobilized, Jan. 26th, 1919.

RUSSELL, R. G., Pte. : Malta, Alex., Gal., S. Egypt, France. Transferred to 1/4 London Regt. from Rouen. Hebuterne, July 1st, 1916 ; Somme, Arras, March, 1917. Aug. 22nd, 1917, hospital. Demobilized, Dec. 12th, 1918. Wounded, injured back.

RUSSELL, A. J. : Malta, Alex., Gal., S. Egypt, France. Transferred to 1/4 Batt. London Regt. from Rouen. Died of wounds received in action, Sept. 14th, 1916, at 22nd General Hospital, Camiers, France.

SAGAR, H., Cadet, R.A.F. : Malta, Alex., Gal., S. Egypt, France. Feb. 25th, 1916, attached H.Qrs. Highland Mtd. Bde., Minia. Transferred to 121 London Regt., Rouen, and served with unit until he left to take up commission, Nov. 11th, 1917. Awarded M.M.

SAMBRIDGE, A. H. : Malta, Alex., Mudros, Gal. Jan. 17th, 1916, invalided to U.K., H.S. " Glengorm Castle."

SANKEY, T., Cpl. : Malta, Alex., Gal., S. Egypt, France. May 6th, 1916, transferred to 1/4 London Regt. from Rouen to Dec., 1917. Invalided U.K., L.C.D., to June, 1918, and then to 1st Res. Discharged Jan., 1919. Wounded twice, back and leg. Awarded D.C.M. Div. Card of Honour (56th Div.).

SARD, T., Sergt. : Malta, Alex., Gal., S. Egypt, France. Transferred to 1/4 Batt. London Regt. from Rouen. Sept., 1916, invalided U.K. Returned to France, March, 1917, to Labour Coy. 151. Transferred to 13th Inniskilling Fusiliers, May, 1918, and served with it to the end of the War. Wounded, arm and chest, Leuze Wood, Sept. 9th, 1916.

SAREL, R. A., L/Cpl. : Malta, Alex., Gal., S. Egypt, France. May 23rd, 1916, drafted to 1/13 London Regt. from Rouen. Reported missing, presumed killed, Aug. 25th, 1918.

SARGANT, F. : Malta, Alex., Mudros. Oct. 15th, 1915, sick at Mudros. Nov. 4th, 1915, invalided to U.K., H.S. " Mauretania."

SAUNDERS, A. A., Pte. : Malta, Alex., Gal., S. Egypt, France. May 23rd, 1916, drafted to 1/13 London Regt. from Rouen, and served for three months with this unit. Wounded, April 24th, 1918. Mentioned in despatches, July 1st, 1916.

SAUNDERS, F. M., Pte. : Malta, Alex., S. Egypt, France. May 6th, 1916, transferred to 1/4 Batt. London Regt. from Rouen, and served with the unit until demobilized, Feb. 28th, 1919.

SAUNDERS, F. H. : Malta, Alex. Sept. 13th, 1915, to General Hospital, Alex., Nov. 1st, 1915, invalided to U.K., H.S. " Salta."

SAVAGE, W. A., Sergt-Instr. Signalling : Malta, Alex., Gal., S. Egypt, France. Transferred to 1/4 Batt. London Regt. from Rouen. Gommecourt, July 19th, 1916, shell shock. Rejoined the Batt. again, afterwards being transferred to 3rd Res. Batt. and joined Brigade School in charge of Signallers.

SAVAGE, W. J. : Malta, Alex., Gal., S. Egypt, France. May 6th, 1916, transferred to 1/4 Batt. London Regt. from Rouen. Died of wounds, Oct. 17th, 1916. Buried in Rouen (St. Severs Cemetery).

SAYERS, F. C., Pte. : Gal., S. Egypt, France. Nov. 15th, 1915, draft from Devonport. May 6th, 1916, transferred to 1/4 Batt. London Regt. from Rouen. Present in all engagements ; twice wounded. Killed in action, Aug. 26th, 1918.

SCAGGS, S. : Malta, Alex., Gal., S. Egypt, France. Dec. 29th, 1915, invalided to Malta. March 25th, 1916, rejoined unit. Transferred to 1/4 Batt. London Regt. from Rouen.

SCALLY, W., Sergt. : Malta, Alex., Gal., S. Egypt, France, E. Africa. Transferred to 1/4 Batt. London Regt.

from Rouen. Embarked for E. Africa, K.A.R., Sept., 1918. Wounded in face, Cambrai, Nov., 1917.

SCOTT, L. E., L/SERGT. : Malta, Alex., Gal., S. Egypt, France. May 23rd, 1916, drafted to 1/13 London Regt. from Rouen. Invalided, U.K., Sept., 1916. Posted 3rd Res. Batt. until March, 1918, when joined 1/4 Batt. in France. Remained with that unit until demobilized, Feb. 20th, 1919. Wounded, Sept., 1916.

SEATON, W., SERGT. : Malta, Alex., Gal., S. Egypt, France. Transferred to 1/4 Batt. London Regt. from Rouen, and served with unit to Sept. 20th, 1916, when invalided home to L.C.D., Shoreham. Reported to 1st Res. Batt. and drafted to P.O.W. Camp, Canterbury.

SEATON, L. H., SAPPER : Malta, Alex., Gal., France. Nov. 1st, 1915, invalided from Gallipoli to Alexandria, Jan. 17th, 1916, to England, H.S. " Mauretania." Drafted to R.E. as a joiner.

SEELEY, J. C., SERGT. : Malta, Alex., Gal., France. Transferred to 1/4 Batt. London Regt. from Rouen. Wounded knee and thigh.

SELBY, J. F., L/CPL. : Malta, Alex., Gal., S. Egypt, France. May 23rd, 1916, transferred to 1/4 Batt. London Regt. from Rouen. Wounded in foot, July, 1916 ; in arm, Nov., 1917. Killed in action, — —, 1918.

SEWELL, C. B., PTE. : Malta, Alex., Gal., S. Egypt, France. May 23rd, 1916, drafted to 1/13 London Regt. from Rouen. Rejoined 1/4 Batt. Killed in action, Sept. 9th, 1916.

SEWELL, G. B., PTE. : Malta, Alex., Gal., S. Egypt, France. May 23rd, 1916, drafted to 1/13 Batt. London Regt. from Rouen. Transferred to 1/4 London Regt. Killed in action near Arras, Dec. 21st, 1917.

SEWELL, H., PTE. : Malta, Alex., Gal., S. Egypt, France. May 23rd, 1916, transferred to 1/4 Batt. London Regt. from Rouen, and served with this unit until discharged disabled, May 28th, 1918. Wounded, G.S.W. left leg.

SHAINAN, J., PTE. : Malta, Alex., Gal., S. Egypt, France. May 6th, 1916, transferred to 1/4 Batt. London Regt. from Rouen. Wounded, left shoulder and arm after three months in France. Eighteen months in hospital. Discharged M.B., Dec. 24th, 1917.

SHARP, G. H., Pte. : Malta, Alex., Gal., S. Egypt, France. Transferred to 1/4 Batt. London Regt. from Rouen. Served with unit for seven months. Invalided U.K. with trench feet after 10 months home, drafted to France to S.W. Borderers. Four months later invalided home for good. Wounded, shrapnel in knee.

SHARP, G. W., C.Q.M.-Sergt. : Malta, Alex., Gal., France. Nov. 4th, 1915, invalided to Malta. Transferred to 1/4 Batt. and served to Oct., 1917. Invalided U.K., 1st Res., July, 1918, and to 34th London Regt. Drafted to France. Invalided U.K., Nov., 1918. Discharged M.B., March 6th, 1919.

SHEA, A. H., Sergt. : Malta, Alex., Gal., S. Egypt, France. May 23rd, 1916, drafted to 1/13 London Regt. from Rouen. Killed in action, Somme, Oct. 9th, 1916.

SHELFORD, H. : Malta, Alex., Mudros.

SHEPPARD, F. C., Shoemaker Sergt. : Malta, Alex., Gal., S. Egypt, France. May 7th, 1916, invalided to U.K. from Rouen. Six months with 100th Provisional Batt. ; 15 months with L.N. Lancs. (disbanded, Feb. 21st, 1918) ; 4 months 14th S. Lancs. Transferred June 19th, 1918, to 16th Manchesters.

SHINKFIELD, E. S., L/Cpl. : Malta, Alex., Gal., S. Egypt, France. May 6th, 1916, transferred to 1/4 Batt. London Regt. from Rouen. Killed in action, May 28th, 1916, at Hebuterne.

SHINKFIELD, L. C., L/Cpl. : Malta, Alex., Gal., S. Egypt, France. May 6th, 1916, transferred to 1/4 Batt. London Regt. from Rouen. Killed in action, July 1st, 1916, at Hebuterne.

SHUTTLEWORTH, S., Pte. : Malta, Alex., Gal., S. Egypt, France. May 6th, 1916, transferred to 1/4 Batt. London Regt. from Rouen. Served with unit to Sept., when invalided to U.K. In Hospital to Jan., 1918. Posted to 3rd Res. Batt. Discharged by M.B., March 1st, 1918. Wounded, G.S.W. arm and lung, Sept. 9th, 1916.

SIGEERS, H. J., Pte. : Malta, Alex., Gal. Dec. 8th, 1915,

invalided from Gallipoli, Jan. 17th, 1916. Invalided to U.K., H.S. " Mauretania." Discharged medically unfit.

SILLETT, W. J., CPL. : Malta, Alex., Gal., S. Egypt, France. Transferred to 1/4 Batt. London Regt. from Rouen. Served 2 years 7 months after Batt. was broken up. Wounded once, gassed once.

SILVEY, J., SAPPER : Malta, Alex., Gal., S. Egypt, France. May 6th, 1916, transferred to 1/4 Batt. London Regt. from Rouen, and to R.E. 4th Surrey Batt. early in 1917. Served all through War in France, then to Germany to relieve a pivotal man.

SIMPSON, G., PTE. : Malta, Alex., Gal., S. Egypt, France. May 6th, 1916, transferred 1/4 Batt. London Regt. from Rouen. Hebuterne, Somme, La Bassée. Platoon runner 168 Brigade. Severely wounded, G.S.W. left arm.

SKINNER, A. L., DRUMMER : Malta, Alex., Gal., S. Egypt, France. May 23rd, 1916, transferred 1/4 Batt. London Regt. from Rouen, and served with unit through War.

SKINNER, —. : Malta, Alex., Gal., S. Egypt, France. May 23rd, 1916, transferred to 1/4 Batt. London Regt. from Rouen.

SKINNER, A. W., SAPPER : Malta, Alex., France. Sept. 20th, 1915, to hospital Alex. Oct. 26th, 1915, invalided to U.K., H.S. " Galeka." 1/3 London Regt., France, Sept. 16th, 1916, to Sept. 1st, 1917. July, 1918, B2, transferred to R.E. (Electrical Engineer).

SLADE-JONES : Malta, Alex., Gal. Dec. 16th, 1915, sick, Gallipoli. Dec. 22nd, 1915, to Malta. Dec. 31st, 1915, invalided to U.K., H.S. " Regina d'Italia."

SMALLBRIDGE, E., SERGT. : Malta, Alex., Gal., S. Egypt, France. May 23rd, 1916, transferred to 1/4 Batt. London Regt. from Rouen, and served all through the War with this unit. Wounded (1st), Gommecourt, arm ; (2nd) G.S.W., Ypres, mouth ; (3rd) Bullecourt, thigh.

SMITH, A. F., L/CPL. : Malta, Alex., Gal., S. Egypt, France. Transferred to 1/4 Batt. London Regt. from Rouen. Reported missing, Sept. 18th, 1916. Presumed killed in action on that date.

SMITH, F., PTE. : Malta, Alex., Gal., S. Egypt, France. May 6th, 1916, transferred to 1/4 Batt. London Regt.

from Rouen. Gommecourt, Somme, 1916 ; Arras, 1917 ; Ypres, Cambrai, 1917 ; Vimy, Arras, Bullecourt, 1918.

SMITH, A. H. A., Sergt. : Malta, Alex., Gal., S. Egypt, France. May 23rd, 1916, transferred to 1/4 London Regt. from Rouen, and in all engagements to Leuze Wood. Invalided U.K., Sept., 1916. Joined 3rd Res. Batt. Marked B2, 1917, March. Joined Labour Batt. to Dec., 1918, when transferred to 189 P. of W. Coy. Wounded twice.

SMITH, H. C., L/Cpl., Bandsman : Malta, Alex., Gal., S. Egypt, France. Joined Base Band, Rouen.

SMITH, E. : Malta, Alex., Gal., S. Egypt, France. May 23rd, 1916, transferred to 1/4 London Regt. from Rouen. Killed in action, Leuze Wood, 1916.

SMITH, F. E., Cpl. : Malta, Alex. Invalided U.K., Sept., 1915, for hospital treatment. Rejoined 4/4 Dec., 1915, and remained on Staff work till May, 1918. Returned to Labour Corps, and in June, 1918, was transferred to 8th London (Post Office Rifles).

SMITH, G. A. : Malta, Alex., Mudros. Dec. 26th, 1915, Invalided to U.K., H.S. " Aquitania."

SMITH, W. B. : Malta, Alex., Mudros. Oct. 15th, 1915, invalided to Mudros. Nov. 4th, 1915, to U.K., H.S. " Mauretania."

SMITH, A. W. : Malta, Alex., Gal., S. Egypt, France. May 17th, 1916, invalided to U.K. from Rouen.

SMITH, A. H., Pte. : Gal., S. Egypt, France. Nov. 15th, 1915, draft from Devonport. May 6th, 1916, transferred to 1/4 Batt. London Regt. from Rouen. Wounded, Oct. 6th, 1916, compound fracture of arm. Eight months in hospital. Discharged by M.B., June, 1917.

SMITH, W. : Malta, Alex., Gal., S. Egypt, France. June 3rd, 1916, transferred to 1/4 Batt. London Regt. from Rouen.

SMITH, R. H. : Malta, Alex., Gal., S. Egypt, France. May 23rd, 1916, draft to 1/13 London Regt. from Rouen. Reported killed in action.

SMITH, H. J., Sapper. : Malta, Alex, Gal., S. Egypt, France. May 6th, 1916, drafted to 1/4 Batt. London Regt. from Rouen. Somme, Arras. Transferred to Field Survey Batt. R.E., Sept. 16th, 1917. Cambrai, Nov. 30th, 1917, in the final advance. Demobilized, Jan. 6th, 1919.

SMITH, R., C.Q.M.S. : Malta, Alex., Gal., S. Egypt, France. Transferred to 1/4 Batt. London Regt. from Rouen, and served throughout the War. Wounded, Ypres, Aug. 16th, 1917, and gassed.

SNASHALL, F. C., CPL. : Malta, Alex., Gal., France. Dec. 15th, 1915, invalided to Malta. Jan. 25th, 1916, to England, H.S. " Formosa." After leaving hospital, joined 151 Labour Coy., France.

SOUTER, F. W., PTE. : Malta, Alex., Gal., S. Egypt, France. May 23rd, 1916, transferred to 1/4 Batt. London Regt. from Rouen. Invalided to U.K., Aug. 13th, 1916. Joined 1/3 Res. Batt. Transferred to Tank Corps, May 3rd, 1917. Drafted to France, Nov. 20th, 1917. Invalided U.K., and drafted to Tank Base, Dorset. Wounded head and shoulder, Cambrai, Nov. 20th, 1917.

SOUTH, A., PTE. : Malta, Alex., Gal., S. Egypt, France. May 6th, 1916, transferred to 1/4 Batt. London Regt. from Rouen. Gommecourt, Hebuterne. Transferred to Hussars, 2nd Cavalry Res., Newbridge, Ireland. Wounded July 1st, 1916, G.S.W., right arm.

SPOONER, W. G., PTE. : Malta, Alex., Gal., S. Egypt, France. May 6th, 1916, transferred to 1/4 Batt. London Regt. from Rouen, and served with unit throughout the War.

STANBROOK, C., LIEUT. : Malta, Alex., Gal., S. Egypt, France. Transferred to 1/4 Batt. London Regt. from Rouen.

STAPLETON, W. A., DRUMMER : Malta, Alex., Gal., Salonica. Nov. 4th, 1915, invalided from Gal. to Alex. Nov. 24th, 1915, to U.K., H.S. " Dover Castle," thence to 4th Res. Batt. Draft to 2/1 Herts., 1917, and sent to Salonica. Demobilized, May 24th, 1919.

STEPHENSON, A. F. J., CPL. : Malta, Alex., Gal., S. Egypt, France. May 23rd, 1916, transferred to 1/4 Batt. London Regt. from Rouen. Wounded, July 1st, 1916, and served with unit until killed in action, Aug. 16th, 1917.,

STERNBERG, M. L., LIEUT. : Malta, Alex., Gal., S. Egypt, France. Transferred to 1/4 Batt. London Regt. from Rouen. Returned to U.K. for commission, R.F.C.

Carried out several tours of duty in France. In Jan., 1918, posted to Lincoln until demobilized, March 11th, 1919.

STEVENS, R. G., Pte. : Malta, Alex., Gal., S. Egypt, France. May 6th, 1916, draft to 1/4 Batt. London Regt. from Rouen. Wounded at Combles. Discharged, July 3rd, 1917.

STEWART, J. W., Pte. : Malta, Alex., Gal., S. Egypt, France. May 23rd, 1916, transferred to 1/4 Batt. London Regt. from Rouen. Mortally wounded, Sept. 8th, 1916.

STOKES, R. F. : Gal., France. Nov. 15th, 1915, draft from Devonport. May 6th, 1916, transferred to 1/4 Batt. London Regt. from Rouen. Missing, presumed killed.

STONE, G. F., Cpl. : Malta, Alex., Gal., S. Egypt, France. May 23rd, 1916, transferred to 1/4 Batt. London Regt. from Rouen. Died of wounds received on Somme, July 21st, 1916.

STOTTER, S. P., Lieut. : Malta, Alex., Gal., France. Dec. 31st, 1915, invalided from Gal. to Malta, and thence Feb. 19th, 1916, to U.K., with 4th Res. Batt. March to Oct., 1916, in France with 1/4 Batt., Oct., 1916, to March, 1917. Invalided U.K., with 3rd Res., Dec., 1917, to Jan., 1919, when posted to Ministry of Munitions. Wounded, Dec. 23rd, 1915, slightly, in Gallipoli.

STOUT, T. J. : Malta, Alex. Aug. 27th, 1915, posted to Embarkation Staff, Alex., for duty.

STUART, J. D., Signaller : Malta, Alex., Gal., S. Egypt, France. May 6th, 1916, transferred to 1/4 Batt. London Regt. from Rouen. Invalided U.K. Posted 3rd Res. Batt. Joined 1/3 Batt. in France, June 1917, until broken up, with 1/2 London Regt. to Apr. 3rd, 1918. Invalided U.K., trench fever. Drafted France, 1/13 Batt. London Regt., Oct. 28th, 1918. Wounded, G.S.W. left shoulder, June 19th, 1916.

STUDDS, E. W., Pte. : Malta, Alex., Gal., S. Egypt, France. Transferred to 1/4 Batt. London Regt. from Rouen, and served with Batt. continuously to Dec. 15th, 1918. Demobilized, Jan. 9th, 1919.

SUGG, F. J. : Malta, Alex., Gal., S. Egypt, France. May 23rd, 1916, drafted to 1/13 Batt. London Regt. from Rouen.

SULLIVAN, R., Pte. : Malta, Alex., Gal., France. Dec.

14th, 1915, invalided from Gal. to Malta, May 29th, 1916. Rejoined unit at Rouen, and transferred to 1/4 Batt. London Regt., and served with unit until Invalided home, May, 1917.

SURRIDGE, E. H., PTE. : Malta, Alex., Gal., S. Egypt, France. May 13th, 1916, invalided from Rouen to U.K. Marked P.M., and discharged for shipbuilding.

SUTTON, J., PTE. : Malta, Alex., Gal., S. Egypt, France. May 23rd, 1916, transferred to 1/4 Batt. London Regt. Invalided U.K., L.C.D., Seaford, Nov., 1916. Drafted 883 Employment Coy., France, thence to 136 Coy. Wounded, July 1st, 1916, left elbow.

SYMES, P. J. : Malta, Alex., Gal., S. Egypt, France. May 6th, 1916, transferred to 1/4 Batt. London Regt. from Rouen. Killed on Somme, July 1st, 1916.

SYME, R. C. : Malta, Alex. Sept. 29th, 1915, embarked for England to take up commission.

TANSLEY, A. E. : Malta, Alex., Gal., Palestine. Dec. 3rd, 1915, invalided from Gallipoli to Cairo. Employed to May, 1917, Clerical Duties, 3rd Echelon, Alex., then marked A1 and drafted to clerical Staff, 75th Div., and remained in Palestine until demobilized, March, 1919.

TAPE, H. J., L/CPL. : Malta, Alex., Gal., S. Egypt, France. May 23rd, 1916, transferred to 1/4 Batt. London Regt. from Rouen, and served with unit for two years. Wounded three times.

TAPLEY, V. C., DRUMMER : Malta, Alex., Gal., S. Egypt, France. May 23rd, 1916, drafted to 1/13 Batt. London Regt. from Rouen. Transferred to 1/4 Batt. London Regt., and served with this unit 1 year 9 months. Taken prisoner, March 28th, 1918, at Oppy.

TAPPENDEN, T., PTE. : Gal., S. Egypt, Italy. May 15th, 1916, invalided to U.K., H.S. " St. George." Transferred to 16th Essex, thence to R.A.F., Italy.

TARRANT, A., PTE. : Malta, Alex., Gal., S. Egypt, France. May 6th, 1916, transferred to 1/4 Batt. London Regt. from Rouen, and served in all engagements to Apr. 16th, 1917, when wounded right arm and knee. Discharged, Nov. 12th, 1917, to munitions.

TAYLOR, A. T., Sergt. : Malta, Alex., Gal., S. Egypt, France. May 23rd, 1915, drafted to 1/13 Batt. London Regt. from Rouen. Transferred 1/4 London Regt., Sept., 1916. Somme, Arras, Ypres, to March, 1918, when wounded left knee. Joined 3rd Res. Batt. Demobilized, Jan. 10th, 1919.

TAYLOR, F. A., L/Cpl. : Malta, Alex., Gal., S. Egypt, France. May 6th, 1916, transferred to 1/4 Batt. London Regt. from Rouen, and remained with unit until wounded, March 28th, 1918.

TAYLOR, B. : Malta, Alex., Gal., S. Egypt. Dec. 7th, 1915, nominated for commission, and left Batt. March 15th, 1916 ; proceeded to U.K.

TEDDER, J. W., Sergt. : Malta, Alex., Gal., S. Egypt, France. May 23rd, 1916, drafted to 1/13 Batt. London Regt. from Rouen. Wounded, March 2nd, 1917, and discharged as unfit for further service.

TEETGEN, H., Bandsman : Malta, Alex., Gal., S. Egypt, France. Joined Base Band, Rouen.

TENTORI, F. J., Drummer : Malta, Alex., Mudros. March 22nd, 1916, embarked for U.K. from Alex. to serve with a Reserve Unit.

THEARLE, F., L/Cpl. : Malta, Alex., Gal., S. Egypt, France. May 6th, 1916, transferred to 1/4 Batt. London Regt. from Rouen. Wounded, Hebuterne, May 30th, 1916, right thigh (H.E.). Discharged M.B., July 26th, 1917.

THOMAS, P. F., L/Cpl. : Malta, Alex., Gal., S. Egypt, France. Transferred to 1/22 London Regt. from Rouen. Served all through the War with this unit.

THOMAS, C. H., Lieut. : Malta, Alex., Gal., S. Egypt, France. May 6th, 1916, transferred to 1/4 Batt. London Regt. from Rouen. Gommecourt, Hebuterne, Les Bœufs, 1916 ; Arras, 1917. Gazetted Worcester Regt., Nov., 1917. Taken prisoner· St. Quentin, March 21st, 1918. Awarded M.M.

THOMAS, W. S., 2nd Lieut. : Malta, Alex., Gal., S. Egypt, France. May 23rd, 1916, transferred to 1/4 Batt. London Regt. from Rouen. Sept., 1916, invalided U.K. In hospital and home service to Sept., 1917. Gazetted to 3rd

London Regt., Aug. 29th, 1917 ; in France, Oct., 1917, to Apr., 1918. Wounded, Leuze Wood, Sept. 9th, 1916 ; Amiens, Apr. 25th, 1918.

THOMPSON, L. L. : Malta, Alex., Gal. Dec. 31st, 1915, died of wounds received in action.

THORNE, F. : Malta, Alex., Gal., S. Egypt, France. May 6th, 1916, transferred to 1/4 Batt. London Regt. from Rouen. Accidentally injured, June 29th, 1916. Discharged by M.B., May 31st, 1917.

THORP, C., Cpl. : Malta, Alex., Gal., S. Egypt, France. May 18th, 1916, invalided to U.K., from Rouen.

THRUSSELL, E. : Gal., S. Egypt, France. Nov. 15th, 1915, draft from Devonport. May 6th, 1916, transferred to 1/4 Batt. London Regt. from Rouen. Wounded once.

THURLOW, V. H. : Gal., S. Egypt, France. May 6th, 1916, transferred to 1/4 Batt. London Regt.

TIFFEN, E., Bandsman : Gal., S. Egypt, France. Nov. 15th, 1915, draft from Devonport. Transferred from Rouen to Base Band.

TOBIN, M. : Malta, Alex., Gal., S. Egypt, France. May 6th, 1916, transferred to 1/4 Batt. London Regt. from Rouen.

TOMS, G. G., Drummer : Malta, Alex., Gal., S. Egypt, France. May 23rd, 1916, drafted to 1/13 Batt. London Regt. from Rouen. Killed in action, 1916.

TOOME, T., Pte. : Gal., S. Egypt, France. Nov. 15th, 1915, draft from Devonport. May 6th, 1916, transferred to 1/4 Batt. London Regt. from Rouen. Wounded both legs and right arm. Discharged by M.B., March 30th, 1918.

TOVEE, H., Sergt. : Malta, Alex., Gal., S. Egypt, France. Oct. 26th, 1915, invalided to Mudros, dysentery, to Alex., Nov. 3rd, 1915, and thence to U.K. Nov. 4th, 1915, H.S. " Mauretania." Transferred to 677 Labour Coy. Acted as Secretary P.R.I., 1st Res. Batt.

TRAYNER, A., Pte. : Malta, Alex., Gal., S. Egypt, France. Transferred from Rouen to 1/4 Batt. London Regt. Hebuterne, Somme. Wounded, shell shock. Discharged M.B., Feb. 27th, 1917.

TRAYNER, H. : Malta, Alex., Gal., S. Egypt, France. May 23rd, 1916, transferred to 1/4 London Regt. from Rouen.

TRAYNER, H., PTE. : Malta, Alex., Gal., S. Egypt, France. Drafted to 1/13 London Regt. from Rouen to July, 1916. Transferred to 1/4 Batt. London Regt. to Oct. 7th, 1916, when wounded. In hospital five months. Joined 3rd Res. Batt. In France from June, 1917, 2nd Corps G.H.Q. Wounded G.S.W.

TREACHER, J. S., A/SERGT. : Malta, Alex., Gal., S. Egypt, France. Nov. 19th, 1915, invalided Gal., Nov. 26th, 1915, thence to U.K., H.S. "Aquitania." Aug. 1916, transferred to Royal Berks Works Coy., served in France with this unit, also with 13th Devon Rgt. and R.E. Invalided U.K. Mar. 1918, and served in C.R.E.'s Office, Salisbury Plain, afterwards D.O.R.E 's Office, Codford, until demobilized Mar. 1919. Wounded, right leg.

TREDINNICK, S. O. : Malta, Alex., Gal. Nov. 17th, 1915, invalided from Gal. Embarked for U.K., Apr. 18th, 1916, to take up commission.

TREND, F. W., 2/LIEUT. : Malta, Alex., Gal., S. Egypt, France. May 13th, 1916, from Rouen to hospital, Havre. Joined 13th R.F. Somme Hospital, Nov., 1916, trench fever, Joined 5th R.E., Feb., 1917, No. 3 O.C.B. Oct., 1917, transferred R.F.C., Reading. Graduated as Pilot. Gazetted, Oct. 15th, 1918.

TREVENA, H. : Malta, Alex., Gal., S. Egypt, France. Transferred to 1/4 Batt. London Regt. from Rouen.

TROWBRIDGE, A. A., PTE. : Malta, Alex., Gal., S. Egypt, France. Transferred to 1/4 Batt. London Regt. from Rouen, and served with unit to Nov., 1916 ; went to hospital, passed by M.B. as unfit for service in line. Drafted to A.P.C. to March, 1918. Discharged, July 16th, 1918.

TUCK, E. H., PTE. : Malta, Alex., Gal., S. Egypt, France. May 6th, 1916, transferred to 1/4 Batt. London Regt. from Rouen. Transferred to A.S.C., 381 Coy., Southampton. Wounded once Gallipoli.

TUNNICLIFFE, W., SERGT. : Malta, Alex., Gal., S. Egypt, France. Drafted 13th Batt. London Regt., April, 1916. Transferred 1/4 Batt. London Regt., Aug., 1916, to

Eastern Command, Labour Centre, Sutton, Surrey, June, 1918. Wounded, Laventie, Feb., 1917. Cambrai, Nov., 1917

TURGEL, R. : Malta, Alex., Gal., S. Egypt, France. May 23rd, 1916, transferred to 1/4 Batt. London Regt. from Rouen.

TURNER, H., 2ND LIEUT. : Malta, Alex., Gal., S. Egypt, France, Italy. Transferred to 1/4 Batt. London Regt. from Rouen, Apr., 1917, to July, 1917 ; 10th O.T.B., Aug., 1917, to Oct., 1917 ; 5th Queen's. Oct., 1917, to July, 1918, to 2nd Queen's. France, Dec., 1918 to 1919. M.G.C., Belgium.

TUTHILL, S. T., SERGT. : Malta, Alex., Gal., S. Egypt, France. May 23rd, 1916, drafted to 1/13 Batt. London Regt. from Rouen. Wounded at Ypres.

TYLER, T. A. : Malta, Alex., Gal., S. Egypt, France. May 23rd, 1916, transferred to 1/4 Batt. London Regt. from Rouen.

TYLER, A., PTE. : Malta, Alex., Gal., S. Egypt, France. May 23rd, 1916, transferred to 1/4 Batt. London Regt. from Rouen until Feb., 1917. Invalided U.K. Draft to 1/3 Batt., June 6th, 1917, to 1/2 Batt., Jan., 1918. Demobilized, Jan. 8th, 1919. Wounded twice and gassed once.

TYRRELL, G., BANDSMAN : Malta, Alex., Gal., S. Egypt. Apr. 12th, 1916, sick at Sidi Bische.

WAGSTAFF, A., SAPPER : Malta, Alex., Gal., S. Egypt, France. May 6th, 1916, draft from Rouen to 1/4 Batt. London Regt., and served with that unit to Apr. 8th, 1917, when transferred to 1st Field Survey Co. R.E. Wounded Somme, Oct. 7th, 1916. Bethune, July, 1918.

WAIN, W.O., L/CPL. : Malta, Alex., Gal., S. Egypt, France. May 7th, 1916, invalided to U.K. from Rouen : stationed at Aldeborough, Windsor, and L.D.D.C., Peckham. Wounded once.

WALSH, F. W., C.Q.M.S. : Malta, Alex., Gal., S. Egypt, France. Transferred to 1/4 Batt. London Regt. from Rouen until Oct., 1916. 3rd Res. Batt., Torquay, Dec., 1916, to May, 1917. Discharged M.B., March 27th, 1917. Spinal injury. Vol. Long Service Medal.

WALBOURNE, S., PTE. : Malta, Alex., Gal., France. Nov. 1st, 1915, invalided to Malta, thence Dec. 10th,

1915, to U.K., H.S. " Nevassa." Transferred to Essex Regt. in France. Demobilized Dec. 31st, 1918.

WALE, A. J., PTE. : Malta, Alex. Sept. 27th, 1915, admitted Hospital, Alexandria, enteric ; Oct. 25th, 1915, invalided to U.K., H.S. " Delta." Joined R.D.C., back to 1st Res. Batt., June, 1918. Discharged M.B., Jan. 22nd, 1919.

WALE, E. H., 2/LIEUT. : Malta, Alex., Gal., S. Egypt, France. May 23rd, 1916, transferred to 1/4 Batt. London Regt. from Rouen. Wounded at Hebuterne, July 1st, 1916. Invalided U.K. with 3rd Res. Batt., March, 1917. Newmarket 12 O.C.B., April-August, 1917. France, with 1/4 Batt., Sept., 1917, to March, 1918. M.G.C. at Grantham, July 7th, 1918, to date. France 14 M.G. Batt.

WALKER, E. N., PTE. : Malta, Alex., Gal., S. Egypt, France. Transferred to 1/4 Batt. London Regt. from Rouen and served with unit to end of war. Wounded twice.

WALKER, F. W., CAPT. : Malta, Alex., Gal., France. Jan. 14th, 1916, embarked for U.K. to take up commission H.T. " Olympic." At Reserve Batt. to June, 1917 ; with new 2/4 Batt. in France from June, 1917, till Apr., 1918 ; also from June, 1918, to Aug., 1918, when badly wounded. Wounded shell, neck, Apr. 25th, 1918, M.G. Bullets right arm, right leg, left thigh, Aug. 8th, 1918. Awarded D.S.O. Mentioned in despatches for services rendered on Sept. 25th, 1917, at Ypres.

WALKER, R. T. : Malta, Alex., Gal., France. Jan. 3rd, 1916, invalided to U.K., H.S. " Britannic." Posted in France to 1/4 Batt. Wounded both legs Apr., 1917. Joined 3rd Res. Batt., then to 2/3rd Batt. Injured Ypres, 1917, and discharged by M.B.

WALL, D.M., LIEUT. : Malta, Alex., Gal., S. Egypt, France. 1/4 Batt. London Regt., Apr., 1916, to Sept. 9th, 1916. Wounded on Somme, Sept. 9th, 1916. Joined 2/1 Batt. London Regt., July, 1917, on Somme as an officer. Went to Ypres Salient, Aug. for three months. Attached to 2/3 London Regt.

WALLACE, A. W. : Malta, Alex. Oct., 8th 1915, invalided to U.K., H.T., " Malena."

WALLDER, H. W., SERGT. : Malta, Alex., Gal., S. Egypt, France. Transferred to 1/4 Batt. London Regt. from Rouen until taken prisoner, Oppy Wood, March 28th, 1918. Wounded slightly Jan. 4th, 1916. Awarded M.M.

WALLER, H., Pte. : Malta, Alex., Gal. : Nov. 14th, 1915, accidentally killed in Gallipoli. Buried at Pink Farm.

WALLIS, S. W., 2/Lieut. : Malta, Gal., France. Nov. 7th, 1915, invalided to Malta with fever, Dec. 28th, 1915, thence to U.K., H.S. " Soudan." Served in France 3rd London Regt., 1916 to 1917. Granted commission 6th R.F. Drafted to 1st R.F., France, Aug. 1917-1918.

WALLIS, J. H. : Malta, Alex., Gal., S. Egypt, France. May 23rd, 1916, drafted to 1/13 Batt. London Regt. from Rouen.

WALSH, F. W. : Malta, Alex., Gal., S. Egypt, France. Transferred to 1/4 Batt. London Regt. from Rouen.

WARNE, A. E., Pte. : Malta, Alex., Gal., S. Egypt, France. May 23rd, 1916, drafted to 1/13th Batt. London Regt. from Rouen. Killed in action, July 1st, 1916.

WARNER, G., Pte.: Malta, Alex., Gal., S. Egypt, France. May 23rd, 1916, drafted to 1/13 Batt. London Regt. from Rouen. Lost an eye in action.

WARNER, J., Pte. : Gal., France. Nov. 15th, 1915, draft from Devonport, March 9th, 1916, invalided to U.K., H.S. "Dwarrha." Drafted to 1/3 Batt. London Regt., Arras, 1917. Wounded G.S.W., left leg.

WARWICK, G.: Malta, Alex., Gal. To Hospital from Wardan.

WASH, R. J., Lieut. : Malta, Alex., Gal., S. Egypt, France. Transferred to 1/4 Batt. London Regt. from Rouen. Gazetted to a commission, Dec. 27th, 1916. Attached 221 P of W. Coy. Wounded shrapnel ball in right foot.

WASTELL, R. J. : Malta, Alex., Gal., S. Egypt, France. May 23rd, 1916, drafted to 1/13 Batt. London Regt. from Rouen. Wounded four times.

WATERS, B. S., 2/Lieut. : Malta, Alex., Gal., S. Egypt, France. Transferred to 1/4 Batt. London Regt. from Rouen. Buried in shell explosion Gommecourt, July 1st, 1916. Killed in action May 3rd, 1917, Arras, Cambrai Road.

WATSON, B. : Gal., S. Egypt, France. Nov. 15th, 1915, draft from Devonport, May 6th, 1916. Transferred to 1/4 Batt. London Regt. from Rouen and served with the unit until wounded Aug. 16th, 1917. Discharged by M.B. Oct. 11th, 1918. Wounded left hand.

WATSON, T. W. N., 2/LIEUT. : Malta, Alex., Gal., S. Egypt, France. Transferred to 1/4 Batt. London Regt. from Rouen and served with unit until Dec. 2nd, 1917. Posted to O.C.B. and gazetted July 30th, 1918, 2nd London Regt. In France with 1/2 Batt. Sept. 19th, 1917, to Sept. 13th, 1918, when taken prisoner. Repatriated Dec. 29th, 1918.

WATSON, R. W., PTE. : Malta, Alex., Gal., S. Egypt, France. Transferred to 1/4 Batt. London Regt. from Rouen until June, 1917, then attached to 6th Corps School.

WATSON, F. E. G., L/CPL. : Malta, Alex., Gal., S. Egypt, France. May 6th, 1916, transferred to 1/4 Batt. London Regt. from Rouen. Reported wounded and missing July 1st, 1916 ; since presumed dead.

WATSON, E. E. : Malta, Alex., Gal., S. Egypt, France. Transferred to 1/4 Batt. London Regt. from Rouen.

WATSON, D. W., PTE. : Malta, Alex., Gal., France. Nov. 11th, 1915, invalided to Alex. with enteric. May 6th, 1916, transferred to 1/4 Batt. London Regt. from Rouen. Wounded July 1st, 1916. After joining 3rd Res. Batt., transferred to 6th Somerset L.I. In France to end of War. G.S.W. right shoulder.

WATTS, J. E., PTE. : Malta, Alex., Gal., S. Egypt, France. Transferred to 1/4 Batt. London Regt. from Rouen, and served in all engagements to Sept., 1916, when wounded Leuze Wood. After discharged from hospital drafted to Labour Corps for recruiting duties.

WATTS, F., PTE. : Malta, Alex., Gal., S. Egypt, France. Transferred to 1/4 Batt. London Regt. from Rouen. In all engagements to Apr. 4th, 1917, when wounded right leg and arm.

WATTS, H., PTE. : Malta, Alex., Gal., S. Egypt, France. Drafted to 1/13 Batt. London Regt. from Rouen, and later transferred to 1/4 Batt. London Regt. Wounded Sept. 9th, 1916. Returned to France, and was wounded when serving with new 2/4 London Regt. Sept. 22nd, 1917, drafted to 2nd Royal Irish, May, 1918. In France to end of War. Wounded third time Nov., 1918.

WEBB, W. J., SERGT. : Malta, Alex., Gal., France. Dec. 27th, 1915, invalided from Gallipoli to Malta. May 29th, 1916, rejoined unit at Rouen and transferred to 1/4 Batt.

London Regt., and served till Oct., 1916. Spent six months in hospital, and two months at L.C. Depôt, Seaford. Joined 3rd Res. Batt., Blackdown. Transferred to R.A.F. Left England May, 1918, until March 26th, 1919.

WEBB, C. R., BANDSMAN : Malta, Alex., Gal., S. Egypt, France. Joined Base Band at Rouen.

WEBB, A. E., PTE. : Malta, Alex., Gal., S. Egypt, France. May 6th, 1916, transferred to 1/4 Batt. London Regt. from Rouen, then to 11th R.F. Was wounded and sent to 13th R.F. ; was wounded again at Arras, then joined 1/2 London to end of War.

WEBSTER, E. F., PTE. : Malta, Alex., Gal., S. Egypt, France. May 6th, 1916, transferred to 1/4 Batt. London Regt. from Rouen. Wounded at Hebuterne, July 5th, 1916. After leaving hospital joined 3rd Res. Batt. at Torquay, drafted to 1/3 Batt. in France, June, 1917. Dangerously wounded Aug. 13th, 1917 ; discharged by M.B. Apr. 18th, 1918.

WEBSTER, S. R., CPL. : Malta, Alex., S. Egypt, France. May 23rd, 1916, drafted to 1/13th Batt. London Regt. from Rouen, and served two years in France. Demobilized Jan. 17th, 1919.

WELFORD, J. W., L/CPL. : Malta, Alex., Gal., S. Egypt, France. Transferred to 1/4 Batt. London Regt. from Rouen. Wounded on Somme, spent three months in hospital, and then joined the new 2/4 Batt. Killed in action Feb. 10th, 1917.

WELLAND, H. A., CORPORAL : Malta, Alex., Gal., S. Egypt, France. May 6th, 1916, transferred to 1/4 Batt. London Regt. from Rouen. Passed 1st Class I. of M. ; rejoined Batt. Reported wounded and missing, March 23rd, 1918. No further news of him.

WEST, O. W. : Malta, Alex., Gal., S. Egypt, France. May 23rd, 1916, transferred to 1/4 Batt. London Regt. from Rouen, and served through the whole War to Jan. 10th, 1919, a fine record indeed.

WHEELER : Malta, Alex., Gal., S. Egypt, France. May 23rd, 1916, transferred to 1/4 Batt. London Regt. from Rouen.

WHITBREAD, A., PTE. : Malta, Alex., Gal., S. Egypt,

France. May 23rd, 1916, transferred to 1/4 Batt. London Regt. from Rouen. Killed in action Oct. 30th, 1916. Buried Laventie Cemetery.

WHITE, H. H., PTE. : Malta, Alex., Gal., S. Egypt, France. May 23rd, 1916, transferred to 1/4 Batt. London Regt. from Rouen and took part in all engagements except Cambrai. Wounded right knee March 30th, 1918.

WHITE, M. W., 2/LIEUT. : Malta, Alex., Gal., S. Egypt, France. May 6th, 1916, transferred to 1/4 Batt. London Regt. from Rouen until Nov. 28th, 1914, when returned to U.K. Household Brigade, O.C.B., Bushey. Wounded Les Bœufs, Oct. 7th, 1916, G.S.W. left hand.

WHITE, A. : Malta, Alex., Gal., France. Nov. 10th, 1915, invalided from Gallipoli to Malta with enteric. Dec. 21st, 1915, to U.K., H.S. " Braseli."

WHITE, W. H. : Malta, Alex., Gal., S. Egypt, France. May 23rd, 1915, drafted to 1/13 London Regt. from Rouen, and then transferred to 1/4 Batt. Wounded Sept. 9th, 1916 ; discharged by M.B. May 14th, 1917.

WHITFIELD, W., PTE. : Malta, Alex, Gal., France. March 23rd, 1916, invalided to U.K., H.S. " Dunluse Castle." Wounded Nov. 22nd, 1915, serious G.S.W. legs. Leg amputated.

WHITEHEAD, H., LIEUT. : Malta, Alex., Gal., S. Egypt, France. May 6th, 1916, transferred to 1/4 Batt. London Regt. from Rouen until May, 1917 ; received Commission Oct. 31st, 1917. Drafted to 1/24th and continued to end of War. Wounded Jan., 1917, face, Neuve Chapelle, Oct. 2nd, 1918, right foot. Awarded Military Medal, July, 1916.

WHITER, S. L. : Malta, Alex., Gal., S. Egypt, France. Transferred to 1/4 Batt. London Regt. from Rouen. Wounded in Gallipoli, Dec. 20th, 1915.

WHITNELL, A. J., L/CPL. : Malta, Alex., Gal., S. Egypt, France. May 6th, 1916, transferred to 1/4 Batt. London Regt. from Rouen. Wounded June 30th, 1916. Returned to France June, 1917, and wounded again Sept., 1918.

WHITNEY, C. F., PTE. : Malta, Alex., Gal., S. Egypt, France. May 23rd, 1916, transferred to 1/4 Batt. London Regt. Returned to U.K., reported to 3rd Res. Batt.

Drafted Buffs Garrison Batt. Rejoined 1/3 Batt. in France. Wounded Aug. 12th, 1917, G.S.W. left thigh and head. Discharged by M.B. Sept. 5th, 1918.

WIGGINS, W. H. : Malta, Alex., Gal., S. Egypt, France. May 31st, 1916, rejoined unit at Rouen and transferred to 1/4 Batt. London Regt. Wounded Gommecourt, drafted to R.A.S.C., Feb., 1917, and to 1/2 East Lancs, F. Amb. Returned to U.K. March 30th, 1919. Discharged Apr. 7th, 1919.

WILCOX, H., PTE. : Malta, Alex., Gal., S. Egypt, France. May 6th, 1916, transferred to 1/4 Batt. London Regt. from Rouen, and served in France to March 28th, 1918. Wounded and missing. Reported killed on that day.

WILKINS, A., PTE. : Malta, Alex., Gal., S. Egypt, France. May 23rd, 1916, drafted to 1/13 Batt. London Regt. from Rouen. Badly wounded July 1st, 1916 ; lost left arm.

WILKINSON, H. W., CPL. : Malta, Alex., Gal., S. Egypt, France. May 6th, 1916, transferred to 1/4 Batt. London Regt. from Rouen until wounded at Leuze Wood, Sept. 9th, 1916. Right thigh smashed. In hospital at Dublin. Discharged by M.B. Nov. 9th, 1917.

WILLETTS, T. L., L/CPL. : Malta, Alex., Gal., S. Egypt, France. May 23rd, 1916, transferred to 1/4 Batt. London Regt. from Rouen, until Aug., 1916. Wounded and returned to U.K. Rejoined 1/4 Batt. March, 1917. Wounded Apr. 18th, 1917. Returned to U.K. Rejoined new 2/4 Aug., 1917. Killed in action, Sept. 20th, 1917.

WILLETTS, J. D., SERGT. : Malta, Alex., Gal., S. Egypt, France. May 6th, 1916, transferred to 1/4 Batt. London Regt. from Rouen to Aug. 16th, 1917, when returned to U.K. wounded. Wounded twice.

WILLIAMSON, H., PTE. : Malta, Alex., Gal., S. Egypt, France. Transferred to 1/4 Batt. London Regt. from Rouen to Sept. 17th, 1916, when invalided to U.K. Joined 3rd Res. Batt. at Torquay, March 5th, 1917. Joined 13th, afterwards known as 151 Labour Coy., until end of War.

WILLIAMS, A. : Malta, Alex., Gal., S. Egypt, France. Dec. 18th, 1915, invalided from Gallipoli ; rejoined unit Apr. 18th, 1916. May 23rd, 1916, transferred to 1/4 Batt. London Regt. from Rouen.

WILLIAMS, E. : Malta, Alex., Gal., S. Egypt, France
May 23rd, 1916, transferred to 1/4 Batt. London Regt.
from Rouen. Killed in action Combles, Sept. 25th, 1916.

WILLIAMS, H. E. : Malta, Alex., Gal., S. Egypt, France.
Transferred to 1/4 Batt. London Regt. from Rouen.

WILLIS, F. : Malta, Alex., Gal., S. Egypt, France. Jan.
4th, 1916, sick Gallipoli ; March 23rd, 1916, invalided
to U.K. in H.S. " Dunluce Castle."

WILSON, A., L/CPL. : Malta, Alex., Gal., S. Egypt,
France. May 6th, 1916, transferred to 1/4 Batt. London
Regt. from Rouen with unit to Jan., 1917 ; then posted
to " Z " Sound Ranging Section, 1st Field Survey Batt.
R.E.

WILSON, J. : Gal., S. Egypt, France. Nov. 15th, 1915,
draft from Devonport. Joined unit Dec. 11th, 1915, sick
Dec. 18th, 1915. May 6th, 1916, invalided to U.K. from
Rouen.

WINDLE, G. : Malta, Alex., Gal., S. Egypt, France. Nov.
14th, 1915, invalided from Gallipoli to Malta. March 8th,
1916, rejoined unit at Alexandria. May 6th, 1916, transferred to 1/4 Batt. London Regt. from Rouen. Killed in
action June 30th, 1916.

WINGROVE, A., PTE. : Malta, Alex., Gal., S. Egypt,
France. May 5th, 1916, transferred to 1/4 Batt. London
Regt. from Rouen. Killed in action July 1st, 1916.

WINSLOW, H. : Malta, Alex., Gal., S. Egypt, France.
June 1st, 1916, invalided to U.K. from Rouen.

WISE, G. F., L/SERGT. : Malta, Alex., Gal., S. Egypt,
France. Transferred to 1/4 Batt. London Regt. from
Rouen as Provost Sergeant until killed in action on Somme,
Sept. 9th, 1916.

WISE, F. C., PTE. : Malta, Alex., Gal. Feb. 6th, 1916, invalided to U.K., H.S. " Neuralia," through bomb wounds
in Gallipoli and discharged from service. Wounded Dec.
10th, 1915.

WOLFE, A. E., PTE. : Malta, Alex., Gal., S. Egypt, France.
May 23rd, 1916, transferred to 1/4 Batt. London Regt.
from Rouen. Wounded Sept. 7th, 1916, in foot, and unfit
for 12 months ; joined 23rd R.F. Gassed Aug. 21st, 1918,
Three months in hospital, and discharged Jan. 5th, 1919.

WOOD, A. A., Pte. : Malta, Alex., Gal., S. Egypt, France. May 23rd, 1916, transferred to 1/4 Batt. London Regt. from Rouen until May, 1917, then transferred to 88 Labour Coy. until end of War. Sept. 30th, 1918, wounded twice slightly.

WOOD, W. J. : Malta, Alex., Gal., S. Egypt, France. May 23rd, 1916, drafted to 1/13 London Regt. from Rouen.

WOOD, J. : Malta, Alex., Gal., France. Jan. 8th, 1916, invalided to Malta. May 29th, 1916, rejoined unit at Rouen, and then transferred to 1/4 Batt. London Regt. Wounded Dec. 31st, 1915, by shell head and arm.

WOODFIELD, J. W., Pte. : Malta, Alex., Gal., S. Egypt, France. May 6th, 1916, transferred to 1/4 Batt. London Regt. from Rouen. Severely wounded July 1st, 1916 ; died Aug. 9th, 1916.

WOODING, T. H., L/Cpl. : Malta, Alex., Gal., S. Egypt, France. May 3rd, 1916, transferred to 1/4 Batt. London Regt. until March 14th, 1917 ; invalided to U.K. through wounds March 7th, 1917. Joined 3rd Res. Batt. Boarded, marked B1, and drafted to R.A.O.C., Woolwich.

WOODROOFFE, A. S. : Malta, Alex., Gal., S. Egypt, France. May 23rd, 1916, drafted to 1/13 Batt. London Regt. from Rouen, and three months later transferred to 1/4 Batt. Wounded severely in hand, and discharged the service by M.B.

WORTH, H. B., Pte. : Malta, Alex., Gal., S. Egypt, France. May 23rd, 1916, transferred to 1/4 Batt. London Regt. from Rouen. Wounded Sept. 26th, 1916. Mortally wounded May 10th, 1918.

WRIGHT, H., Pte. : Malta, Alex., Gal., France. Dec. 22nd, 1915, sick, Gallipoli. Jan. 15th, 1916, invalided from Cairo to U.K., H.S. " Salta." Drafted to France, March, 1917, until wounded March 28th, 1918. Wounded G.S.W. leg.

WRIGHT, G. F., Pte. : Malta, Alex., Gal., S. Egypt, France. Dec. 22nd, 1915, invalided to Malta. Apr. 13th, 1916, rejoined unit at Alexandria. May 23rd, 1916, transferred to 1/4 Batt. London Regt. from Rouen and drafted to Labour Batt.

WRIGHT, F. T., Pte. : Gal., S. Egypt, France. Nov. 15th,

1915, draft from Devonport. May 6th, 1916, transferred to 1/4 Batt. London Regt. from Rouen, and then served with 1/3 Batt. until disbanded, then with 1/2 Batt. until wounded. Wounded three times, left thigh, right arm, right hip.

WRIGHT, J. C., PTE., DRUMMER: Malta, Alex., Gal., S. Egypt, France.   ιy 23rd, 1916, drafted to 1/13 Batt. London Regt. fro.. Rouen, then transferred to 1/4 Batt. Served 20 months in France ; had trench fever and drafted to A.S.C., M.T.

WRIGHT, W.: Malta, Alex., Gal., S. Egypt, France. Dec. 19th, 1915, invalided to Alexandria.

WRIGHTSON, S. H., PTE.: Gal., S. Egypt, France. Nov. 15th, 1915, draft from Devonport. May 6th, 1916, transferred to 1/4 Batt. London Regt. from Rouen. Wounded and lost left leg and a finger.

WYBOURNE, A.: Malta, Alex., Gal., S. Egypt, France. May 6th, 1916, transferred to 1/4 Batt. London Regt. from Rouen.

WYNCOLL, V. H., PTE.: Malta, Alex., Gal., S. Egypt, France. May 6th, 1916, transferred to 1/4 Batt. London Regt. from Rouen. Drafted to 4/1 Cambridge Regt., and then to Agricultural Labour.

YATES, E.: Malta, Alex., Gal., France. Nov. 16th, 1915, invalided from Gallipoli to Alexandria, thence Dec. 6th, 1915, to U.K., H.S. " Glengorm Castle."

YATES, F.: Malta, Alex., Gal., S. Egypt, France. May 7th, 1916, invalided from Rouen to U.K.

YOUNG, W. A., PTE.: Malta, Alex., Gal., S. Egypt, France. Transferred to 1/4 Batt. London Regt. from Rouen. Wounded Aug. 16th, 1917, and left leg amputated. Discharged Nov. 7th, 1918.

ADDENDA.

OFFICERS.

CHAPMAN, L. R., Lieut., A/Capt. : Malta, France. Invalided from Malta, June 27th, 1915. Served in U.K. with 4th Reserve Batt. until Feb. 4th, 1916. Joined 1/4 Batt. in France, Feb. 5th, 1916. Invalided to U.K. July 4th, 1916 ; served with 3rd Res. Batt. until Aug. 1st, 1917. Re-embarked B.E.F. Aug. 4th, 1917. Joined G.H.Q. 3rd Echelon, Aug. 6th, 1917, and served continuously until May 24th, 1919, when demobilized. Wounded July 1st, 1916. Mentioned in despatches Nov. 8th, 1918.

N.C.Os'. AND MEN.

BLAND, A. H. : Malta, Alex., Gal. Invalided to Alex., Dec. 23rd, 1915.

LEE, R. R., Pte. : Malta, Alex. Oct. 21st, 1915, invalided to U.K., H.M.T. " Aquitania."

MOOTHAM, D. G., 2nd Lieut : Malta, France. Oct. 1915 to Nov 1917. Lt. & Q.M. to Ghain Tuffieha Convalescent Camps, then reverted to Private and returned to U.K. and sent to G.O.C.B. Cambridge. Commissioned May 19th, 1918, and posted in France to 201 P. of W. Coy. Oct. 1918 appointed Q.M. to Troopship and Trooptrain to Malta, then released Jan. 14th, 1919, in France.

PARSLOW, W. H., Lieut. : Malta, Alex., Gal., S. Egypt, France. Transferred to 1/4 Batt. London Regt. from Rouen. Left for U.K. for Commission. Returned to France with draft and subsequently killed in action.

SMITH, H. G., Pte. : Malta, Alex., Gal., S. Egypt, France. Transferred to 1/4 Batt. London Regt. from Rouen.

ADDENDA II

OFFICERS.

SIMPSON, A. H., CAPT. : Malta, Gal. Proceeded from Malta July 9th, 1915, for duty with 2nd Battn. Royal Fusiliers in Gallipoli, where he was severely wounded.

N.C.O's. AND MEN.

SMITH, G. E. F., 2/LIEUT. : Malta, Alex., Gal., S. Egypt, France. Transferred to Machine Gun Corps. (Heavy Branch) ; then commissioned in Tank Corps and served in France with this unit.

BARR, R., PTE. : Malta, Alex., Gal., S. Egypt, France. Transferred to 1/4 Batt. London Regt. Wounded July 1st, 1916. Discharged unfit Oct. 8th, 1917.

BORNE, L. W., PTE. : Malta, Alex., Gal., S. Egypt. Transferred to R.A.S.C. on medical grounds.

CORRECTIONS AND ADDITIONS
N.C.O's. AND MEN.

BROWN, W. G., PTE. : Malta, Alex., Gal., S. Egypt, France. Transferred to 1/4 Batt. London Regt. in France. Wounded in hand ; transferred to R.A.F. as B2, and served with that force till demobilised Feb. 9th, 1919.

CLARKE, A. W., SERGT. : Malta, Alex., Gal., S. Egypt, France. Transferred to 1/4 Batt. London Regt. Served on Staff as Instructor at the London Command Depot, Sept. 1917—Sept. 1918. Nominated for Commission and sent to O.C.B. until Feb., 1919, when demobilised.

BUDGEON, C. W., PTE. : Awarded French Croix de Guerre.

www.ingramcontent.com/pod-product-compliance
Lightning Source LLC
Chambersburg PA
CBHW030404100426
42812CB00028B/2829/J